the TALE comes to an END

the INCREDIBLE memoir of a life together that has no EQUAL

JOHN (JACK) ALEXANDER

The Tale Comes to an End © 2025 John Alexander

All Rights Reserved. No part of this book may be reproduced in any form or by any electronic or mechanical means including information storage and retrieval systems, without permission in writing from the author. The only exception is by a reviewer, who may quote short excerpts in a review.

No generative artificial intelligence (AI) was used in the creation of this book. The author expressly prohibits the use of this publication as training data for AI technologies or large language models (LLMs) for generative purposes. The author reserves all rights to license uses of this work for generative AI training and the development of LLMs.

This book is a work of non-fiction. This publication is designed to provide accurate and authoritative information in regards to the subject matter covered. It is sold with the understanding that neither the author nor the publisher is engaged in rendering legal, investment, accounting, or other professional services. For privacy reasons, some names, locations, and dates may have been changed.

These are the memories of the author, from their perspective, and they have tried to represent events as faithfully as possible.

Printed in Australia

Cover by Lizza Creative

Internal design by Alana Lambert

Images in this book are copyright approved for use by author

First printing: November 2025

Paperback ISBN 978-1-7640189-2-0

eBook ISBN 978-1-7640189-3-7

 A catalogue record for this work is available from the National Library of Australia

Distributed by Lightning Source Global

Also by John (Jack) Alexander

A Lie in the Tale
The Tale Gets Longer
The Tale Comes to an End

Acknowledgements

I must mention three delightful patient ladies who persevere with me to enable this trilogy to be written. I am indebted to Sam Elley, my editor, who was fun to work with and her skill in keeping the story as written. Dear Alana Lambert, who answered all my questions and managed to put the books together for marketing. Finally, Elizabeth McCracken who painstakingly put up with me in designing the last two covers of *The Tale Gets Longer* and *The Tale Comes to an End*.

Author's Note

Why would I write this, our personal family history for the world to read?

I feel we have had an extraordinary life coping with natural disasters, life threating medical emergencies and human interference in our lives.

It is in the hope, we may be able, in some way, to help readers who go through some of the above problems, that they may find comfort in not being the only ones and they see each day is a new day. Life can be tough and hard to understand and life does end, but we have had a fabulous journey of love and adventure and, through reading our story, we wish yours will be much richer.

*This book is dedicated to Jack's heroine,
his darling wife, Helen.*

PROLOGUE

1962

Just a happy girl with her two brothers and a sister, living on a Victorian dairy farm with a struggling family, trying to make ends meet. It was a happy family and love was always present in their small wooden farmhouse. But the girl had an embarrassing moment at 13 years of age. She had an accident where she couldn't reach the toilet in time.

This event was now happening all the time. A rush to the toilet, sometimes she made it, other times it was too late. She hid her panties in the corner of the garage until she had the chance to secretly wash them. It was so embarrassing to this young girl, she told no one, until she injured her knee at 16 years old and had to stay home. This was when her mother found out.

Her mother took her to the doctor and was horrified at his suggestion of a serious operation on her young daughter. She went to a naturopath, who suggested the main diet should be eggs: poached, fried, boiled, in milk drinks and raw. Sadly, after two years of this diet and no relief of her running to the toilet, the young girl's weight went down to less than 40kg.

Her body collapsed and she remembered floating. Everything was wonderful and all was at peace, except for the yelling and the banging. This noise brought her back as the doctor said, "We thought we lost you then."

At 18, she had an operation that had never been performed on such a young person. The operation was an ileostomy. This is where the large bowel is separated from the small bowel or ileum and joined to her abdomen, hopefully to be joined up later on, if possible. So, now our girl had an appliance and an external pouch for her continual running faeces, at the right side of her abdomen. Not a pleasant thing for an 18-year-old to cope with.

As she was recovering in hospital, a social worker came to see her with some forms.

"Please sign these as they will enable you to receive an invalid pension for life."

That was not going to happen, as our girl had decided, after she was able to manage her new body, she would do nursing.

And nursing she did. After rejection, a fight and a good doctor, she was given a three-month trial. She excelled, with an impressive record and her full registration as a nursing sister. Studying, ward duty and the normal worries of a young lady, she still had to manage her appliance, leakage and associated problems.

She fell in love with an airforce chap from Perth. They were keen on each other till his mother interfered and said, "Drop the girl. She will have problems all her life."

And so, he did. She was devastated. Again, sometime later, she fell in love with a Queensland chap. His mother said, "Drop the girl. She is a medical problem."

So, what did he say?

"I love her so much and we will marry."

And so, they did. The girl was thankful for her life and each day was beautiful. No matter what, she was always happy and smiling. Her name was Helen.

THE BEGINNING

1968

Jack and Helen were driving into the future, with all its twists and turns and ups and downs. With love in their hearts, excitement in their souls and adventure on their minds.

Having just married in Melbourne, our two lovers were driving to Queensland. For Jack to start his new job as a manager of a large sheep and cattle property for the first time as manager. It lay just east of Cunnamulla in western Queensland. While Helen was looking forward, with some apprehension, to her new life as the station missus, it was going to be a new experience for both of them.

Jack, originally from Melbourne, had left years before to start his career in the pastoral industry in Queensland. Occasionally, he would go back to Melbourne to catch up with family. On one of those return trips, he met his lifetime love at a friend's 21st birthday party.

After two years of separation, where he had left for Queensland a week after he met Helen, Jack decided to go back to Melbourne and marry the girl of his dreams. They had written every day to each other, till the price of stamps went up.

(You can read about it in Jack's books: The Lie in the Tale and The Tale gets Longer).

Helen, who had finished training as a registered nurse and midwife at the Royal Melbourne Hospital and the King George Hospital, Sydney, was only too happy to leave the career she loved, for love and adventure with her Jack. After quite a few months in Melbourne, which had not been kind to the loving couple: robberies, car accidents and unpleasant incidents, they were both pleased to leave that city behind and start a new life in the west.

They felt sad saying their goodbyes to family and friends and the familiar places, especially the farm Helen grew up on and the Royal Melbourne Hospital, which was an establishment that had saved her young life and also given her a great nursing career. Jack was just pleased to get out of that city and back to the bush, which he loved.

A wave goodbye to family, in the drizzly early Melbourne morning and Helen snuggled up to Jack. They drove their near new Holden car, with their few possessions in a covered trailer, heading for sunshine, adventure and fun.

C.1

Ardglen Station
May 1968

They drove from Melbourne, some 1400 kilometres to Cunnamulla, then a further 75 kilometres to Ardglen station. The last 60 kilometres were on very rough, sandy, red dirt road. They arrived at the large, tall, white boundary gates. Jack said to his new missus, "What have I got myself into?"

They drove through the gates and Jack was thinking, "I'm the new station manager. I hope I can wing it."

He felt nervous and unsure of himself. It was his first manager's job, looking after 80,000 acres with stud and commercial sheep and cattle. His dear, new bride just smiled saying, "I know you will manage because you are a manager now. Of course, darling, you will be magnificent."

That was not what he felt. He had a feeling of nausea and apprehension as they drove the further 10 kilometres to the homestead.

Three years previously, Jack had worked on the property as a leading hand and knew it well. He had left, due to the then manager taking a month's wages from him. This was because he and the other workers had accidentally damaged the veranda floor in the shearer's quarters, doing extreme gymnastic manoeuvring over tables. Even though Jack had reported the damage and, on the weekend, they had repaired it, he had still lost the month's wages. Jack and the other ringers walked off the property that morning, never to return.

It was a typical Queensland homestead, built in the late 1880s. It had one major central room as a dining room / lounge with a fireplace and a pressed tin ceiling. A gauzed veranda surrounded most of the house, with the main bedroom in one of the corners which, thankfully, was closed in. Another building, attached by a walkway, was built of corrugated iron. This housed the kitchen, bathroom (hot water by a chip heater), cooks' bedroom, a spare bedroom and a thirty-two-volt lighting plant and batteries for power.

The kitchen contained a large table, that accommodated six people, the normal pale green cupboards and benches. A green monster, the Sampson wood stove had two large ovens on each side of the fire box. It wasn't a combustion stove or even built in. This is what the new missus worked with to feed six or eight hungry working men. On the walkway were two kerosene fridges. No gadgets like electric frypans, toasters, Mixmasters, freezers or anything that was 240 volts.

Around the homestead was an overgrown garden and lawn, surrounded by a chain wire fence. A water tank sat on a high stand, beside a windmill pumping water from a bore. When they arrived, there were hundreds of cats. I kid you not. They were on the windmill, on the tank stand, on and under the veranda and up the trees. They all mysteriously disappeared after a month. The missus thought Jack may have been responsible; the owner said the cats had to go. Jack loved animals but wild cats in the Aussie bush, he believed, didn't belong. In the corner of said garden was the butcher shop and laundry with a 32-volt washing machine and a hand wringer.

Outside the fence, next to the laundry, was a large shed consisting of a tool room/workshop and four large open truck and machinery bays. Opposite that, 20 metres away, was a two-storey building, housing the office and a large storeroom. Underneath was the oil/fuel shed and garage for the 64 XM Ford Falcon station ute. A shearers' / workers' quarters was nearby and further down the road were the shearing shed and yards and further still the cattle and horse yards. So, there you have it, their new residence and workplace.

The owner of the property Jack's new boss, Mr Griffiths, a tall, fit-looking man in his 50s with a pleasant face, greeted them as they arrived. No pleasantries like, 'You must be tired after a long trip' or 'Would you like a cup of tea?'

After the introductions, Mr Griffiths said to Helen, "There is a shoulder of mutton in the butcher shop. You have three men to cook for, plus yourselves, for dinner. I'm taking Jack to show him the property and what I want done, the book work I require, plus signatures for the bank and other legal papers he must know. I want to leave here this evening to get back home to Toowoomba tonight."

Talk about being thrown into the deep end with a fast learning curve. No unpacking the car and trailer, no familiarising themselves with the house or meeting the working men. From standing beside their car, to getting into the passenger side of the Falcon ute and out into the paddocks, his new boss showed Jack stock watering places with their windmills, how to check the stock and a confusing, nonstop chatter on what he wanted Jack to do and what was expected of him.

The property, in years gone by, was one of the biggest in the area with hundreds of thousands of leasehold acres. In the 1950s, the government broke up the leases on large properties to 40,000 acre lots. This, it was realised, was too small a block to be profitable in the Mulga country. The property of Ardglen now had two 40,000-acre blocks, separated by another 40,000 holding, managed by a Mr Tweet and his family.

They ended up at the bore paddock at the top of the property, with a large flowing, near boiling, bore. Surprisingly, it had tiny, transparent fish at its discharge, only staying a metre at the bore head. This bore delivered permanent stock water to much of the two blocks, plus the neighbour's holding, by bore drains.

Not far from the bore, the drains ran into a sandy, porous soil; it was like a huge spring mattress. You could jump on the ground and it would wobble, feeling very weird. You could walk on it but riding a horse could be dangerous. Worst still would be to drive near or on it. That is what the boss did. He bogged the tractor up to the seat, went and got another tractor to pull out the other but bogged that too. Was the lesson learnt? No, he bogged the grader as well.

This was what the boss really wanted to show him.

"Jack, the first thing I want you to do is get all the machinery out of the bog and make sure they are in good working order."

Jack just looked at the disaster, thinking, *How am I going to rectify this mess?* Then they drove straight back to the homestead, into the office for the paperwork, then off he went back home to Toowoomba.

If you thought Jack had it rough, poor Helen had it much worse. Her priority was to familiarise herself with the Green Monster, the huge two oven stove. She tried to light it, to start organising dinner for five, as well as boiling the kettle for a badly needed cup of tea. She was thankful there was wood, kindling and an old Country Life newspaper in the large wood box beside the stove.

Getting the monster alight was a difficult matter. She had never lit a stove like this before. She thought once she struck a match to the newspaper and kindling, it would stay alight. After the third attempt, it seemed to be burning. Then, she filled and put the large kettle on, fetched the shoulder of mutton from the butcher shop, found where the vegetables were and explored the kitchen for utensils, cutlery and crockery. All she needed to do was cook and serve dinner that night.

What was that burning smell? Opening the fire box, she found her fire was out. She cleaned out the smouldering wood and started again to get the monster alight. A slight panic ensued as she tried again for some success. This time, she kept the fire box door opened so she could monitor the flames and keep feeding it with kindling, till it was well alight.

Helen decided she would roast a shoulder, bake the vegetables and see if she could make gravy. So, while shelling peas, preparing the vegetables and keeping an eye on the fire, the kindling was running out. She tried small pieces of wood, hoping they would catch. She put her finger in the kettle water to find it was still cold. *Oh, for a gas stove*, she thought. This was real. How was she going to get dinner ready and served for five by seven o'clock?! Then, she remembered that Jack said the men had to have a pudding or sweets. *What will I do?* she thought, *I cannot even get the damn stove hot enough.*

At last, the wood was starting to burn and there was hope that dinner might be done in time. It was getting onto four o'clock as she put the shoulder in one of the ovens. She thought, *Will the monster be hot enough to cook dinner?* And she was still dying for that cup of tea.

But Helen was not leaving the kitchen. She was keeping an eye on that stove. She desperately wanted to unpack some things from their trailer to make a bed for themselves and check out the chip heater in the bathroom, as another priority was to have a hot shower to get clean again after travelling hundreds of kilometres on dusty roads. No, she was staying close to the monster, just to make sure dinner would be cooked.

At last, she heard a car arriving.

Thank God, Jack is back, she thought. But no, 'Griffo' was leading him into the office. "Oh dear, its nearly 5.30 and I need some light and I desperately need Jack home as the stove is still not hot enough to cook dinner," she pondered.

A car had driven away and then she heard an engine start thump, thump, thump and, all of a sudden, the lights went on in the kitchen. Jack had switched them on, as he walked in. Helen looked a bit teary-eyed and hugged him saying, "I need you desperately. I have been having so much trouble with the stove and I am sorry but dinner won't be ready in time."

Jack was also tired, exhausted with the journey and a million new instructions. He was glad that Griffo had gone, so they could be on their own to sort things out. Then he noticed the fire box door open on the stove and a sad little fire burning within.

"Darling, you must keep the fire box closed as you are losing all the heat."

Helen then went into detail about the terrible time she'd had to get it going and was not game to shut the fire box door because she wanted to make sure it did not go out again.

He stoked the fire up and, when it was going well, Jack noticed the water in the large kettle was just warm.

"Love," he said, "I don't think we are going to have tea by seven. Have you seen the working men yet?"

"No, I've been too busy with the stove."

"I know," Jack said, "let's call it the Green Monster." To which she readily agreed.

Jack went out and started unpacking the trailer and car, looking for essentials like clothes, pyjamas and toiletry bags. The station supplied all food, furniture, linen, blankets, towels soaps etc. but they wanted their own items.

Helen rang the bell for dinner. It was an old school bell on a small tower which stood in the back yard. Not long after, three men tramped into the kitchen. Jack introduced himself and Helen. They offered their names in a cranky way.

"I'm Arthur," said a solid built bloke with a kindly face but a bit rough round the edges. He looked in his early 50s. "This is my son Greg," he said, pointing to a late teenager, thin and not the strongest looking lad.

"I'm Harry," a man in his mid-30s said. A tough-looking individual, who looked fit and very capable of looking after himself.

They shook hands and, as they started to sit down at the table, Harry said, "We have been fencing all day and expected our dinner at seven, not bloody nine o'clock."

Jack apologised and said, "Dinner was delayed by the owner and there was trouble with the stove but I can assure you from now on, all meals will be on time."

Jack felt, as the new manager, he had to stamp on his authority. He looked Harry in the eye and added, "Swearing, including 'bloody' in front of or in hearing of, the missus, will not be tolerated. If you could apologise to her, I am sure she will apologise for the late dinner." And so, it was.

It was important for Jack to establish that he was the boss from the start, for several reasons. They were on an 80,000-acre property, miles from any town or neighbour, let alone police, ambulance, doctor etc. Being isolated, it was important that discipline prevailed. It must be remembered that Jack was only 26, hardly shaved, looked extremely young and was short of stature, although he had the experience and toughness to handle situations that may arise from men of all persuasions. Jack had mentioned to Helen that they would always eat separately from the workers, to have time to themselves, keeping that bit of independence from the men.

The roast and rice pudding had passed, just. They were not

her usually fantastic culinary delights. Helen was an excellent cook but never had cooked on a large wood stove.

That night, while cuddled in bed, Helen asked, "They called me missus, not Mrs Alexander."

Jack explained, "The missus was a name of the highest regard, as was the term 'cook' on a station. A station could never operate successfully without either."

He started at 4.30 the next morning, to light the monster, for breakfast to be cooked by 7am. Jack decided breakfast would be his job. At six o'clock, Arthur came in with the mutton chops for breakfast. He had killed the night before, hanging the carcass in the butcher shop and cut the sheep down that morning, putting the rest of the mutton in the kerosene fridge. Greg came in with a full bucket of milk, fresh from the house cow that morning. Harry was on the wood heap, splitting wood and kindling, to keep the wood box and the wheelbarrow full to feed the monster. The monster only slept between 9pm and 4.30am.

After a good breakfast of cereal, chops, eggs, tomatoes and toast, cooked on the monster with the fire door opened, Jack gathered the men together to sort out the chores and jobs. Arthur was happy to do the killing every fourth day; Greg was happy to milk the house cow during the week and Harry said he would keep the wood box full every day. So, that was sorted.

It was mentioned that they needed to work a good five-day week. In emergencies or sometimes during shearing, they were expected to help. Jack also mentioned his alcohol policy. He did not have a problem with them having a drink at night but anytime he smelled, heard or saw it, he would not be very pleased.

He asked them about the jobs they had been doing. They said they had been fencing and collecting firewood. Jack mentioned that the boss wanted all the machinery out of the bog and sand up at the bore.

"Do you know about it?" he asked.

"We sure do. What a dumb thing to do," said one of the workers.

"Well, it's our job to get them out," said Jack, "so, your new job is to get yourselves up to the bore drain and start making a new one to change the flow away from the bogged machinery."

Jack said he would come and check how the job was going after lunch, adding, "Do you think you can give it a go?"

They were not very enthusiastic, but they all agreed that they would try.

That gave Helen and Jack time to unload their car and trailer and sort themselves and their gear out. Helen found the chooks and collected the eggs. Jack, now the boss, showed her how to start the Southern Cross Y.B single cylinder lighting engine. They took stock of the store and what food was needed. Fuel, bread, newspapers, mail and orders came on the mail truck once a week. They had a few hours getting organised and finding where everything was. Jack didn't ask Helen if she enjoyed herself the first day on a Western Queensland station, He was wise sometimes.

After lunch, Jack went out and checked how the men were going. They weren't. They had tried to dig one of the tractors out but it was hopeless under those conditions, and not what he wanted them to do.

He marked out a new drain which was well away from the original, although still on sloping ground. It was a start. Once they understood what he wanted, that the ground had to dry before trying to get the machinery out and not to let water into the new drain until he gave the say-so. They got to work. They managed to divert the water and get the machinery free from their prison, after a lot of energy and frustration. It took over a month to free the two tractors and one grader and get them operating again. That was between other stock and station work.

Normal station life began. Helen started a veggie garden and, as Ardglen had a running bore drain at the back of the house, there was plenty of water. There were no complaints from the men, instead, they congratulated her on her meals which were always on time. After a while, they accepted their young boss, even though Harry was testing him all the time to see what he could get away with.

A few days after arriving, it was decided to check out the working horses. Being the boss, Jack wanted to make sure he would pick the best for himself. He caught the night horse, which was usually white or grey, so they could be seen in the early morning light or dark, depending on the season. The night horse was usually a quiet horse, easy to catch and kept in the house paddock.

He was surprised at how many horses there were, mustered from the front paddock. Thirty in all. Many more than three years ago when he had first been there as a leading hand. They had not been looked after well. Knotted manes and tails, and bad feet.

From the beginning, it did not start well. Jack had a hell of a time trying to catch, bridle and saddle those horses, doing one at a time, then trying to ride them. To save you the pain of what he went through, all he would say was, all the horses were difficult as he was trying to mount. He'd have to screw the ear of the horse as he swung into the saddle to try and steady the plunging steed.

How many times did he get bucked off and thrown, landing on his right shoulder, his back, his left shoulder, and all parts of the body? Jack couldn't remember. But he did not give up when thrown. It was just a matter of get on again, thrown again, probably two or three times, then try another horse and it all happened again.

When Jack came home for lunch, worn torn and sore,

Helen asked, "What have you been doing? Whatever It is, it's not healthy for you."

"Having a bit of trouble riding the station horses," he said. "I would have been bucked off a few times and cannot seem to find any good stock horses for myself or the men. I might have better luck after lunch and a nap."

"You know what you are doing dear, but please be careful."

"I'll do my best love," he promised her.

That afternoon, his best was not good enough. Eventually, he found four, barely suitable, horses out of the 30. He did not try them all, only about 16 of the mob. It must have been a good exercise for him as the following year, he was successful in winning the saddle buckjump at the Cunnamulla Rodeo.

Days later, Griffo, (Mr Griffiths to you), rang up and said, "I forgot to tell you, there are a few bulls in the front paddock. I want you to sell the lot at the next cattle sale. I also want you to contact a horse dealer and sell those 30-odd horses also in the front paddock. They are all unridden rodeo horses and unbroken stuff that have been gathered up around the district by the last manager and I want them all gone." Jack timidly asked him where the station horses were. "Oh, they are in the ram paddock. Haven't you found them yet?"

The horses were sold without the slightest regret. Indeed, there was a great feeling of pleasure as the loaded truck disappeared down the road. Also sold were the bulls, which received excellent prices. A few weeks later, the manager of an adjoining property came to see Jack and mentioned he was missing a couple of bulls and asked if he had seen them. Jack had an odd feeling in his stomach as he was describing them. No, he had not seen his bulls. Thank goodness he was not at that cattle sale when the station bulls were sold, along with the neighbour's two. It was a good, new manager making his boss a profit.

Routine station work kept them busy, which included:

delving bore drains, windmill and fence maintenance, checking waters and general maintenance. Then, of course, there is the stock work: branding, earmarking, weaning, shearing, pest and parasite control and pasture management. There was also the horrid bookwork: ordering supplies, parts, fuel, keeping the store full and so on. Do not forget, before breakfast there were the day's chores of milking the house cows, killing a sheep for meat, getting the horses in, feeding the chooks and the wood for the monster.

The most important of all routine jobs was what the missus had to achieve: keeping the monster alive, baking and cooking for smokos, lunches and dinners. Then there was looking after the vegetable garden and the house yard, normal everyday housework and the million and one extra things a man would not know or appreciate about women's work.

This particular, lovely, spring day, with the bluest of cloudless skies and a slight southerly breeze, it was decided the boss would spend the day on his horse, checking the stock and familiarising himself with some of the property. Riding home in the late afternoon, after a great informative day, he noticed an emu strutting towards him. His mount seemed to be getting nervous, increasing his walking pace. The emu now started running directly towards them. The horse increased its pace to a trot. Do emus get rabies? The thought occurred as this very strange event was unfolding.

The emu increased its pace and the horse went from a trot to a canter. The emu was catching up to them. The boss was feeling a bit apprehensive. The horse was galloping with its head turned so it could keep an eye on the emu. Jack started to lose complete control of his steed. The emu caught up and, incredibly, managed to jump on to the back of the horse. The boss bailed out and rolled on to some soft grass, noticing the emu riding the galloping horse in the distance.

Walking home with this experience in his head, he couldn't believe what had happened. *Did it occur? Who would believe an emu riding a horse? That is ridiculous. Did I get too much sun? Am I having hallucinations or a mental breakdown?* Helen and everyone else, did not need to know.

He arrived home to find the poor horse standing at the yards, sweating and very unsettled. The boss unsaddled and gave him a good rub down and brush. After making sure the horse had settled down, he released him into his paddock.

After giving Helen a good hug and kiss, asking how her day was and what was for tea, the boss told her about the emu hopping on to the back of his horse. She replied with an incredulous look in her eye, "The men are back from doing the bore drain and you had better have a shower and be ready for tea." She made no comment about the adventurous ride that day.

That evening, he rang Cliff, who managed Clestrain Station nearby. Jack knew Cliff when he was minding a station next door to him for a short while a few years ago. Cliff was a World War Two veteran: tall, thin, dropped his aitches, a Chips Rafferty look-alike, bushman, horseman all his life except his four years of service and a real character who could talk a locomotive off its rails.

Jack told him about his experience with the emu that day. He roared with laughter. After recovering, he told Jack that the last manager of the property, Gordon, raised an emu chick, which ended up as his pet. For a bit of a lark, when it was half grown, he would put it behind him on the back of his horse. As time went by, the chick had grown to full size. It would jump on to the back of any horse when ridden. This caused a lot of accidents, with horses bolting and stockmen having busters. Cliff further said that he thought Gordon had gotten rid of the emu months before he left the property.

Jack was pleased he had rung Cliff. He was not going mental

or having hallucinations, after all. Though, it was obvious the emu was dangerous for him and his workers. There were a lot of emus on the property, so it was thought one less should not be a problem. Later on, the bird was helped to a better life in heaven.

C.2

The Workers
Ringers, Station Hands, Jackeroos

Station work went on and, to keep things maintained, employees were needed to help with fencing, yard building, mechanics, windmills, boar drains, maintenance, plus countless little jobs that must be done. Yes and the all-important stock work.

Men and women come in all shapes and sizes. Highly educated, some limited, some little schooling with no reading or writing. Good workers, some lazy. Bushmen, city folk, loners, criminals, old or young, black or white. They came and they went.

Old Arthur, his son, Greg, and Harry, did not stay long. Arthur was poisoned by a mulga stake and had to be rushed to Cunnamulla hospital 65kms away. He had a swollen arm, fever, vomiting and a red stripe up his arm. When did this happen? In the middle of a flood.

It was a dramatic drive into town in his ford V8 ute across flooded creeks and gullies turned in to boiling rivers. The word spread on the party telephone line, with people getting their tractors and trucks waiting on the Cunnamulla-Bollon Road to help Jack and his worker get through to the Cunnamulla

Hospital. The Wedgeegoar Creek was the main problem as they had to be towed through the torrent by a high suspension truck, then finally, a few kilometres further, they hit the tarred road to town. Arthur, in a critical condition, was made comfortable at the hospital where he was treated for a quite a few days.

Driving Arthur's truck back to the station that day, there were troubles ahead. All the station neighbours had taken their trucks and tractors back to their homesteads, not thinking that Jack had to come back on that same flooded road. Instead of the Wedgeegoar Creek slowly going down, as he thought, it was much higher than it should have been. It was found out later that a large dam had broken its banks up stream, which greatly increased the water level.

Just to be sure, Jack took the fan belt off and covered the radiator with a corn bag, so water would not wet the engine. He was glad he did. Crossing the flooded creek, he put the clutch in a bit to keep the engine revving. The water came over the wheels, the bonnet and even partially over the windscreen.

It was not a wide crossing and, as he came out the other side, the petrol engine spluttered, then died. It takes a lot to dry an engine. Jack put the fan belt back on and took the bag off the radiator, all while getting drenched in the pouring rain. He did get home late that night, skidding and slipping all the way on that red soil.

Arthur's son, Greg, took their truck to town to see his dad and that was the last Jack saw of those two. Harry left with a bad attitude three weeks later.

Jack needed men and started phoning around the stock agents and asking around the pubs to find workers. It was Tom that was picked up from the mail truck at the station turn off. He was about 50-odd years old, scruffy with an unshaven face but a friendly, smiling grandfatherly look. He had hardly any personal belongings but what he had was in a small plastic airline bag. He told Jack he had lost his suitcase at the Brisbane railway station. Jack was suspicious about his story as the boss was starting to get a good idea of a person's character, even though he was just 26.

Tom was a good worker for the first week or so but slowly got more and more tired. Helen thought he was wonderful because he went to town regularly and brought home a Women's Weekly for her. She said Jack couldn't sack him but it was taken out of boss' hands when the local police phoned. They informed him that Tom had a few warrants out and when would it be convenient to come out to pick him up? The cops were told Tom was going to be let go anyway, so the sooner they could come, the better.

Police arrived the following week, putting Tom, who was very casual about it all, in the back of the police car. The police then gave the information that Tom was wanted for robbery in Perth, Western Australia, trespassing in a girl's college dormitory in Adelaide, rape in Victoria, and some other crimes in NSW.

They knew Tom was working at Ardglen but did not advise of his record until they had all the warrants. They thought it better that he stayed on the station instead of keeping him in town, housing and feeding him. So much for the boss' darling bride, who occasional ran in the nude along the veranda to the bathroom. Even though Tom was lazy while there, he had behaved like a proper gentleman.

Another employee was Herb Scantlebury, who lived in the shearers' quarters with his wife, Liz. Herb, an Englishman, was a thin, medium built man, always with a five a clock shadow and always talking with ridiculous yarns and information about nothing. But he was a handy employee. Liz was a very large woman and had decided to lose her abundant layers. She answered an advertisement in the Australasia Post magazine for a slimming suit that was guaranteed to help the wearer lose pounds off their weight.

It arrived by post and she unpacked a clear, plastic body-covering suit with elastic around the ankles and wrists. Now, in summer, the heat can reach well into the 40s, which is a dry heat but not dry enough for Liz. Wearing this suit under her clothes during the hot days, it would be filled with fluid from her glands and you could hear the fluid squelching as she walked around. I do not think she lost much weight as the suit was discarded after a fortnight.

It was their first Christmas and dear Helen thought she would cook a traditional English Christmas dinner: roast, plum pudding, Christmas cake, the works, for us and the men. She worked in a hot, corrugated built kitchen, attached to the house by a small breeze way veranda.

How she did it, what with that large green monster stove throwing out tremendous heat and the fiery sun belting down on the iron roof, I don't know. Helen did her best, cooking in 50 degrees or more. She managed a beautiful, delicious Christmas dinner but they were all so hot sitting in that overheated kitchen that no one could eat or enjoy the benefits of all Helen's labour. Helen said from now on, it would be salad for Christmas lunch and so it has been.

That afternoon, Brian, one of the workers, a strong, hard man in his early 40s with a 'do not mess around with me' demeanor, called out to the boss while he was trying to have a nap.

"What's the problem?" Jack asked.

Brian said in an angry tone, "I want to finish up now."

"What? Now? Its Christmas. You have had a couple of days off and you want to leave now and lose a week's wages?"

"It's that Herb Scantlebury. I can't stand it any longer, annoying me with his stupid stories and lies. He never stops and he is driving me crazy," said Brian.

"We'll go over to the quarters and sort this out with Herb," said Jack.

"Herb!" the boss shouted as they approached the shearers quarters, where he and Liz lived on one side and Brian on the other. "Me and Brian want to have a yarn with you now, if you don't mind."

Herb sheepishly came out with Liz in tow, saying, "My missus is coming out with me."

The two were standing on the veranda while Brian was below on the ground. The boss said, "Herb, Brian here wants to leave his employment now as he is not happy with you interfering with his privacy. He states he is sick and tired of you yakking at him all the time, especially on his days off, with your stupid exaggerated stories and lies, leaving him no peace at all."

Then the real reason that was upsetting Brian came out.

"Herb, what's more, the boss has been working us hard the last month, and I cannot get to sleep at nights since you and your missus have been rooting every night and your bed is banging on the corrugated iron partition wall and I can't stand it a moment longer," a very angry Brian shouted.

Showing surprise and astonishment, Herb and Liz said nothing.

A suggestion was made that Brian move his bed and belongings to the far end of his side of the quarters and Herb would keep away from Brian and respect his privacy.

"And, what's more, move your bed well away from the wall and stay your side of the quarters as far away from Brian as you can, will you do that?" asked Jack.

Herb and Liz meekly agreed and returned to their quarters.

"Brian, you still want to leave today?"

"No boss, thanks for sorting that out. I'll stay and see if Herb keeps his end of the bargain."

Brian did leave, three weeks later; Herb and Liz stayed another six months.

Years after, it was believed Herb went to jail for a considerable time, allegedly for a sex crime. Twenty odd years later, he ended up managing the Cunnamulla garbage tip and starred in a TV documentary series called, 'Cunnamulla'.

Men came and went. Rarely did workers stay more than six or 12 months. Some were sacked, some could not stand the boss and some were just drifters.

This day, there was an early muster in Coventry Lake paddock. Freezing cold, frost everywhere, Sun just up. They loaded the horses into the truck and drove out to the paddock. It was easier to truck than spend the time riding out. The boss gave the men their orders, how he wanted the paddock mustered and arranged the three of them to meet him at the dam in the southwest corner. Two turned up with sheep, one man they waited for, for over half an hour. Anything could have happened to him: lost, fallen from his horse, hit his head on a low branch. The boss told the two men to wait there while he looked for the missing man.

An hour or so searching, the missing man was found at the entrance gate into the paddock, sitting beside what was once a large fire but now only a few dwindling flames. The boss enquired as to why he had not met them at the dam, as requested. He answered, he could not find any sheep and did not feel like riding all the way to the dam because he was cold. It was obvious he had not moved since they arrived.

Angrily, the boss said, "You have stuffed up the muster and the day for us. You have not done what you were told. You have let me and the men down. You are no good to me at Ardglen, put your horse in the truck, while I ride and tell the men what happened, then I will transport you back to the homestead where you will finish up."

Jack took the bludger back and paid him the wages due. Wages were paid once a month by cheque at stations. Then he was told he was to be taken to the Bollon-Cunnamulla Road to be picked up by the mail truck.

He said, "You can't do that. You owe me an extra week's pay in lieu of a week's notice and I'm going on strike."

At that, he sat on the office steps and refused to move. A sit-down strike. What could be done? The boss could not physically shift him as he was a very big man: six foot two and well built. By that time, the men had arrived home. They were told about their work mate's bludge and his strike. They suggested he be left to starve. So, they all trotted off to have lunch, leaving the striker still on the office steps.

Seeing the day was stuffed, they all did chores around the homestead, while the striker did not move from sitting on the steps.

By 4.30 that afternoon, he was still on the steps and the boss was getting slightly concerned about his behaviour. Then, to his surprise, a travelling vehicle pulled up at the homestead. A suited man wearing a tie got out of the car, and said, "Is it all right to pass through to the next property?"

"Go right ahead, but who are you?" Jack asked.

"The name is Jack Smyth, the industry inspector." Reaching out his hand to be shaken, he continued, "I am on my way to sort out a bit of trouble at Heywood Station." This was a neighbour's property managed by Sid Tweet.

"As a matter of fact, you, Mr Smyth, have just come here at the most appropriate time. I have a dismissed worker here who has gone on strike and will not move from the office steps."

"Do you mind if I have a talk with him?"

"Go ahead," said the boss, pleased Mr Smyth had arrived right at the time when the situation was starting to be a big problem.

Ten minutes later, Mr Smyth came back.

"The man admitted he was wrong and deserved to be sacked and you were right to pay him fully up to the time he was dismissed. But you cannot take a person to the main road, hoping he will get a lift. It is your duty to take him to town, even though it is about 70 miles away. However, under the circumstances, to save you a long trip, I will take him to town after I have finished my business at Heywood station.

"By the way, you look very young to be running a large commercial and stud sheep and cattle property out here."

The boss answered, "Everyone says that."

It was a fact and it caused the boss some trouble with employees. His baby face features, limited whiskers and appearance of a young tenderfoot, men thought they could try and get away from doing jobs and constantly tried him out. They soon realised their mistake as he had the experience and toughness to handle any situation that arose.

Looking so young also caused Jack problems with the shearers. As you may be aware, shearing is the busiest time on a sheep station. With mustering in large acreage paddocks, drafting, resting sheep for four hours before they're shorn, the dipping, spraying and marking, and returning to the paddocks. We won't mention all the gear and supplies the boss has to have on hand when shearing starts.

For instance, mattresses for shearers had to be 100mm thick. So, Jack, deciding to save time and money and, with plenty of fibre mattress on hand, put two mattresses together to make up the 100mm. Strike action was threatened, as the rule was: it must be one mattress, 100m thick, not two or three.

This meant a race into town to buy 20 foam mattress and load them into the truck before shearing started.

Jack thought, *Okay, if I have to play by the rules, so must they.*

Common practice was a five-minute break every hour for shearers. At the start of each hour, the boss often heard the shearing stop. Then it would take a good 15 or 20 minutes before he heard them back at work. This was not good. The sheep must be shorn.

The next time the boss heard the machinery stop, he raced up to the board, where the shearers were lounging, pulled out his pocket watch and paced up and down for the five minutes. It was an awkward moment. They swore but went back to their shearing.

That night, two shearers approached the boss and said, "Mate, the cockies let us have more than 10 minutes on the hour. Why are you being just a shit?"

"Because," replied Jack, "I'm just a manager and if I don't get the job done in time, I get the sack. The cockies own their own place and let you blokes get away with these stops. Let's just abide by the rules and we can get on well together." A shake of the hands and the deal was made.

Another time, the only employee Ardglen had was a young man the agents sent out. He was tall, skinny, a droopy expression on his face, long hair he kept flicking his head to keep off his face. His name was Gordon and you could only describe him as thick.

The boss asked him if he knew how to check a car for fuel, oil, and water. This was something that must be done every morning. He answered he did it regularly with his dad's car. Being suspicious of his statement, Jack asked again, describing the radiator cap, dip stick and fuel gauge. He looked at his employer as if he was stupid and said, "I do know what to do."

Sometime later, he came back saying, "Just as well I checked the oil, it took six litres of the stuff."

"What? That cannot be correct!" Jack marched out of the office to check what he had done. Yes, he had filled the car with oil, right up to the filler cap on the tappet cover. He hadn't bothered to check the dipstick.

After draining out the good oil down to the correct level, Jack showed him the dip stick and the marks, low and max.

"Oh, I didn't know that. My, you learn something new every day," he exclaimed.

"I am learning patience, I am learning. It's better than murder," the boss muttered under his breath.

This day, they had to muster the front paddock, consisting of a few hundred acres. Reluctantly, the boss took Gordon with him as he still had not managed to get any more working men.

At the entrance, Jack drew a mud map of the paddock, outlining the boundaries, features, dams, scrub patches, clay pans and so on. Then slowly and carefully, he explained what he wanted Gordon to do.

"Gordon, all I want you to do is ride around the fence line, always keeping the fence on your right, in sight. If you see any sheep, just yell as loud as you can and chase them to the left of you, towards the centre of the paddock, always keeping the fence line in sight and I will be picking them up when I hear you yell." The boss was explaining this as he drew on the mud map. "Now Gordon, do you understand what you must do?"

"Yep, I just ride around the fence and any sheep I see, I just shoo them into the paddock."

"That's right but always keep the fence in sight as I do not want you getting lost and we will meet here at this spot."

After explaining everything in detail more than once about mustering and what he had to do, Gordon mounted the safest station horse and started to ride the fence. He turned his head towards the boss and spoke, "What else am I supposed to do?"

Jack with a sigh, said, "Oh, just count the fence posts."

Practically mustering the paddock by himself, with Sparkle, Jack's devoted sheep dog, they waited with their mustered sheep at the designated meeting place for Gordon to turn up. It was with relief after some time, he arrived.

"Did you see any sheep?"

"No," he said, "I was too busy counting fence posts. There are 533 posts."

Did the boss say he had patience with Gordon? I think he could have screwed his head off.

As Jack didn't have other employees, Gordon was useful to fetch and carry, hold a fencepost straight, thread some wire, pass a spanner or bring a horse. Better than no one.

It had been a hard, exciting, educating year for the missus and the boss. They went on holidays, driving to Melbourne to catch up with family. Griffo, the owner, was minding the place while they were gone. When they returned, there were no men for the missus to cook for.

Jack asked, "What happened to Gordon?"

"That useless idiot. I sacked him."

"What did you sack him for?" Jack asked.

"He had his jumper on after lunch. Any man with a jumper on after lunch has not been working hard enough, so I sacked him," said Griffo.

Jack did end up with some good workers but you will hear about them in another chapter, headed Aboriginals and Stories.

C.3

Their Personal Life on Ardglen

Helen was settling in well, managing the green monster, cooking wonderful meals. The men never wasted any time coming to the kitchen when called and all thought she was great. Talk about busy. The vegetable garden and the flower garden she started, were something to behold. The row of colourful marigolds along the front fence were a rainbow in the stark sandy outback surrounds.

She loved watching her man on a horse; she thought how magnificent he looked and how well he managed everything. She rarely missed her nursing life, as she was so busy and happy, whistling happy tunes throughout the day. She loved her man and couldn't wait to put her arms around him. Jack felt exactly the same. He always enjoyed coming home to his beautiful wife. Every day they said to each other, "I love you."

Helen was enjoying her new life but she did miss 240-volt electric power, freezers, gas cooktops and ovens and all modern conveniences. But her sewing machine, that Jack managed to convert to 32-volt power, was always in use. She made red night shirts and matching hats with bon bons on top, for her sister and husband and Jack's sister and her husband one Christmas. She made flannel work shirts for Jack and a beautiful outfit to wear at the Cunnamulla races.

Helen's joys, beside sewing, were gardening and cooking. Jack thought he probably came next. And how could we forget the other part of the family: Cammie the corgi pup the boss had bought his bride just before coming to Queensland.

Jack knew, for a woman on an outback station, it could be a very lonely life, with no neighbours within cooee, no radio and a limited party line phone. A lot of time the men would be gone by 7am and home at 5pm. A long, lonely day for any person.

Cammie was a delight for Helen and they had a very strong bond together. If Helen put the garbage out near the door for Jack to incinerate, Cammie would guard it because it belonged to Helen. When Jack went to fetch it, a growl and bared teeth would ensue. If one of the working dogs came into the yard, Cammie would get hold of their ear and not let go until the boss released it.

Helen loved helping Jack when he was short of men, with the drafting of sheep, Of course, she brought Cammie along to help. She would put the dog on the yard post and she would help Helen run the sheep through the drafting race, barking excitedly and making the sheep run. Every now and then, she got too excited and fell off the post in among the running flock. Being pummelled and rolled by the sheep, she would have to be rescued, panting and thinking it was all good fun.

Even though a corgi is a cattle dog, she was not a paddock dog. When Helen helped Jack to muster a small paddock on a horse, things were different with Jack's sheep dog, Sparkle. If he asked Helen to drive the sheep down the fence line, with Sparkle's help, so he could go and find more sheep, no way would the dog let Helen move the sheep. They belonged to Jack. So, when Jack eventually found them, they were exactly where he had left them, with poor Helen frustrated and near tears, because the dog would not let her move the sheep. However, Sparkle was happy with herself because she thought she was doing the right thing for the boss.

Talking about dogs, Helen asked Jack what an old telephone generator was doing bolted on to Jack's bedside table. Jack said the last manager had put it there and it was connected to a wire that went under the floor and continued on to all the working dogs' chains. If the dogs started a barking frenzy in the middle of the night, the manager would just roll over and wind the handle furiously on the little generator, which gave all the dogs an electric shock to entice them to be quiet. Helen suggested, quite firmly, not long after they arrived at Ardglen, that the generator had to go or there might be wires switched to the person lying beside it. Jack dismantled the generator immediately.

They did things together on the station as much as possible. But it must be remembered, back in the sixties, women were not welcome in a man's working world, especially on stations. Women were not even allowed to go into hotel bars. But it never stopped Helen helping her man when needed. At shearing time, Jack had to get the wool away to town in the truck late in the evening. Who was the woman rolling the large 300lb wool bales out of the shed to the truck? It had to be Helen.

Helen and Jack never ate with the men. They were in the kitchen, while the missus and the boss ate in the dining room. This gave them privacy so they could talk over the day's joys, fun and problems. This was their time together. After dinner, Helen would organise the washing up with the men, while the Boss nicked off to the office, to do the dreaded paperwork and work out the next day's jobs. Then two tired humans would crawl into bed and cuddle up, ready for the dawn and another exciting day in western Queensland.

The weather was a mixture of dust storms, extreme heat, floods and fires in the long summer months and below freezing, frosty, cold westerly winds in the winter. But they came and went. Usually, the weather was beautiful, with blue skies and warm sunny days.

Helen's mother-in-law was coming to stay, the first time since they were married. Helen was busy cleaning the homestead as best she could. It was a very old Queenslander and open to the elements. Then Jack and Helen drove to pick Jack's mother up in Cunnamulla, leaving a beautiful clean house, with flowers in the spare bedroom, new sheets, the works. But alas. While they were away, a large dust storm decided to leave inches of dirt in every room, crevice, cupboard and wardrobe.

The mother-in-law's bedroom and bed were covered with the fine dust, as was all the kitchen, plates, cups and cutlery. It was an unholy mess when they arrived home. Helen was so embarrassed. She wanted to give a good impression, to show what a good wife she was but now this. But Jack's mother, Beth, was not fazed and the three of them got busy with shovels, brooms, wet rags and mops till the place was gleaming again. And Jack's mother was impressed with Helen, for living under such conditions, just so she could be with her man.

They did have a social life. Who could not in the bush? There was the Slim Dusty Show, the Cunnamulla Show, and friendly nights at one of the neighbours, playing card or board games or just having a social evening.

Our couple decided to have a swimming party. At the back of the homestead, the bore drain ran into a dam, which only contained bore water. It was clear, with a deep firm bottom but Jack had not exactly immersed himself in it. Occasionally, Helen would float around on it with an old tyre tube with Cammie splashing about.

So, it was thought, *What a great place for a swimming party*. They called all the neighbours around and with plenty of food and drinks supplied, a party they had. Until Harold decided to be the first one to break the water and dived in. He came up with a sheet of corrugated iron. Then Phil went in and brought some timber up and then it became Helen and Jack's dam cleaning party.

Jack thought perhaps he should have checked it out prior to having the swimming party. At the end of the day, everyone had a great time and, thank God, there were no injuries. The hosts ended up with a nice, cleaned out dam. Jack took a fully loaded trailer with the rubbish from the dam to the station garbage heap.

It was early days for motor bikes on stations as it was all horses. But Jack managed to talk Griffo into buying a Suzuki two-stroke motor bike, so he could check stock, make sure paddocks were mustered clean and waterholes inspected. It saved fuel and time.

He thought it would be a good idea to teach Helen how to ride it. He gave very careful instructions about the accelerator, gears, clutch and brakes, making sure she fully understood his instructions. He was informed, quite strongly, she knew what do and she wasn't stupid. She managed to put it into first gear and took off, turning her head towards Jack with a wave.

It took a bit of time to find her amongst the mulga scrub, some 200 yards down the road. Luckily, neither the bike nor Helen were hurt. Perhaps some dented pride, some dirt and a few scratches. A few lessons later, that day ended up with a very competent rider.

All the working dogs had been left off their chains by the men, as usual, in the afternoon to give them a run when not working. On this horrible afternoon, as Jack was arriving home from a day out in the paddocks, all the dogs came rushing around the car, barking excitingly to meet him. He felt a bump. He heard a dog yelp in pain, so he stopped the car. In front of Helen's eyes, Jack had inadvertently run over her precious corgi, Cammie.

Helen raced out to pick up Cammie, who was dragging her legs behind her. Her lower back and pelvis were severely fractured. Helen and Jack were devastated. The little dog he had bought for her in Melbourne. Jack could not stand to watch this poor little dog in such pain and wanted to put her down. But Helen said, "She's my dog and I will nurse her until she is better."

During the day, Cammie was on a soft bed beside the green monster stove. At night, she was on her bed in their bedroom. Helen massaged her constantly, working her back legs and continuously nursing and loving her. It was six months of tender, loving care that helped Cammie manage to walk again, even though her back legs were wasted and did not look right. But she did manage to walk and later run, though she was never 100 percent again. Helen had that lovely companion dog for eight years before Cammie passed away.

Coming home from the paddocks, the boss noticed Helen chopping wood. He was furious.

"You must not do that. I pay men to chop the wood," he said.

Helen replied, "But there is no wood to cook dinner as the wood box is empty."

"No wood, no dinner for the men," the boss said.

"So, it looks like no dinner for the men," she muttered as she put the axe down and walked off to the kitchen.

Jack did a few chores, some office work then went to see how Helen was getting along. She had the table nicely set for dinner as always but, this time, there was a difference. On each setting, there was a knife, fork and spoon and on each plate was a block of wood.

"Ring the bell for dinner and we will see what happens," said Helen with a mischievous smile.

The bell was rung. The men came over for dinner after a hard day's work.

"Hey missus, what's this block of wood on the plate?" they exclaimed.

Helen said in her sweetest voice, "That's all for dinner, as there is no wood to cook your meal on a cold stove and there is only bread and jam and no hot water for tea."

Suddenly, the men were out of the kitchen, to the wood heap with axes swinging. From that day on, the wood box and barrow were full of wood 24 hours, seven days a week, with never a problem since, even with replacement workers. There must have been a sign somewhere in the men's quarters about getting a log of wood for dinner!

The men would take the large trailer on the tractor and pick up timber in the paddocks to be sawed into the right lengths of blocks, for the wood stove, which then had to be split for the wood box. Now, a bench circular saw was used, run by a large belt, driven by the PTO (power take off) on the tractor. No shields, no workplace safety in those days and the use of such a saw had its dangers.

This day, while sawing wood, out of the corner of his eye, Jack saw Helen gesturing wildly. By all accounts, this was a no-no, as she knew that disturbing the boss while he was sawing, could be very dangerous. Slightly annoyed, Jack stopped sawing, put the PTO into neutral and strode over to Helen.

Excitedly, she said, "Guess what. I'm pregnant."

"That's good," Jack said. He gave her a half-hearted hug, still cross that he had been disturbed while sawing.

Jack started the sawing job again and then it struck him, what Helen had said.

"She is pregnant! My god! We are having a BABY! It could be a son. WOW!"

He finished the wood sawing as soon as he could, put the tractor away, raced to the kitchen, threw his arms around Helen and said, "We are having a baby! We are having a baby!" as he whirled her around excitedly.

They both laughed with happiness and joy but Jack had the feeling this should have been his reaction a half hour ago. Well, what was done, was done. He knew he needed to be more attuned to a woman's feelings and never delay again. *No matter what*, he said to himself.

It was a good year that year. Jack was riding well. As a matter of fact, he won the bronco ride at the Cunnamulla rodeo. Some say the rodeo is cruel and some parts are. But with the horses then, they were usually wild horses or running on the local common for the year. And a half day a year for 10 seconds is not a bad life. These days, rodeo horses are trained, expensive and well looked after.

For Jack, it was a contest between man and beast, where the beast had the advantage over the man. *Can he stay on my back? Can I get rid of this annoying human as soon as possible?*

The nervous excitement and adrenalin that coursed through Jack's body when, over the loudspeaker, his name was called for chute four. He thought, *This is it, I can't chicken out, so I'm riding this outlaw the best I can and put on a show as well.*

The most dangerous part was in the chute. As Jack gently eased into the saddle, held the halter rope the right length, the horse was already jumping about, trying to get out. When he was sure he had a good seat and his position was right, Jack yelled, "Let's go!"

The gate opened to the very large, hard-packed ground show arena. Nowadays they ride in a nice, sandy round yard.

How long is eight seconds? Long enough. Jack could feel huge muscles bunched up underneath him, the hard jolt as the four hooves hit the ground. The twisting, the thrown forward and back, in the air and down again. Eight seconds were more like eight hours. Jack kept his head in line with the horse's head. Where the horse went, so did Jack's body and balance.

Where are the pick-up men? Jack thought, *time must be up.*

The crack of the whip or ring of the bell meant time was up. Jack had ridden the outlaw. *Where are the pick-up men?*

"Give us ya shoulder, mate," as Jack was lifted from the plunging bronc and gently put on the ground.

His legs were wobbly and his breath had been knocked out. He did the cowboy limp back to the chute to, "Congratulations, good ride mate, you stuck that one" and so on. Of course, he was so bloody pleased with himself that he managed the ride and wasn't turfed on to the hard ground.

Injuries? No, not really for Jack. He had been thrown quite a few times on station and rodeo horses but never seriously hurt. Okay, big bruises, soreness for a week, muscle aches and pains but no broken bones. The worst incident was when he was knocked out at the rodeo at Kynuna when the poll of a bullock he was riding, hit his head. Lying on the ground, he came to and was dazed.

He heard the chute boss say to someone else, "We cannot leave him here, it's bad for the show. Drag him off behind the chutes and let him die there."

Jack, still dazed, said, "I'm all right; I can walk back," which he managed.

The successful ride at Cunnamulla was, sadly, Jack's second last. The last one was at Bollon, a couple of weeks later, when, unfortunately, the horse fell on him and he wasn't given a reride, which should have been done as he wasn't hurt. It was then decided, mainly by Helen, that he should give the rodeo up as she was pregnant, and he should think about his future health and family. And so, it was.

Rodeo time at Cunnamulla was a big weekend as the Slim Dusty show came to town and everyone went. The front was always reserved for the Aboriginal children and adults, while whites could sit anywhere, other than the front. Everyone enjoyed the Slim Dusty Show. At interval, everyone rushed out to be refreshed and, guess what, the entertainers were now serving them all chips, sweets and drinks.

Life was good. Jack and Helen worked hard, loved each other madly and enjoyed the life and people. The heat could be well over the 40s, though it was a dry heat with no air conditioners. In winter, there was frost on the rails and taps. It was freezing cold but they did have the green monster to keep them warm. Sunny, balmy days and windy days; it was all there. The mulga looked the same all year round. The other trees: the gums, iron bark, leopard woods and wilga changed slightly. The fauna and flora also changed with the seasons, which always surprised Jack as how nature lived and coped under hard conditions. The sunsets and sunrises, the stars and the moon were their delights. God, it was good to be alive and in love.

C.4

Aboriginals Stories

White, black, brindle-coloured, they were all the same. Good, lazy, devious, thieving, short, fat, tall and thin; All just the tribe of human beings. The boss had found most Aboriginal workers were honest, open and gave a fair day's work when there was a mutual understanding.

A young, dark chap, called Freddie, refused to muster a particular paddock. When questioned why, he replied, "There are spirits in that paddock, and I will not muster there, boss."

The paddock mentioned was called, The Blackfellas Playground. It was an unusual paddock. It had a lake on the western side, thick mulga scrub on the eastern side and in the middle was a sandy, stone flat with some large holes in it, which a human could fit in, and an array of smaller holes. Beside the lake was a knoll with a tight grouping of four date palms. How they grew there was a mystery. It was not uncommon to find Aboriginal artefacts lying about if searched carefully.

It was suggested to Freddy he never needed to muster that paddock if he could show or explain the reason why. On some rare occasions, to get out of work or have a day off, a worker would tell a cock and bull story about some religious, heritage or sacred ground story.

So, Freddie decided to get in to the Falcon ute and show the boss. Once they got to the paddock gate, he was very nervous, so much so, the boss had to open and shut the gate to drive through. As they drove along the station road, the boss could see his passenger crouching down in his seat, window up and door locked. They came to the thick mulga scrub against the sandstone flat. After driving for a short time, Freddie said, "Stop."

The boss was told to get out quickly and shut the door. Walking around to Freddie's side of the car, Jack was given instructions from the young man, yelling as he peeped from the bottom of the car window ledge.

"Boss, get down on your hands and knees. Keep your head well down and move backwards and forwards looking at the scrub base."

Jack felt like an idiot, crawling on his hands and knees, bulldozing the ground with his right cheek, backwards and forwards. Was he being set up by Freddie? He thought so, until he saw it. A thin, narrow, straight line continuing out of sight through the thick mulga vegetation. A spirit path. A track walked by thousands of feet over thousands of years. The track was so hard packed by the foot traffic that no grass, root or shrub could penetrate that thousand-year-old path.

Getting up, Jack made a big deep cross in the dirt with his boot so he could show Helen this spirit path later. As he got in the car, he said to Freddie, "Fair enough, I will never ask you to come in this paddock for any reason."

Freddie was much relieved when the boss closed the gate on that paddock.

They drove straight home. There were some chores to be done by the lad, while Jack raced inside to Helen.

"Quick, come with me. I'll show you a blackfella spirit path."

Hopping in the car, they both took off to The Blackfellas' Playground paddock. They never did find the spirit path. The deep marked cross, made by Jack's boot, could not be found. They searched for a good length of time but had no success. Every time Jack went into that paddock, he never saw that historical path again.

That night, the boss looked in the old employees' register. A thick leather-bound volume of all employees, dating back to the late 1880s, had been recorded in copperplate writing, in ink, by past managers. The register contained dates, names of employees, their wages, store accounts etc. Jack searched for any surname of Freddie's relatives or ancestors that had worked on Ardglen but he could not find anyone. How did he know about the spirit path? How did he know where it was? Maybe it's in the memories.

A story was told to them by an old Aboriginal bushman, who lived in the traditional camping ground in Cunnamulla that had been there for centuries. Sadly, it had been destroyed for a tourist caravan park. Jack did not know if the story was completely true, but he did know the victim died six months after the event.

A valued Aboriginal stockman was sick. He had visited the local, Dr Greg, who could find nothing wrong. His boss, a well-to-do grazier, sent him to Sydney to a specialist, who could not help him either. The stockman got sicker and weaker until he died five months later from some undiagnosed illness.

The Story: They were drinking grog around a campfire in their traditional camping ground when someone spied two strange Aboriginal men in the vicinity.

"Hey, you two come and join us for a drink," which the two strangers did.

As the group were getting more inebriated, one of the strangers put some Yama Yama, or ground up human bone, into one of the fella's drinks. Then they left the camp site and went on their way.

The old bushman told Jack, "Them two strange fellows walked through the nights from the Northern Territory to Cunnamulla (an incredible 1,000+ kilometres) to sing that fella. (To point the bone or put a death wish on someone) That fella, he had been mucking about with some sheilas in the Northen Territory, so he had been sung."

Questions were asked. How did the victim know he had been 'sung', and why did he die five months later? It took months to get the answers. After the strange fellas put the Yama Yama in the drink, they went in search of his wife and told her, her man had been 'sung' and he would die. When the victim came home that night, his wife screamed at him, "You been 'sung'. You bring bad spirits to the family, you must not stay here, you die."

He knew then, as they had known from time immortal, he would die. His mind and soul told him so. Five months later, he passed away.

Another old Aboriginal bushman, Billy Button, could predict when rain would fall. In the late 1960s, when it was very dry, he informed the locals that four inches of rain (100 mm) would fall on a particular day in July. This forecast even reached the Brisbane papers and the forecasters at that time, said it was impossible. Lennox Walker, long-range forecaster, said there were no sunspots that would give any indication of rain in that month. It seemed a contest between the weather bureau and long-range forecasters and an old Aboriginal man in Cunnamulla. It did rain the four inches on the day and date in the Cunnamulla area, much to the joy of the locals and red faces from the city experts.

Billy Button was the celebrity of Cunnamulla and constantly

shouted drinks at the local hotel by the graziers, who wanted to know when the next rain was due. Unfortunately, Billy Button died six months later from, it's believed, alcoholic poisoning. Talk about killing the goose with the golden egg.

George and Barry were two of the best Aboriginal workers from Cunnamulla, to have worked at Ardglen. Honest, hard-working and a pleasure to work with. They'd had a hard day's work one day and, after dinner, the boss had to load the truck up with wool bales. Helen had helped at the last shearing and the bales needed to be taken to the town railway.

George and Barry had come down to the shearing shed and said, "Hey boss, we will give you a hand."

"No, you have had a hard day and you knocked off work for dinner," Jack said.

"If you can work after dinner, so can we." With that, they started rolling wool bales to the truck.

The boss informed them he was not allowed to pay overtime, but they insisted, "If you have to do it, it's all right by us to help. Money is not a problem."

Jack was thankful as he had to get up at 4am to cook breakfast for 5.30 and an early start mustering the next morning.

They worked for six weeks or so and, on one particular Friday, said, "Boss, we want to finish up, can we have our pay cheque?"

They were paid monthly, the basic wage with holiday pay, including full board and keep. Paying them off, Jack's only hope was that they would come back after their walkabout and binge.

The mailman came once a week, arriving at Ardglen at about 10pm. Not only did he bring mail but bread, fuel, fencing gear, wool packs and anything that was ordered from town. Sometimes, inebriated workers would get a lift back to their stations to resume work and they would be lying amongst the merchandise on the tray of the truck.

"Any of these yours?" asked the mailman, pointing to four or five bodies lying there.

"Yes, these two are mine. Barry, and George."

The mailman would roll them off the truck with the drums of fuel and other goods and there the items would stay till morning, except the bread and food perishables.

Today, if a video was taken, people would be horrified at the images of the two Aboriginals rolled off the truck and left on the ground for the night. That was the way it was then. It suited everyone. The mailman was happy to give workers a lift to their employment for free. The managers were pleased to get their workers back and the cold night helped George and Barry sober up. Enough so they could stand and wobble back to their quarters, to be seen the following day for breakfast or dinner when fully recovered from their hangovers. Then back to work until the urge came to go walkabout again.

They always gave the boss a week's notice before taking off again, before getting a mate or mailman to give them a lift back to town.

One day, the boss took George to town in the forward controlled Bedford truck. On their way, a stone flew up and broke the huge windscreen, which shattered all over them. Jack looked at George. He was a pasty grey colour. Jack said, "Gee you look white."

George replied, "Not as white as you are."

At a previous station, they had a black sheep in a mob of 1500 ewes. Jack's old boss said to Bill, the Aboriginal stockman, "What have you been up to, Bill?" pointing to the black sheep.

Bill waved his arm over all the 15,000 white ewes and said, "Not as much as you, boss."

George and Barry loved the missus, especially her cooking, and she loved their stories and humour. When Jack and Helen eventually left Ardglen, they met them in town and the tears flowed as they hugged Helen and begged her not to leave.

C.5

Dramas, Accidents, Hospital

On a sheep station, shearing is the busiest time. There are sheep to muster, draft, spray, brand and take back to their paddocks. Then there was the organisation of supplies, equipment, food for the shearers, shed hands, experts, tar boys, wool classers and skirters. It was like running a full production industrial factory for a month in a year.

The boss was busy in the shed weighing and documenting the stud sheep clip, when Helen came rushing into the shed. In those days, for a woman to come into a shearing shed, without permission from the shearers, was a "no-no". She was holding a towel over her hand and explained, "I have cut my thumb"!

"Okay love, give us a look at it and I will bandage it," said Jack.

"No, you don't understand. I have cut the tendon in my thumb."

"Oh dear, it looks like I better run you into town to the doctor when shearing is finished for the day."

"No, I must go now or I will lose the use of my thumb."

"What? Now? In the middle of shearing?"

"Yes now, it will be an hour before we get to the doctor in Cunnamulla and then it still could be too late."

Jack did not realise the seriousness of the situation but, as Helen seemed very worried, they left straight away after telling the wool classer he could also do Jack's job, which he agreed to do.

At the doctor's an hour later, he asked Helen how she did it. She replied, "I was slicing the meat off the bone when the knife slipped and cut my thumb."

"No worries, my dear. I have done hundreds of these," he said, as he worked on her tendon and stitched the thumb up. Then he requested the nurse to plaster her hand, which was to stay on for three weeks.

Back home, while finishing the shearing, Helen still managed to cook for the boss and the station men, with the left-hand out of action. Three weeks later, back to Cunnamulla to the surgery, where the doctor cut off the plaster and asked Helen to move her thumb. There was the tiniest of movements, more a twitch than anything else.

"Move your thumb again." Yes, a slow twitch of movement. The doctor sat back in his chair with an incredulous look. He yelled, "Nurse, nurse, come here quickly." A nurse rushed in, expecting some disaster. "Watch this. Move your thumb again, Helen." Helen did. "You see that, nurse? It works. The thumb works. I have done hundreds of them and this is the first one that works!"

If Jack had known this, he would have driven a couple of extra hours to Charleville. Helen had full use of her thumb but it took time to heal.

Helen always left early, driving the HR Holden car 200 kilometres, over rough dirt sandy roads to Charleville and her doctor, for her pregnancy check-ups, then back again to cook the men's dinner.

On this dreadful day, after her doctor's visit, she didn't look right at morning smoko.

"Are you feeling alright, love?" Jack asked.

"Yes, dear. I think so but I have a bit of pain in my belly. As a matter of fact, I think I will lie down," Helen replied.

Just before lunch, she was crying and rolling around, holding her five and half months' pregnant belly in great pain. Jack called her doctor, Dr Dorothy Herbert. She sounded cross.

"I told that girl to leave immediately and fly to Melbourne to see her surgeon for an urgent abdominal operation."

Helen had not mentioned anything to Jack about having to go to Melbourne for an urgent operation.

The young doctor said, "I am flying down immediately in my little Cessna 172 aeroplane to pick Helen up. She needs emergency treatment. Is there a nearby airstrip and where can I find it?"

Jack informed her, they had a good serviceable airstrip at the station, as the owner flew in and out for visits. The property was 75 kilometres from Cunnamulla and 105km from Bollon on the Cunnamulla-Bollon Road. Ardglen station was 10 kms north off that road.

"We will put the Bedford truck at the entrance, with a red cloth attached to the top of the crate to indicate where we are," he said.

Jack found some red material from Helen's sewing drawer, gave it to one of the men and told him to take the truck immediately to our entrance on the main road and tie the red material on top of the crate so it was visible from the air.

"It needs to be so a plane can see it. It will be urgently taking the missus to hospital."

Jack then got the other two men to follow him and Helen to the airstrip in the ute. Bundling Helen in the car and gathering a few of her things for hospital, they took off for the air strip. Poor Helen was as white as a sheet, sweating and moaning in great pain.

Twenty minutes later, they could hear a light plane in the distance, searching for them. It was getting late in the afternoon and Helen needed urgent medical care.

"You blokes get that tin of fuel out of the ute and splash some on that big old pile of wood that's at the end of the strip. Then being very careful light it, we must attract the plane, showing it where to land," said Jack.

The fire was lit; smoke started to rise; they heard the change of the aircraft engine as it came nearer to them. They saw it and waved frantically. It saw them; it was descending; it was landing. The doctor was here. The first thankyou to God.

The first thing Dr Herbert did was give Helen a morphine injection, then they all helped the patient into the back seat of the little plane, with Jack in the front. They taxied to their take off position, did the checks, the throttle opened and the little plane climbed into the sky.

Helen started to vomit into the bag, due to the morphine injection. She was still writhing in pain on the tiny back seat of the Cessna. But Jack's attention was drawn to the windscreen. Because it was getting dark, there were no landmarks, just mulga and more mulga, for hundreds of miles. The plane had no instruments for night flying. They all could be in serious trouble, with a very sick patient, a very stressed and worried husband and a pilot very concerned she might not find the airfield in Charleville.

"Jack, could you please scan the sky from left to right and see if you can see a red light or beacon, which is on the top of the water tower in town?" said Dr Herbert.

Jack scanned until his eyes watered. He thought of nothing else except a red light. *Will we see it? Will we miss it?*

"I see it, I see it," Jack yelled excitedly, "It's about 11 o'clock on the left of us."

"Yes, I can see it now," said the doc.

There was a feeling of relief from the two in the front of that plane but not from the poor girl in the back, who was still moaning with excruciating pain in her belly.

They landed safely. The second thankyou to God. The aircraft taxied to an ambulance that was standing by. Two ambulance officers helped the ailing Helen out of the little plane and put her on a stretcher. The doc said, "I will put the aircraft away and I will see you at the hospital."

Jack got in the front of the ambulance, holding Helen's full sick bag. They went at a fair speed, arriving at the Charleville hospital soon after. Two hospital staff were waiting at the entrance as the ambulance pulled up. The two officers got out, swung the back doors open and poor Helen, on the stretcher, was raced inside with Jack following close behind, forgetting the full bag of puke left in the ambulance. One of the staff pointed to a waiting room and suggested Jack made himself comfortable there, as they continued to the operating theatre.

It was some time of anxious waiting till Dr Herbert and Dr Ariotti came to see the very worried Jack. He stood up to greet them. They were discussing Helen's condition in medical jargon which Jack could not understand. After about five minutes, Jack could take it no longer, "For God's sake, don't stand there talking, just operate on my wife now."

Dr Herbert answered, "That's what we were explaining and waiting for you to give us the go ahead to operate." Off they went to save a beautiful lady.

Was it three hours or four? Maybe it was four. Nurses scurrying up and down the passageways urgently. What is happening? Is Helen all right? Will she survive?

Being left alone with no other people to talk to, no tea, coffee or biscuits, Jack's mind was not in a good place. He remembered when he was in Cunnamulla Hospital years ago with a badly infected right hand which had nearly been amputated. During that visit the nurses had been racing hither and thither. Jack found out later, a woman had died on the operating table. Was Helen dying because of the activity of the nurses? Jack's hand had been saved as the emergency of the woman dying had meant the flying surgeon had no time left to do the operation on his hand. Thankfully, the infection was treated with penicillin and other drugs and Jack's hand healed nicely.

Still waiting. A numb bum from sitting for a long period, walking and pacing up and down, very concerned about his and Helen's future and, my God, the baby. He forgot about the coming baby. Would it survive the anaesthetic and the long operation? His world could crumble. What was happening? He needed to know. Could someone tell him? Where was everyone? He felt like he could be on a deserted island. Jack felt very frightened and his mind was full of terrible thoughts. How long had he been waiting? Two, three or more hours?

After enduring a long stressful wait, Dr Herbert walked down the passageway in her scrubs. Jack stood up and was about to run to her but managed to contain himself.

"It all went well; it was a very big operation but Helen will be fine. The nurse has booked a room at the motel and has ordered a taxi for you."

"Will Helen have complications? What about the baby and what will the end result show?" Jack asked.

"I can answer all your questions in the morning. For now, Helen is comfortable and the operation was successful, so the best thing you can do is have a good night's rest. You have had a big day and I will see you in the morning," a very reassuring Doctor Herbert said.

For the third time, Jack thanked God as he laid on his bed. The drama, Helen in terrible pain, organising the men, Dr Herbert, the plane trip, the hospital, the waiting, the stress of it all. No wonder he fell into an exhaustive sleep.

The next morning, Jack woke up to a knock on the door.
"Breakfast."

Don't remember ordering any breakfast, Jack thought, as he got up and answered the door.

"I did not order any breakfast," he said to the motel owner.

"Doctor Herbert ordered the breakfast for you. She said you would need it."

Jack thanked her as he took the laden tray and mentally thanked the good doctor for her kind thought.

Breakfast was just what he needed: cereal, eggs and bacon, tomatoes, sausages, baked beans, toast and tea. He did not realise how hungry he was as he had not had lunch or dinner the day before.

After a full tummy, a beautiful shower and dressing in yesterday clothes, without the underpants, Jack's thinking was to buy some more clothes and some toiletries as he wasn't sure how long his stay would be.

Then the shock. No money! Jack had forgotten his wallet. Perhaps he could plead and bargain with the bank, if they could advance him some money from another branch to his. He had been so worried about Helen that he had forgotten his wallet, change of clothes and necessary toiletries.

Being very anxious at how Helen was this morning, he quickly walked the few kilometres to the hospital. Jack, still madly in love with his wife of two years, just had to be by her side.

It was great to see her propped up in bed, smiling as Jack walked into her room. He kissed her, wanting also to give her a big hug.

"Be careful, Darling. I am so sore, even with the drugs they have given me. Look," she said, "they have cut me again," as she revealed the large scar from chest to pelvis. The new fresh scar, with its stitches, followed the old scar.

"They told me, as the baby was growing, it had caused my remaining bit of bowel to be caught which caused the excruciating pain. The operation released that bit of bowel so the baby could grow."

"How are you feeling? Have you any pain at all?" Jack asked.

"No, but I am very tired and sore." Helen said.

Just then, Dr Herbert walked in, followed by her two corgi dogs, which went with her everywhere. The hospital did not seem to mind and all the patients loved it.

"How are you feeling this morning, Helen? And how is the pain?"

Helen told her the same as she had told Jack. Dr Herbert said the operation had gone well but, at some time in the future, Helen would need a proctectomy. But for now, everything was fine and, being young and fit, Helen should be out of the hospital in a week or so.

"We will see how you progress in the next day or two," said the doctor.

"Dr Herbert, will the baby be all right after such a long and serious operation?" Jack asked. "And, by the way, thanks so much for the breakfast this morning. It filled a very vacant place."

"That's fine, Jack. I thought, after your hectic day yesterday, you would need it. And yes, the baby should be fine. We even saw some of the foetus during the operation. Helen, you will still need to keep up your monthly checks. Now, is there anything else I can do for you? If not, I will drop in this evening to see you."

"No thanks, doctor, the nurses are looking after me and I am sure they will give me pain relief when I need it," said Helen.

"All right, I will see you later on and, Jack, you look after yourself."

"I will. Did you know Helen has a corgi? Her name is Cammie," Jack said.

"They are lovely dogs," said the doc, "and I am glad you

made the right choice." A lovely smile and the good doctor, Dorothy Herbert, left.

Fancy a very experience GP/surgeon, Dr Ariotti, and a young GP, Dr Dorothy Herbert, managed a complicated operation with limited equipment in a small country hospital. If Helen's operation had been in a major city hospital, it would have had specialists, colectomy surgeons, assistant surgeons, an anaesthetist, theatre staff and the latest equipment for such a large operation. Meanwhile, in Charleville, the limited staff performed a successful abdominal operation. Jack thanked God for the fourth time.

"Darling, would you please pass me some water?" said Helen, "I'm very dry in the mouth and I think I will have a sleep now, as I feel a bit worn out."

"Okay love, I will leave you in good hands and will call in later. I better get you some toiletries. Is there anything else I can get you?" said Jack.

"You work it out darling, I'm too tired to think."

First thing Jack had to do was visit the Commonwealth Bank to get some much-needed money. He had no wallet, licence or any type of identification and his money was at the branch in Cunnamulla. A phone call to the branch manager, a discussion on the dire situation his customer was in, the manager was requested to approve an urgent payment to him through the Charleville bank. Under the circumstances, it was agreed and Jack left half an hour later with enough cash to buy some clothes, toiletries for both of them, payment to the motel, lunch and some flowers for Helen.

Without a car, a lot of walking ensued with the parcels but, managed he did. Helen improved rapidly and, after a week, it was agreed she could go home but she was not to travel on 200 kilometres of rough dirt roads. If so, she would have to stay for another week.

Jack used his resources as he had heard of a Mr Schmitt at Wyandra who had just bought a light aircraft. Jack asked him if he would be so kind as to fly Jack and his recovering wife from Charleville back to Ardglen station. He readily agreed as he was keen to use his new toy any chance he could. So, it was arranged for the next day.

The hospital and Dr Herbert allowed Helen to be discharged as she would be flying home. Then all Jack had to do was find a casual cook to give his missus time to recover back at the station.

The benefit of living in the country is, everyone knows someone and, once an enquiry is made, results usually happen. And so, it was. The cook at Boatman Station had a daughter who was looking for a casual job and they were both in town at that time. No time for an interview. A phone call was made where Jack asked if she was available to do some cooking at Ardglen station. Yes, she was, so she was to meet at the Paragon café at 12.30 the next day, ready to fly out to the station for a fortnight's work, cooking for the men. She was very excited and said she would meet at the café at that time.

The next day was an exciting day. Jack picked up a renewed Helen from the hospital, still wearing the clothes when she had arrived, except for the new underwear that had been bought. A very gracious thank you to Drs Ariotti and Herbert and to the great nursing staff. Then they took a taxi to the café as Helen was still stiff and sore from the stitches and operation to her tummy.

They had a bit of lunch at the café, waiting to meet their new employee and to be ready at the arranged time of 1pm at the airstrip for Mr Schmitt and his new aircraft to fly them home. Helen nodded towards a few booths behind them.

"Don't look around but I think that's our new cook with her mother."

"How do you know that?" Jack asked.

"Because it's the only mother and daughter here."

Jack, desperate to look around, tried to sneak a look.

"Don't look around I said."

"And why not?"

"Because I could be wrong and if I'm not, we are in trouble."

"And why would that be?"

"Because she, the daughter, is hogging into a large sundae with the works and washing it down with a chocolate milkshake."

That was too much for Jack. He turned around and groaned, saying "I think your right."

At that, he got up and walked up to the two, saying to the young girl, "I'm Jack Alexander. Are you Shirley, the one coming to help us at Ardglen?"

She acknowledged that she was, with chocolate sauce at the corners of her mouth. Her mother said, "I'm glad it was you; I wasn't sure who she was going to work for but I know you will look after her."

They both knew each other as Jack was an overseer at a property near where she worked as a cook and they had met a few times on different occasions. A small discussion took place: the weather, the Nebine open community centre and do you know such and such. Jack mentioned that they would be catching a taxi soon to the airstrip and would Shirley be ready in ten minutes for the trip there?

And so, it was. Mr Schmitt, with a big smile, was waiting for them beside his new Cessna 182 aircraft. Strapping themselves in, Jack in the front with the pilot and the two girls on the back seats. The pilot did his checks, made sure they were properly belted in correctly and taxied to the holding point. Before taking off, a few more safety checks, a talk on the radio and brakes off, picking up speed for take-off.

Then it happened. In a brand-new aircraft belonging to someone doing them a favour, Shirly spewed all her stomach contents of her breakfast, sundae and chocolate milkshake all over the new smart leather upholstery of the aircraft.

There was the stink of the vile vomit while the other two passengers and the pilot concentrated on their bodily functions, so they would not add to the colourful, smelly sick.

The flight took a mere half an hour to reach Ardglen. We circled the homestead to let someone know to come and pick us up in a car. Safely landing on the station strip, we all quickly removed ourselves from the plane, waiting for a lift back to the homestead. Jack kept apologising to the pilot about the spew in his new plane and would try and clean it up when the car arrived. Mr Schmitt was very gracious about it all, saying it was going to happen sometime and that it now reminded him to purchase some sick bags for the aircraft.

When the vehicle arrived, they got some water and rags to get some of the vomit cleaned up, so the pilot would not have a smelly trip back to Wyandra. Did the perpetrator help? No way, she was busy checking her handbag for a tissue or something. Jack offered to pay for the trip and cleaning charges but Mr Schmitt would not accept any payment. He said he was just glad to help after he had heard about the whole emergency we had both been through.

Jack was now back as the boss and Helen as the missus. Now safely back into their own bed, they were very tired after her first day out of hospital. Herb and his wife were still there, as well as young Greg from Eulo and Simon. The boss thanked the three men for their help in the emergency trip and for looking after the station while they were away.

"The missus and I really appreciate your cooperation and all that you have done. Now what has happened while we were away?" asked Jack.

Herb stated the fire had burnt itself out and, seeing the boss was not about, the boys went to town for a few days while he looked after the place.

Then Simon piped up, "We thought you might be back, so we did the chores, chopped wood, filled the wood box up."

Herb said, "I have milked the cow and I killed last night, so we would have some meat."

Thanking them again and seeing the day was nearly done, the boss told them to knock off and indicated work would start in the morning.

Back in the homestead, the boss checked up on Helen, then checked on Shirley to see what she was up to. She was lying down on the bed in the cook's bedroom with the door opened.

"Excuse me, Shirley, what are you going to cook this evening for the men and us? The stove has to be lit as it takes an hour or so to heat up."

She replied, "A Sao biscuit will do me."

"Well, so it might but you are employed to cook and there are four people to cook for, excluding yourself, so what are you going to do?"

"I feel sick and I don't cook much, anyway."

"Right young lady, up you get. I will get the stove alight and going, then you are going to peel five potatoes and onions, shell peas, peel the carrots and pumpkin ready for me to cook. I will put the vegetables on the sink and I want this done by four."

The boss was feeling very disappointed and angry, as he started to get the stove alight, thinking she took the job as a cook and now the girl said she doesn't cook. The boss got the vegetables, putting them on the sink as well as the shoulder of mutton, hoping the girl actually got the work done that was asked of her.

A quick check on Helen.

"You don't need to worry, darling. I am fine you just do what you have to do," she said.

"Okay dear, as long as you're resting and feeling all right."

Leaving the missus, the boss went outside. After he checked

the green monster was well alight, he then checked the vehicles and that all was good to start work in the morning.

Jack was back at 3.30pm to stoke up the stove and there was the missus peeling spuds. The boss was furious.

"What are you doing? You're supposed to be resting," he said.

"I just can't lie in bed and do nothing and the men have to be fed."

"We have employed someone to cook and, my God, she is going to cook."

At that, a very sheepish Shirley approached around the corner. How long she had been there and what she had heard was of no concern to the boss.

"Helen, Shirley is now here to start preparing dinner for the men and she has to learn because she will be cooking for the next fortnight to earn her wages. This is what she was employed for, right Shirley?"

"Now that I have started, Shirley can help me do the preparation, so she knows what to do," said Helen. "And dear, I imagine you have plenty of work to do, seeing we have been away for a week and I can manage, with Shirley's help, so off you go and leave me and Shirley to do the night's dinner."

The boss left the kitchen to let the women get on with their work.

All was going well. The missus recovered quickly from her operation, her garden was blooming and so was she. For example, the boss, the missus and Griffo went to a Santa Gertrudis cattle sale in Charleville. It was a big sale as the Santa cattle were really making their mark in Queensland. As a matter of fact, with Griffo's permission, Jack was starting a commercial Santa Gertrudis stud at Ardglen.

Now, as it were, the missus and the boss were walking back across the sale ring to their seats. A hush fell over the crowd as they all stared at the missus. She looked outstanding, very pregnant and with a glow that radiated around the sale ring. She was at the peak of womanhood and the boss was the proudest husband ever to be walking beside her.

Even though the missus was doing extremely well after the operation and carrying the baby was a joy to her, the boss was worried and mentioned his concern to her.

"Look darling, I'm a bit worried about the coming birth. You have had a huge operation and been under anaesthetic for four hours. This could have affected the health of the baby and we could end up with a child with physical or mental damage."

"Well, whatever will be will be," she said. "We can't do anything about it, so it's not worth worrying about."

But the boss, a born worrier, was not satisfied with the missus' answer and continued to be apprehensive about what was in store for them on the baby's arrival.

The boss was busy running the station during the day but at night he was painting the baby's room, a pastel blue and singing the Paint Your Wagon song, *I was born under a wandering star*. He was also busy acquiring cots, prams, bouncinettes etc, while the missus was busy cooking for the men and gardening, as well as doing a lot of sewing and crocheting.

It was time. Country women had to go to a town three weeks before the due date of a birth. In this case, the missus went to Charleville to a private house that took in women about to give birth. The boss strongly advised Dr Herbert, that he wanted to be at the birth. Seeing as he was there when it went in, he was jolly well going to see it come out. This was not conventional in 1970, for a husband to be at his wife's side as she gave birth. But that is what the boss was going to do by hell or high water.

The phone rang.

"This is Dr Herbert. Helen is starting labour and if you want to be here, you better get moving." And moving the boss did. He already had contingency plans in place and Griffo was coming to hold the fort.

There was 200km of rough, sandy, dirt road to negotiate, to get to Charleville in time. You betcha he would make it. Though, trying not to speed, his feet seemed to have a fair bit of weight on the accelerator pedal at times. He prayed he wouldn't hit a 'roo or pig, let alone a wandering cow, as it was the worst time to drive, just as the sun was going down.

Did he make it? Of course he did. As it happened, poor Helen was in labour for 32 hours. Jack helped Helen with the relaxing and breathing but ended up falling asleep and carted himself away to a spare bed, warning that he must be woken up for the birth. And so it was, in his jeans, shirt, leather vest and riding boots, Jack watched as the miracle of birth took place, as a wet and red baby boy was pushed out. What a joy. Helen was smiling as she held her newborn son, while Jack kissed her, saying he loved her and what a clever girl she was.

But what was this? Oh no, he knew it would happen. The baby had, what Jack thought was, a huge tumour on the left side of his head. Devastation. Did Helen know? Jack dragged his feet out of the hospital, a tired and worried man, and slowly drove to the motel that had been booked previously.

What was he going to do? How was he going to console his beloved wife? What was the future going to hold for this young family? Why was he upset? He had envisioned that a problem could occur with his new son. He was not in a hurry to go to the hospital the next morning. The crying, the consoling over the devastation of having an abnormal baby. The confrontation of it all made Jack reluctant to even turn up to see his wife and baby but he did as he knew Helen would need his love and comfort.

"Excuse me, where is the Matron?" asked Jack, then when he saw her asked, "Oh, Matron how is Helen?"

"She is fine."

"Yeah, well, what about the baby?"

"It's just a lovely 7lb 13oz baby boy."

"Now, look here, you can tell me the truth, I can take it. I'm from the bush, now really, how is Helen and the baby?"

"For goodness's sake," said Matron. "Go into her room, she is feeding the baby now and they are both healthy and fine."

Jack walked into the room and beheld a beautiful, contented mother feeding a very healthy baby boy. Relief washed over him as he kissed his wife and beamed at his handsome son.

"Darling, what happened to the large tumour at the side of his head?"

"That's just a scalp hematoma. It happens when a baby is too long in the pelvic area but it disappears a quarter hour after birth. It's quite normal, didn't I tell you this sometimes happens?"

"No love, I thought it was a tumour and that we had a disabled child."

"Sorry, darling but all is well. Are we still going to call him Damon?"

"Yes, my sweet. It will be Damon John Alexander, a healthy baby boy."

They kissed and hugged and, within a week, were back to work at Ardglen, with their special gift.

What joy but Cammie didn't think so. *What's this bundle my mistress is spending so much time with? And the noise it makes. What is happening to my family?*

Yes, the poor dog, who had always had the missus' attention, now felt second fiddle, even though the missus spent times making a fuss over the dog. It took time for Cammie to adjust, like all of the family, but she always guarded the baby as she knew it was special to her mistress, even though she always ignored the baby itself.

A new boss in the family and everyone had to toe the line

to his demands: the feeds, nappy changes, the be quiets, and play times. It was all a new ball game. Hungry, he was always hungry. Not only did the missus breast feed him, he also had to have a bottle or two a day, as well. Night became a worry. He would exercise his lungs, even though he had all his feeds, clean nappies, no pins or bites, lots of cuddles and walking in the pram. They did everything good parents would do for their pride and joy.

The boss had a brilliant idea. It was very cold in Cunnamulla that May and it was hard to get out of a warm bed in the middle of the night.

The boss said to his wife, "Stay in bed dear. I'll do the midnight feed," and so he did but with a slight difference. There was some Farex cereal in the cupboard used to feed orphan joey 'roos. The boss crushed up some grains into tiny pieces, mixing it with warm baby's milk. He placed a bit on the tip of a teaspoon and fed it to the hungry baby. From then on, it was a midnight feast for baby Damon and no more crying, which meant his parents got a good night sleep.

But, alas, a week or so later, he was caught by his midwife wife.

"What in the blazes are you doing? You cannot feed a three-week-old baby with solids."

"Darling, my sweet, I have been doing this for well over a week and it has not had any effect on him or us. We have enjoyed good night sleeps. He was just a hungry boy."

What's it like living out west? As an example, Helen wrote a letter to the mother-craft nurse in Charleville with some problem she was concerned about with her baby. Whatever the problem was, it was solved weeks before she got an answering letter with the solution.

C.6

Incidents, Fights and Exit

The boss and the missus were enjoying their life at Ardglen but nothing was perfect and so there were, what you would call, a couple of hiccups during their time there.

First, there was Mr Sydney Tweet, the manager of the property next door. For some reason he had immense dislike of Jack. He would ring him up about every third night on the private line between the two stations and abuse him: swearing, going to kill him and all manner of objectional threats. Jack would never say anything until Sid had exhausted himself, then he would simply say, "Have a good night, Sid," and hang up.

Once, he saw Jack and Helen in town, driving down the main street. He drove his car across the road and stopped just before crashing into them and the abuse started. Jack could or should have gone to the police about it but he ignored his behaviour completely.

Jack could not understand Sid's behaviour. Maybe he didn't like a young chap taking over the management of Ardglen from his mate, which had nothing to do with Jack or was he an alcoholic or had mental problems. There was nothing Jack did consciously or unconsciously that incited such behaviours.

Then the situation started to get serious. Now, the bore drain ran through Ardglen's top block then through Sid's block and then into Ardglen's lower portion of the property. The sheep from those two properties were completely dependent on that water.

Checking the waters regularly, Jack noticed a somewhat restricted flow coming down the bore drain. A few days later, he checked again and noticed the drain was dry. He drove up to the top block and there was plenty of water there, so why wasn't any water getting into the lower block? A walk into Sid's property, for about a kilometre up a dry drain, showed why.

In a pipe, placed in a paddock roadway crossing, was a man-made block to stop the water going through. The bore drain, before the block, was flooding the paddock for some distance with so much water backed up,

Jack rang Sid up that night and said, "Sid, I am not getting any water in my lower paddocks. There must be a break or block somewhere, so could you please delve your part of the drain, which is your responsibility so I can get some water?"

"You go to hell," was the response. "You have no right to tell me what to do."

"Well, actually Sid, it's our bore and I can ask you to help keep the drain running. So, if you're not willing to delve or clean your part of the drain, then we are going to delve and clean out the drain from the bore, right through your place in the morning, so we are able to get the water into our block."

"Well, good on ya, Jack."

"And Sid, we will charge you for our time: tractor hire, shovel handles broken and anything that costs Ardglen money."

"You little %$#@&**," and he hung up.

The next day, miraculously, the bore drains were running as they were meant to be.

Jack and two employees had a big day lamb marking in the

top block, starting at 6am and finishing at five. To get through to the Ardglen's lower block and the homestead, they had to pass through Sid's place, an understanding between the two property owners that Ardglen and their staff had the right of passage.

On this momentous day, as Jack and his crew were on the way home, they were blocked by a flimsy barricade, with Sid, his son, his overseer and employee, standing at the obstruction.

"I wonder what's this all about," Jack said to his men as they stopped the truck and got out and walked towards the barricade. Jack said, in his normal tired voice, when it came to dealing with Sid, "What's the trouble, Sid?"

Then, without warning, a barrage of punches rained down on Jack, started by the four men. Jack did his best to defend himself but, in the fray, he noticed his two employees sitting in the truck watching the unprovoked fight. Jack thought, *I can't fight the four of them on his own*, so he made his way back to the truck with punches still flying.

Jack drove the truck through the flimsy barricade, while noticing Sid holding a very squashed bloody nose that gave Jack some satisfaction. He asked his two men why they didn't help their boss. They replied, they were not employed to fight and were not staying on a place where a range war was taking place and gave a week's notice.

Two weeks later, Griffo flew up in his little Cessna and wanted to know about the fight. Jack was surprised as he had told no one about it. Eventually, Sid's overseer felt guilty about it all and left his employment. But first, he told Harold, another neighbour, about it all, who then informed Griffo about the few headaches Sid was causing his manager.

Griffo said, after Jack told his story, "You should have told me you were having trouble with Sid; I need you to manage this place without you copping these types of incidents. Anyhow, you won't have to worry about Sid anymore as he has been dismissed and a new manager, Mr Cliff Herring, is taking his place."

Jack was excited, not that Sid had left, but Cliff was an old mate of his and they got along well together.

Poachers started to cause concerns and were becoming a problem. They left gates open that should be shut. They would mistakenly shoot stock instead of feral pests and kangaroos and no one wanted someone sneaking around their house at night. So, the poachers had to be stopped.

Cliff was now Jack's next-door neighbour. He was an ex-World War Two veteran, injured in New Guinea, could talk a leg off a cow and a no-nonsense man. He had shot a spotlight out with a .303 on some poachers' moving vehicle.

The plan was hatched. All gates out of the two properties were locked with thick chains and padlocks. Only one entrance was unlocked. This meant that anyone would have to pass the Ardglen's homestead to enter into Cliff's property and the only way out was back the same way.

It was at 1am on New Years Day when Jack heard a car slowly driving around. Then a shot, a non-revving engine started to cruise around, another shot. Jack jumped out of bed, dressed quickly and grabbed his new licenced Smith and Western .22 revolver. When he heard the poacher's car rev up and drive at pace through the open gate into Cliff's place, Jack got on to the inter station phone and said, "Cliff, the poachers are in your place near our boundary."

A sleepy Cliff, still in his pyjamas, said, "I'll just get me hat, boots and spurs on and I'll be on me way".

Jack was ready. He hid behind the office building, revolver at the ready. Then he heard, in the still midnight air, the poachers say, "Quick, there is someone coming."

He could hear Cliff's ute on its way. The poachers flew

through the boundary gate into Jack's property, where Jack stood out from his hiding place, straight into the path of the poacher's car, with revolver pointed at the centre of their wind screen.

They screeched to a stop. Jack, still pointing the revolver at them, asked their names and what they were doing trespassing on the property. There were two men and a woman in the front and three in the back, all from the Aboriginal camp in Cunnamulla.

Jack made them unload the five dead roos, saying they didn't belong to them. The woman screeched that they were to feed the chooks. Jack had never heard of chooks eating 'roo meat. He wondered how the eggs would turn out. Ignoring the comment, Jack said, "I hear a car coming. I suppose it's some of your mates?"

"No, it's no mates of ours. I'm turning the lights and engine off," said the driver.

Cliff pulled up in a swirl of red dust behind the poacher's ute. Yes, he still had his striped pyjamas on but he also had his sweat-stained Akubra stockman's hat, as well as his RM Williams riding boots with attached Willoughby spurs.

Cliff gave them a good talking to, threatening them with what would happen if he ever caught them on his place again. Then turning to Jack, he said, "They're on your place now, deal with them."

Jack said, still pointing the revolver, "Right you mob, we'll give you ten minutes to get off the property or I'll come after you shooting."

Well, did they take off? It's a wonder the three in the back didn't fall out with the acceleration of the vehicle.

Cliff said, "Jack, let off a few shots." Which Jack did, emptying six shots into the air.

As Cliff and Jack walked around the office building, they

were surprised to see Helen in her nightie, holding a shot gun, crouched down behind the garden fence in amongst her marigolds. Noticing the surprised looks on her Jack and Cliff's faces, she explained, "Darling, I was worried about you facing all those men with high-powered rifles and I wanted to protect you."

Jack jumped over the fence, gave Helen a big hug and kiss and said, "Darling, you better go and get a dressing gown on before Cliff sees everything you have."

The three of them had a cup of tea, talked about the night's events and wished a Happy New Year to each other.

A footnote: not long after the event, the telephone party line went out. A distant neighbour rang Jack and said he could not ring town. He had checked his line and could find nothing wrong with it. His neighbour closest to town could ring but he couldn't. He knew the trouble was between his and his neighbour's place. Could Jack bring his field phone and help find the problem?

Ardglen station was responsible for the party line between Bendena and Cunnamulla, a line of some 180km long. Jack did not know why Ardglen was responsible for the whole line, but it was.

With field phones, Jack and his neighbour worked their way, clipping the field phones on till they came to a dead spot. At first glance, they couldn't see anything wrong with the line till the neighbour said, "Have a look at this Jack."

Looking very closely, Jack could see a piece of copper wire, tied to the telephone line next to the insulator. It ran down inside a crack into the post and then into a small glass of water sunk into the ground. That was more than enough to make the line not operational. After removing the problem, Jack wondered who would do such a horrible thing, as it would deny at least 15 families from contacting emergency services or even town.

Out in the isolated bush, it was a severe criminal offence. Jack wondered if it was payback from the poachers.

The police turned up one night. Knocking loudly on the door at 2am in the morning, they woke, not only Helen and Jack, but the baby as well. Bang, bang.

"Police here."

Jack got up to see what the police would want at this hour. He opened the door and saw a constable, immaculately dressed, standing there with a clipboard.

"What do you want at this hour?" Jack asked.

"I have come to check if you are on the electoral roll."

"What!? You have woken my whole family up, at two in the morning, to see if we are on the roll? Give us a look what you have there," said Jack as he took the clipboard from the policeman.

Reading it, he exclaimed to the man in uniform, "This is not the area you should be in. This roll is for west of Cunnamulla, not here. You have caught the wrong mail truck," said an angry Jack, who then turned his back and went to bed to let the copper rectify his mistake.

It was found out, much later, that the police sergeant was so fed up with this particular officer, he sent him on the western mail truck to see if people were on the roll, just to get rid of him. Helen had heard he used to go to the hospital to charm the nurses and, while he was doing so, another nurse would run out and take the rotor button out of the police car to disable it. Of course, it ended up very late in the evening when he had to ring the sarge to fix the police car. The rotor button was found just beside the distributor cover. There were many stories about this particular copper, whether all true or not, but he was fondly remembered as 006.

There were a few problems with companies and investors that had not much experience of the land and would ask their managers to do unrealistic activities, such as, "We are sending two semi-truck loads of hay. We want you to distribute it to the drought-stricken sheep immediately."

And here would be their manager throwing good hay on to excellent feed to fat sheep. There was no drought or starving sheep in the district. The company must have read of a bad drought but did not bother to find where it was.

One company told the manager when to shear, when to join the rams and when lambing was to be. Therefore, the sheep would be lambing on the board while they were shorn. This was a terrible thing to happen.

The manager sent an urgent telegram to the company saying, "Permission to withhold shearing to carry out lambing."

The reply came back, "Withhold lambing, carry on shearing."

The manager felt like answering that telegram by suggesting the company send three thousand champagne corks.

One of the problems Jack had with Griffo was the order, "We don't drench sheep. It's just pouring money down their throat."

Hence, the two thousand sheep he wanted Jack to sell, were unsalable, as the buyers would not touch wormy animals. It all came to a head, when Sid rang up, (before he was dismissed) with glee in his voice, "All your sheep are dead in the paddock next to our place."

Jack raced up to the paddock and saw groups of dead weaner sheep huddled together in small, groups under various trees. Jack's first thought was, Sid, his problem neighbour, might have somehow poisoned them. Jack took samples of liver, kidneys, stomach and heart from several of the sheep, raced home and put the samples in plastic bags in the kero fridge.

Then, he rang the DPI (Department of Primary Industries,) to see if they could come out as soon as possible, after explaining what had happened. They came out that morning, looked at the dead young sheep and said, "Jack, it's not your fault. What it looks to us, is that you recently had shorn these weaners, then we had an unusual cold snap of weather and, being poor and wormy, they just died of hyperthermia."

Jack said, "I knew they were wormy but the company policy was not to drench."

"We know that. It's well known that Ardglen has wormy sheep."

"Well, could you do us a favour and write a detailed report on what you have seen? That the sheep died because they hadn't been drenched, then in explicit detail about different drenches, their different costs and the improvement to the health of the animal and better wool clip and send the report to me," asked Jack.

After a big fire to get rid of the dead sheep and a clean-up, the report came to Griffo from the DPI. It was a beauty. Six foolscap pages and brochures of drenches. It was just what Jack had ordered. He and Helen happened to go down to Griffo's place in Toowoomba the following week, with some old horses in the station truck. It was good for Helen to see a city again and make purchases of fabric and all sorts of haberdashery. Jack thought the truck would be fully loaded going back to the station.

Jack handed all the monthly papers to his boss, along with the DPI report stuck in the middle. He dropped Helen off to the shops, (brave fella) and went to let the horses, he'd brought down the previous night, out of the yard. The horses would not go out of the yard into a lush green paddock. Why? The yard was on a piece of flat ground; the paddock was a deep slope. The poor horses from the flat country couldn't find any firm ground under their feet. It was air. They did not think of stretching their legs to find a firm footing. After an hour of trying to get them out, Jack left them with the gate open to work it out themselves.

At four o'clock in the morning, there was a loud banging on their motel door, which woke the couple up. Jack accused Helen of ordering breakfast too early. She pleaded innocence. Another loud bang on the door.

"Sounds like someone needs us rather urgently," said Jack, as he got up and opened the door and saw an angry Griffo, shaking some papers in his hand.

"Have you seen this report and read it thoroughly?"

Jack, keeping a straight face, said, "I have and it's rather concerning."

"Yes, I want every sheep on the property to be drenched with Coopers Ripercol immediately and I mean immediately." Then he stormed away.

Jack hopped back into bed with Helen and she said, "Looks like you are going to be a busy boy now your plan has worked out."

"Gosh, what a man has to do to look after someone else's flock," said Jack as he turned around to encourage more sleep.

Now, Jack's boss, Mr Griffiths, was a kind chap. He gave Jack his first manager's job, looking after his large investment and making sure that investment was profitable. Jack wanted to prove to Griffo he had made the right choice and did more than his best to be a successful property manager.

But there was a slight conflict between the two. One was very young to fully manage a large enterprise and the other, with wealth and a town upbringing, wanted to influence his young manager, as he'd had troubles with his previous older employees.

Griffo would fly in, right on lunch time. He would buzz the homestead, then Jack would race out to the air strip to pick him up. A shake of the hand, an enquiry of each other's health and how were things, a positive nod to each other and then back to the homestead.

Meanwhile, Helen would be busy making an extra place and food for the newly arrived guest. She would get another bottle of her home-made ginger beer, as she knew Griffo liked it. When he came, it was always about lunch time. Griffo loved Helen and they both got on well together but not so much with Jack.

After lunch, Griffo would drive the ute, with Jack as passenger, for a drive round the property, checking stock, water and feed. No argument there. Then it would start.

"Jack, could you please explain why one of the screws is missing from the hinge on the fuel shed door?"

"I never noticed it was missing," Jack replied.

"Well, you should have. The next thing, all the screws will work loose, then the door comes off, then all the fuel will be covered in dust. For one screw missing, a broken hinge and door, plus contaminated fuel, that would be an unnecessary cost. Fix it."

Then he would move onto the next of his concerns.

"Now, Helen wanted that table moved outside, why wasn't it done?"

"Sorry but I had no idea she wanted it moved," said a puzzled Jack.

All the afternoon it would go on. He found a one-inch nail in the dust.

"What's this doing here Jack? That could cause a puncture and more costs."

Griffo would pick, pick on small things. Nothing said about the now healthy sheep, the cattle in good condition, the bore drain flowing, the windmills all working, the fences in order, or even all the machinery he bogged and had been retrieved. It was all now running and in good working order. No, nothing was said but a screw and a nail. Oh, the injustice of it all.

They sat down to a cordial dinner with conversation mostly

between Helen and Griffo. Jack was upset at the way Griffo spoke to him in an abusive manner. He didn't eat much as he knew what was going to happen after dinner. Bookwork. Every item was scrutinised, one by one, with an explanation required.

"Now Jack, why was this three sixteenth bit bought?"

"I guess it was broken, as it is not with the other drill bits, and had to be replaced."

"Who broke it?"

"I guess, one of the men."

"That is a lack of training of the men. Now explain this, why was this purchase made? What authority was given for this expense?"

And so, it went on and on, till about midnight and, after all the frustrated answers, he would say, "I'm satisfied."

Good. He went to bed satisfied. Jack couldn't sleep, poor chap, he was all screwed up with the total interrogation he had gone through over the last eight hours. And it ended up he had done nothing wrong. This trial and tribulation, Jack had to go through every three to four weeks when Griffo arrived.

It even happened when Helen's dad decided to drive up with them on one of their trips to Melbourne. Griffo went off at Jack in front of the father-in-law. When Griffo walked away, Helen's dad said, "Why don't you tell him to go and stick it?"

Jack said, "One day I will but, at the moment, I like my job, except for Griffo, I'm learning all the time and if I can be patient. I'm sure it will be better for my career."

Jack did have a break where he did not see Griffo for nine months. It was bliss. It came about when Jack bought a Santa Gertrudis bull for the new stud herd that he was starting. The bull was called Dollar and it was the biggest bull Jack had ever seen.

When the bull was unloaded into the Ardglen yard, Jack, to get to know him better, hopped over the rail and talked to him, so Dollar would sense he had come to a good home. The bull charged. Jack ran for the top rail of the yard. Then he noticed the bull wasn't angry but just wanted a pat. Dollar had been a bit of a pet at his previous home. So, Jack slid down the rails and gave the huge bull a good rub behind the ears and on his jaw. He seemed to like that. When Jack walked into the yard again, Dollar would rush up to him. Jack would put his hand out and Dollar would stop for his rub.

On this exciting day, Griffo drove up with his wife to look at the new bull Jack had brought. He was impressed. Jack said, with a bit of mischief in his eye, "Mr Griffiths, jump into the yard and get a good look at him."

"Is it safe?" asked Griffo as he climbed down from the rail into the bull's yard.

Dollar did his thing and went straight for Griffo. He ran to the nearest rails and, when safe, said, "Jack, you bought a wild bull. He will get mongrelly calves. How dare you," shouted a very angry Griffo.

Jack said calmly, "Look Mr Griffiths, I will show you how a real stockman handles bulls."

At that, Jack walked into the yard. The bull charged. Jack's hand went out and the bull stopped and got his rub. Was Griffo impressed?

"Can I do that, Jack?"

"Yes, give it a go."

So Griffo slowly entered the yard and the bull trotted up to him.

Jack yelled, "Don't move, just put your hand out."

The bull stopped and Griffo gave it an attentive pat on the forehead. He was overcome with amazement; he ran to collect his wife and brought her down to the yards and said, "Watch this, I'll show you how a real stockman handles a bull."

He got into the yard and Dollar did his thing. A pat and a look at his wife, hoping for an admiring glance, which didn't happen. But, she was impressed with her husband's stockman ability.

That night, after dinner, when Jack and Helen were in bed, Helen whispered, "You shouldn't play that sort of thing on a city bloke; it could have consequences."

And it did. A few months later, Mrs Griffiths rang and said, "Mr. Griffiths won't be up for some time. He has had a bad accident. He has a broken pelvis, arm and three cracked ribs."

"Goodness," said Jack, in his most sympathetic voice, "how did that awful thing happen?"

"Mr Griffiths went to a cattle sale in Theodore and there was a bull charging everyone, so he tried to show everyone what a good stock man does and he was hit and crushed against the rails. He was lucky to be alive, thanks to a few brave souls who managed to get him out of the yard and called the ambulance."

"Oh, we are so sorry to hear this. I do hope Mr Griffiths will be okay and tell him we wish him a speedy recovery."

Jack was quite happy about the event. Not Mr Griffiths getting hurt but not having to see him for quite a few months.

It started to come to an end when Helen and Jack brought their first-born baby son, Damon, home. As soon as they arrived and put Damon in his new cot in his newly painted room, Griffo appeared and wanted to have a look at the baby. When he did, he was all smiles and said to Helen, "What a beautiful baby you have given birth to." Then to Jack, "I want to see you in the work shed."

Griffo had come to look after the station while Jack and Helen were in Charleville. When in the shed, Griffo pointed to a small three corner tear in the motorbike seat.

"How did this happen?" he asked.

"I'm not sure how it happened, probably while mustering, a bit of mulga caught in the seat and did the small tear. That is easily fixed."

Jack was tired from the 200km trip from Charleville and the birth of their son. The whole experience was too much for him. Right then he could not give a stuff about Griffo and the job. He had all he wanted: a lifetime dream, a beautiful wife and a healthy baby son.

"Mr Griffiths, I'm sick and tired of your constant nick picking. You have never said what a good job I've done with the stock and the property. It is evident that you think I'm a bad manager, so you might as well find a good one, because you now have a month's notice from me. In other words, you can stick your job."

At that and without waiting for an answer, Jack turned around, went back into the homestead, gave Helen a big hug and said, "I just gave Griffo a month's notice."

"Well dear, I'm not surprised. I knew it would come to this someday, what with the trouble Griffo gave you. I knew, one day, you would give notice but what are we going to do now?"

Holding Helen in his arms, he said, "Jack will find something, darling, a new adventure for my family."

Lunch was awkward. Nothing was said about giving notice. Griffo mainly talked to Helen about the baby and her time in Charleville. After lunch, Griffo was surprisingly pleasant and said to Jack, "Let's go down to the sheep yards and have a talk."

They both walked in silence down to the yards, found a spot under a shady tree and sat down.

Griffo, in his kindest of voice, said, "Jack, I would like you to reconsider what you said before. You have done a great job managing the property and I want you to stay. I have to admit that I have, as you said, picked on you for the little things and never commended you on all you and Helen have done since you have been here, looking after my property. But Jack, you're such a young fella and all I was trying to do was teach you that it's the little things that are just as important as the big things."

"Well maybe but every time you come here, without any pleasantries, you just seem to blast me for the whole time you're visiting."

"Perhaps I have been a bit harsh and I'm sorry, Jack. I really like you and want you to stay. How about, for compensation, your start off a Santa Gertrudis stud which, I know you have wanted to do. I'll give you full say on the buying and setting up." Griffo started to rise and continued, "I think it best that I head for home now and let you think things over."

And at that point, he just picked his things up from the homestead and left.

Jack went and told Helen what had just happened.

She asked, "Are we leaving or staying?"

"I really don't know. His whole attitude has changed. I should have told him years ago, how upsetting he was when he came to visit but that's not good now. I do like it here and it would be a great experience to start a Santa stud and doing the buying. What do think my love?"

"Well, we are settled here and I know you like being the big boss and managing. I like it here too. We have so many friends and though I miss nursing, we have our baby and I do like the excitement of station life. But darling, you have given notice and he might be just leading you on till he finds another manager."

"Gosh, I did not think of that. Just let's see how things work out and maybe I put the word out, that if anything really of interest comes along, we could be encouraged to accept. What do you think?"

"Just tread carefully, my love."

Then an event occurred which helped Jack and Helen make an important decision.

In Jack's words:

Well, what I know is an ABC television crew came up when

the Opal Festival was on in 1970 and they filmed everyone having a great time. Whites only. I don't think the Aboriginals were the slightest bit interested in the festival.

They also filmed the Aboriginals at their traditional camp, I don't know how many thousands of years old. They offered to pay some Aboriginal woman to struggle with a 44-gallon drum of water, making out that is what they had to do at the camp. However, the times I went there, there was plenty of taps with town water and septic toilets, which were looked after by the council. At that time, we property owners and managers employed Aboriginal labour at the award rate, as did the council.

But for some reason, the ABC decided to make a film of white people having a good time and the Aboriginal people being treated badly. They made a big racist program out of it, to sell a story, which I think was completely wrong and hurtful to all who lived in Cunnamulla, black and white, at that time. It was a great community which, I thought, did not have any real racist element.

Of course, the southern states were horrified by the showing, believing everything was true, but far from it. However, activists stirred up Aboriginal communities from Bourke, Brewarrina and towns in-between, as far as Boggabilla.

They came and smashed shops and windows and wrote graffiti everywhere, They frightened and threatened the whole town. So much so, the two Greek cafes and the well-known Wiggins clothing store, that had been there for decades, not only did they close, but they also left town within a week. They used to say when the Greeks leave the town, it collapses and, in this case, it did.

It took years before Cunnamulla became a decent, liveable town for whites and blacks again. Unfortunately, the town of Charleville suffered too. The tourist industry ended up helping those two devastated towns to be reborn again.

What a shame that journalists and film crews will do anything to sell a story, whether true or not.

It was at this time that both Jack and Helen decided Cunnamulla was not a safe place anymore, so they gave their month's notice, which caused Griffo some grief, as it did for Helen and Jack. It was sad. Was it the right thing to leave? Only the future could tell.

C.7

Sandgate
(An Interval)
July 1970

They found a little flat behind a motel which was adequate for their needs, both in comfort and price. A good walk to the main shopping centre of Redcliffe, the beach and the long pier. It was a great contrast from Cunnamulla with its mulga and red dust. But the three settled in well. Jack and Damon were overjoyed at seeing a television for the first time. It was all so different but Jack needed the break before the next adventure.

Helen and Jack were sorry to leave Ardglen and all their new friends, who had welcomed the couple so warmly. But they had made their decision, leaving their belongings next-door at Derain Station and Sparkle, Jack's young sheep dog, as it would be cruel to take her to the city. They just took their essential gear for themselves, the baby and Cammie and took off for the big smoke in their new, green Ford Escort G.T.

Oh dear, it looks like I had forgotten to tell you about the new car. After 16 months at Ardglen, the publican at the Warrego Hotel offered to pay cash for their car. They took the cash, as it was 100 dollars less than what they had paid. Their faithful

Holden. They had hardly used it while at Ardglen, because the station truck and ute were always used, as their outings were mostly work related.

The Cunnamulla show was on and Jack noticed a few new car displays and he was taken by the little green Ford Escort G.T. He talked to the salesman and was more enthused, so raced off to find Helen to make his plea. Thankfully, she loved the little green car and gave the go ahead. It was quite reasonable to buy a car now, as they were leaving Ardglen and would need transport and they were cashed up. But the salesman said the car was not released as yet and could not be sold and had been brought to Cunnamulla for display purposes only.

Jack wanted the car and said to the salesman, "I won't accept that. It's quite obvious to me and other show patrons that these cars are for sale. Why would you truck these cars at a cost, all the way from Brisbane and not sell them? That's crazy. What's the best price now? We know there is a show special and will pay cash."

The salesman had to find a phone to ring his employer.

Jack said, "We will be back in an hour."

Jack also had to ring the dealer as an anonymous person to get a correct retail price for the new Ford GT that was coming out. He raced to the post office, rang the Brisbane dealer, whose name and number was displayed with the cars. Surprisingly, he was told that $2,500 would be the full retail price and they wanted to know would Jack be interested? Jack said he would think about it. He raced back to the showgrounds, had to pay another entrance fee, found Helen to get her approval, then waited an hour before going back to the display.

Jack found the salesman, and asked, "What's the verdict?"

He looked at Jack with a strange expression, saying, "In the last hour, we have had another enquiry into this Ford car which seemed strange as its not on the market yet. However, you may purchase the car for $2,300 cash, but you have to wait till the show is over to pick it up."

Wow, thought Jack, *$200 cheaper to what the dealer had said.*

"Well, okay then, as long as it is clean without sticky fingers, scuff marks and dints," he said.

"No, we will detail it for you and we can fix the registration and insurance, but that will cost extra."

"That's fine," said Jack, "so you will have it ready and registered by this Monday morning?"

"Yes, we will but can I have a $500 deposit now?"

Jack opened his wallet, where he always kept a few blank cheques, just in case. Borrowed the salesman's pen, he wrote out a cheque and gave him his personal details for registration and insurance purposes.

Now, an awkward conversation for Jack started in the car on the drive home.

Helen said, "I suppose we both have to go back to town on Monday to pick up the new car. Who is going to drive the new car home?"

A bit of silence ensued as Jack thought about the question. Then said with just a tiny bit of tongue in cheek, "I gave that a lot of thought, darling and, I thought, as a bit of reward, I would get one of the men to drive me to town and he could bring the ute back, while I drive the new car back."

Jack felt "the look" more than saw it and said, "Oh, I didn't think. Do you want to drive the new car home?"

"You darn well know I do, so stop teasing."

Of course, Jack desperately wanted to drive it home but love can make a bloke do strange things.

"Yes, my sweet, why did you think otherwise?" He saw the smile and knew he had made the right sacrifice.

Helen managed to keep a permanent nursing job at an agency. Jack was going to be a house husband. They both enjoyed their new roles: Helen back to nursing, which was her calling and Jack just loved being at home, doing the chores, listening to talkback radio, watching TV while feeding Damon in his lap, going for walks with Damon in the pram and Cammie the corgi limping beside.

Helen worked from 8am to 6pm, leaving for work at 7.15am and arriving home at 6.45pm. This she didn't mind, except she really only saw her baby briefly in the mornings and on weekends. He was two months old then and a good baby, as long as his stomach was full. The weekends were shopping, exploring the beaches and enjoying each other's company, feeling very proud pushing the pram with their beautiful offspring in front of them, so the world could see how clever they were.

Now, as mentioned, Cammie adored Helen but was very jealous of the baby and ignored Damon most of the time but, he belonged to Helen, so she had to protect him, even if it was a smelly, little human. This day, leaving the baby and pram outside a shop, while the parents did a quick purchase, there was a commotion outside. Cammie was barking furiously at a little old lady. It happened the dear lady wanted a peek at the baby and she had leant into the pram, not noticing a little Corgi dog tied and lying under it.

Cammie rushed out to protect Helen's baby, snapping at the old girl's ankles and, with her rush, nearly tipped the pram over. This put the instigator off balance with the shock of a little monster attacking her. Jack raced out, steadied the pram and calmed poor Damon, who had been rudely woken up. The stressed woman, holding her breasts, was pacified by Helen, who sat her down on a nearby bench. What more could you do in a situation like this? Give Cammie a treat for being a good girl and continued with their walk, leaving the old woman muttering to herself, "That's the last time I'm looking into a baby's pram."

Jack loved to watch Helen dress for work. She took much

pride in her nurse's white uniform, which was pressed, with her red and white Royal Melbourne, and her blue King George hospital midwifery badge. She looked so professional, with her red cape and veil. She took time with her veil, the symbol of her qualification into the nursing profession. The care in folding and ironing it, the placement on her head, which took some time as she had long soft, fair hair, reaching just past her waist. She would gather it up and fold a bun on top of her head, securing the veil with bobby pins. With part of it tipped forward on her forehead, she looked a picture of the most beautiful, smiling, caring human and she was his wife.

Of course, it was completely different when she came home from the hospital. A finicky Jack would say, even without a hug or welcoming home kiss, "Get that uniform off immediately, with all its germs and don't forget to boil your hands." He was joking but Jack liked being fit and well and had a bit of a thing about germs and being sick. This was amazing, seeing as he cuddled up in bed every night with his lover, who had an ileostomy bag that could explode and sometimes did. This did not worry him in the slightest. Funny man but then true love does make a difference.

Meanwhile, as a new house husband, Jack had great fun with his baby son. He would pull the rug over Damon's head and the baby would pull it down with a gurgle and a laugh. It was a game repeated often. Damon loved his bouncinette and would rock it so hard, sometimes the body frame would hit the floor. But the best time was at lunch when Jack made up Damon's Farex baby food. He would sit on his father's lap, both watching their favourite TV adventurer program, while having their lunch.

Jack was a bit worried about Damon dribbling food out. Jack would do what he'd seen mothers do and scoop it back into Damon's mouth. He mentioned it to Helen, when she came home one night.

She said, "It's a thing babies do, so don't worry about it." So, he didn't.

Helen did worry, when she came home early one day, due to the death of her elderly patient. She was horrified to see Jack feeding her baby Farex out of a full breakfast bowl.

"You haven't been feeding all that have you? No wonder he is spitting it out; he is overflowing with what you are feeding him. He should only be having a few spoonful at his age, plus his milk."

Damon, when we left Ardglen, was just a normal sized baby but now, he was round as a ball. You could nearly have bounced him.

The Sandgate stay was only temporary as the bush was always calling. Jack had to find a job. He put some ads in the Queensland Country Life advertising as an experienced station manager. This gave him a few interviews in the city, which meant taking baby Damon with him. He had early starts as he had to pack baby feeds, toys and nappies: the expensive disposable ones, although normally they used the cloth nappies. He would drop Helen off to work and find a park in the city.

What a job! Getting the pram out, then all the necessary baby gear, plus the baby. Yes, we know all mothers have to do it but they have hips to hold the baby, boobs for comfort and a special female instinct to be able to handle such things. But Jack had trouble as the baby kept slipping off his narrow hip and trying to boost him back, while with pram and gear, believe you me, Jack had some awkward moments.

For instance, men with babies were not allowed into baby change rooms as they were "Women Only". Where could one change a baby? On the park bench outside the town hall after being refused entrance to the change rooms. While changing, it always happened, some kindly woman would stop by and ask if you knew what you're doing and where was his mother. Bloody busybodies.

Surprisingly, Jack met men in a similar situation, taking care of babies because their wives were at work, in hospital, died or left them, literally, holding the baby. There were no facilities or help for the single, male fathers. It was disgraceful. Men worked, women had babies and that was the way society functioned.

Going for interviews was difficult too, as offices and work buildings didn't cater for prams and babies. Nevertheless, Jack managed.

"I have a baby, and if it is a concern, too bad."

Both interviews that day were a complete waste of time. The first one was a friend of Griffo's and just wanted to see Jack, as Griffo had told him Jack was the best manager he'd ever had. Jack wished he'd known that. He was not looking for a manager, indeed it was not even mentioned whether he had a property or not.

The second interview was at the chambers where the judges and barristers had their offices. This was a manager's job for one of the judges. The son, a barrister, was the interviewer and told Jack his father had a large farm with crops and cattle and was looking for a manager. He asked Jack about his experience and why wasn't the mother looking after the baby, who had found a ruler on the desk and was playing with it while still on his father's lap.

The barrister said they would pay $50 a week.

Jack said, "I would need to be fully found, (which meant all food, furniture and living costs) with decent accommodation for my family, car and at least $75 a week."

"No, we will pay only $50 a week, you will have to found yourselves and we will not supply a car. But we will lend you money to build a house on the property."

Jack got up, taking the now-chewed ruler from his son, putting it back on the desk, hoisted his distressed baby, who had lost a toy, on his hip and said, "Sir, you are not looking for a property manager, you are looking for cheap labour," and walked out with both of them not happy.

A position soon became available at Prairie, a little town and railway siding near Hughenden. Helen asked for a week off, so Jack could check out the job and property. The interview was at Dundee Station, just south of Richmond, Queensland, a trip of approximately 1,500 kilometres, a 3,000-kilometre round trip. It was a long trip, especially the last 147kms of rough, dirt road which, surprisingly, the little Ford Escort handled well.

Mr and Mrs Frazer gave Jack a good welcome, begged him to stay for tea and the night and would show him the property the next day. Jack felt very comfortable with the Frazers and knew they would be a pleasant couple to work for.

After a great roast lamb dinner, with a bread-and-butter pudding, a comfortable bed and a goodnight's sleep, Jack was keen to see the property he could be managing, the conditions and make up his mind about the position and do the long drive back to his little family.

The next morning, after a hearty breakfast, Mr Frazer, who insisted on being called Dick, showed Jack around the Richmond property and his impressive herd of Brahman cattle. They talked about Jack's experience, was impressed when he told him at the last property he had started a Santa Gertrudis stud. Dick mentioned that he wanted Jack to manage and look after his other breeding property, Jireena, south of Prairie, a 50,000-acre property, running Brahman and the new breed, Brangus.

Back at the homestead, after smoko, they took a 240-kilometre drive to Jireena. Jack was not impressed at his initial sight of the homestead. It was about one kilometre off the Prairie-Muttaburra Road. There was a house on a knoll without a garden or shade trees or shrubs of any kind. Helen would not be impressed at all. Jack had his doubts too.

But inside the house, it wouldn't be called a homestead.

It was a new structure with a modern kitchen and a gas stove and oven. Helen would be pleased. There was a nice bathroom, toilet, shower only and two bedrooms with a nice little lounge or sitting room, then a breeze way and two very large bedrooms up a couple of steps, which belonged to the original homestead that had been demolished, leaving just the two rooms. Of course, the only power was 32-volt fridges, kerosene and a large 44-gallon chip heater outside for hot water, piped into the house. There was also a party telephone line, run by the exchange in Prairie.

All in all, it wasn't too bad. Very liveable but not a mansion by any means. There was plenty of water from deep water holes in Towerhill Creek for Helen to quickly establish shade trees and a garden. Wages were $80 a week clear, plus fully found. Sadly, the only car was a VW Buggy, plus an international tractor. There were a few sheds: a large hay shed and some quarters.

Later, Jack found out most of the property was the other side of Towerhill Creek, not only running cattle but also a few hundred sheep with a shearing shed and quarters, about three kilometres from the manager's house.

Besides the cattle and sheep, there was a stockman, Max and his partner, Madge, both in their forties, thin and fit. They both looked as if they could do a round or two. They lived in the shearer's quarters. Other permanent residents were a dozen ducks with permanent diarrhoea, a billy goat with sharp, large horns and an old cattle dog, Biddy, short of a few teeth.

What was Jack's decision? Well, his boss and wife were really nice people, the house and wage weren't too bad and Dick had said, "Run it as your place. I have enough on my plate not to be bothering you."

Jack said, "We will take the job but I will need three weeks before I can get here."

"That's fine. Max can continue looking after the place till

you get here. When you're settled in, give me a ring and I will come over and we will get the paperwork done."

A shake of the hand and they both went their separate ways.

Driving back to Brisbane, Jack, as normal, felt sick in the stomach. As usual, he had made his decision on the spot, instead of thinking about it. It was quite reasonable to say, "I'll talk it over with my wife and I will let you know within the week," instead of rushing in and saying, "I will take the job," without discussing it with Helen. What had Jack done?

As it turned out, it would be the best job Jack could have had, considering what future disastrous events were in store for their little family.

It was a great welcome home as Helen and Damon were so happy to see him and he was excited to be with his little family again. There was a group hug with Cammie, including whirling around the little kitchen and lots of kisses all around. It was just the best homecoming.

"Well," said Helen, "Did you take the job?"

She knew Jack had, as she knew her husband was impetuous and made up his mind without thinking.

Jack said he did and told Helen his new boss and wife were fantastic people.

"It is sort of a new house and, guess what, a gas stove and oven, and there is plenty of water for Helen's Garden. The pay is good and the climate up there is warm all year round."

It was a colourful description by Jack but, as always, he seemed to worm his way out of trouble.

Helen, as a casual, went and gave a week's notice at the agency. Jack went down and saw the publican owner of the flat and asked how much notice he would require, seeing he was getting a job in North Queensland.

The owner of the pub said, "Do you realise, we forgot to take a bond off you, but I know you will leave the flat in excellent condition. Congratulations in getting a job and seven days' notice is sufficient and, Jack, if the job does not work out, you're welcome back here."

Jack said, with of a feeling of relief, "I really appreciate that" and shook the publican's hand. Thinking, if Helen didn't like the place, he always had a place to come back to.

It was a very busy week of cleaning, scrubbing, packing, an excited dog and a cross little baby, as he was not getting the attention he required. Helen had a few more questions about the property and how they were getting their belongings from Cunnamulla to Prairie.

"There is not a lot I know, love, but as I am back to being a manager, I can manage our problems and it will all work out in the end." Jack replied.

"I know it will, dear, but you seem to be avoiding a few of my questions about the property."

"My sweet, I can't tell you what I don't know."

The cost of moving their belongings by removal companies was prohibitive. Then, Jack remembered a car and truck yard, called Cousins, along Ipswich Road. He thought it might pay to make a visit and it did.

There was a late 1950s Bedford truck, with a timber tray and sides, red and black, with a transfer on both doors saying PMG, which stood for Postmaster General. It must have been used for delivering large parcels to business. It was tired and well used, no roadworthy then but had four months registration. It started with a second-hand battery and sounded alright.

"Just get it out of the yard, son and pay me $250," said the owner.

"I will pay the money now if you like but I can't pick it up till next week," Jack said.

"Pay me when you collect it, son."

"Thank you, I will see you early on Monday."

They shook hands on the deal and Jack felt most satisfied with himself.

The family packed and squeezed all their gear into the little Ford Escort and left Sandgate very early that Monday, arriving at Cousins Car and Truck Sales at 7.30am. The truck was ready to go. But Jack realised there was no spare tyre, jack or wheel spanner for the vehicle. After some rummaging around the back of the shed, the salesman found a suitable but rather bald, spare tyre, an old screw up jack and a rusty old wheel spanner that seemed to fit the wheel nuts. Jack paid the $250 but was informed it was another $25 for the extra gear. Jack had no option but to pay the extra.

Helen drove ahead. Jack said he would meet her at the bottom of the Toowoomba range, as he had to fill the truck with petrol. He also bought four litres of oil, a jerry can of water, just in case, and a large tarp and ropes to protect all their gear which they had left stored at Derain Station, next to Ardglen, for their trip to Prairie.

Helen should have been there waiting. The truck was going beautifully but could only do 75km/h. Where was she? She should have been here half an hour ago. Jack had been waiting at the meeting spot for some time when, whoosh, as the little green Ford Escort raced past and kept going. Poor Jack was in a bind. Why didn't she wait? Where now will they meet up? Did she know how to get through Toowoomba and on to Cunnamulla? These were the questions in Jack's worried mind as he put the old Bedford into gear and started to climb the range.

Getting to the top of the range, he looked for her. Where was she? He continued down towards the city centre and, out of the corner of his eye, at the tourist information centre, was their little green car.

"Why didn't you stop at the meeting place and what took you so long?" asked a rather relieved, but cross, Jack.

"Don't growl at me. I had to feed and change the baby and give Cammie a pit stop. That wasn't just five minutes and, anyway, how did I know where the bottom of the range was until I start to climb it?"

"Well, didn't you see the truck at the side of the road patiently waiting for you?"

"No, you didn't have a cranky baby and a restless dog keeping you distracted, while concentrating on the road, did you?"

"Okay, I'm sorry. I was just worried about you and how I would find you. Look, just follow me and we will have an early lunch at the BP service station."

And so it happened, there were a few scary moments when cars had to get in between them, but Jack kept a good eye out and waited at the side of the road till

his darling caught up. They were both relieved to reach the service station, as now, with the city behind them, it was a single road to Derain Station. They decided to stop at their special hotel in St George, which had a precious romantic link. Jack wondered if they could try that romantic link again as he was driving along. The truck had no radio, so he had occasional thoughts.

The 300km to St George was a good, but tiring, run. There were stops for the baby, dog and a wee at the side of the road. They made it to St George at five: a long day of 570 kilometres. Jack lost all thoughts of romance, just a feed and sleep for him. Poor Helen, she was exhausted. The drive with baby and dog was a bit too much. Jack forgot his selfish needs when he saw how tired his poor wife was, after she had done such an excellent job.

He took the baby and dog for a walk so she could shower and freshen up and lie down before going down to the dining room for dinner. They slept like a baby, except the baby had been sleeping about all day in the car and was now restless. So, it was zombie parents who had to attend to Damon's urgent needs.

Tired, but refreshed, they were not looking forward to another nearly 200km trip on a mainly, very rough, sandy corrugated road to Derain Station. They bought a few loaves of fresh bread, fresh fruit and vegetables to give Judy and Phil, the owners of Derain station. It is something you do when visiting outback stations. They had given them notice a week or so ago but rang them again that morning, saying they would be there about 1pm and was there anything they could bring them. They said 'no' and were looking forward to seeing them again and must stay a couple of days. That was nice of them.

There was a great welcome. Baby Damon was not sure about Judy picking him up and hugging him. Jack was pleased to see Sparkle running up to greet him with tail wagging furiously and Cammie, thinking all the excitement was for her, was barking and running around. Helen and Judy were so pleased to see each other; they hugged and talked all at the same time. The two couples had always enjoyed each other's company. Plenty of chatter ensued over a lunch of cold meat, pickles and lettuce and salad sandwiches, followed by a pot of tea, of course.

That afternoon, while the girls were catching up on gossip, Phill took Jack for a drive to show him some clearing he had done and some impressive yard work. Jack told Phil about his new job.

"Don't know about them Brahman cows. They could go wild in this country but the Santa herd you started at Ardglen, seem okay. You know, Jack, that place, only in the three months since you left, the new manager was a disaster and the talk is, that it may be up for sale. A shame you left, we all miss you."

"Phil, to be honest so am I but you knew the strain Griffo put on me and, as the missus says, "If you're not happy, do something about it."

They had a good check out of the PMG truck.

Phil said, 'Besides looks, I can't see anything wrong with it, except the mileage meter doesn't work. So how many thousands of miles it has done is anyone's guess. I think you will need lots of luck to get it all the way up north. It must be 1000 kilometres or more."

"No, Phil, it's approximately 800," Jack said.

A nice dinner, a card came of 500, then the baby was settled and they were off to bed.

The next day, they got ready for the drive up north. Jack borrowed Phil's grease gun and greased all the nipples on the truck, as well as a thorough check of everything, including the tyre pressure. Helen helped Jack get all their stored gear out of the storage room and supervised the packing of the truck, which caused some slight disagreements as to where precious things should be placed. However, the truck was packed, with the new tarp covering it all and the ropes expertly placed and tied, to make sure nothing would move. This left the little green Ford more room for Helen, Damon and Cammie to do the trip in more comfort than before. Sparkle was going in the truck with Jack.

The rest of the day was relaxing, just old friends enjoying each others' company, another game of 500 and perhaps a fair bit of wine enjoyed, as well.

The following day, on the stroke of 8am, our couple with their baby and two dogs left Derain, with hugs, kisses and handshakes, "And don't forget to write."

Helen led the way. She had driven to Charleville tons of times. Jack was left in the dust, following behind. They had arranged to meet at the BP there.

A fill up of car and truck, a morning cuppa and it was off to Barcaldine for the night. The road was just a ribbon of bitumen. If another vehicle came, you had to get off the road, which was sometimes a problem. If it was wet on the heavy, black soil, it became a game of chicken, as the car that gave way was eventually bogged. If there was a Skinner bus or truck heading towards you, you had no hope. The trip, thank God, was without trouble, except for occasional stops for baby, dogs, parents and checking the load on the truck and occasional adjusting the tie down ropes.

Cammie was smuggled into their hotel room while Sparkle was tied under the truck, of course with food and water, in the hotel yard. When they entered their bedroom, Helen got the giggles.

"What's so funny?" asked Jack.

"Look at the room. It's like we are back in the 1940s but take a gander at the bed. It must be four foot off the ground. How will we get into it? And being an old metal frame bed with brass knobs on it, it will rattle all night."

"Well, darling, if you keep far right in the bed and I keep far left, it should be alright. I will give you a boost like I do when you get on a horse," quipped a smiling Jack.

But what worried Helen was how was she going to visit the shared toilet during the night, which was down the passageway, getting out and in of the high bed with her appliance full.

Jack suddenly realised the situation, saying, "I gotta go, be back in five."

Jack scrummaged around in the pub's backyard and found a good heavy solid box.

"And where do you think you're going with that, son?" asked the publican, who had just stepped out.

"Er, I know I should have asked but I need something like this so my wife can get in and out of that high bed during the night."

"Put it back before you leave," said the man with a genuine smile.

The night was survivable, the breakfast was good, the box returned, the car and truck filled to the brim, as it would be the last petrol stop before getting to Jireena. Jack led the way to the

Aramac turnoff and then said to Helen, "Follow this road to Muttaburra, we will meet there. If you have a problem just stop, I won't be far behind".

They all had a rest stop at Muttaburra.

"Now listen, love, from now on the road is dirt, rough, and sometimes just a track through the spinifex," said Jack. "Don't be a hero, heroes don't last in this country. If unsure, stop. There could be other tracks leading off the main track and they all look the same. This road is just a station road and has limited use."

"Jack, I want to follow you now; I have the baby and I am not too sure if I can go first," said Helen.

"Okay love, I will lead but give me five minutes start, then you follow, as you don't want your vision hampered by my dust. I will stop every now and then for you to catch up, then we will do the five-minute thing again."

Helen was thinking, *I hope I don't get lost in this awful country and Jack wasn't too clear about the place and job. I just have to rely on him. He has been so good to me but honestly, I wish he wouldn't make decisions on the run. I suppose, so far, everything ends up well. But what am I thinking? I do love him and will follow him anywhere.*

Jack was thinking, *I hope Helen is coping with this shocking road or, as a better description, track. I do love her so much, and why am I bringing her to this Jireena. Surely, I could have found a better job and accommodation for my family, which means more to me than anything else. A property near a hospital so we could both enjoy our careers. Gosh, is she going to like this place miles from anywhere? Maybe I should have given her more details about the place. Oh well, if things go pear shaped, we can always find something else.*

C.8

Jireena
September 1970

"Why have you stopped and how much further is this place?" asked Helen, looking very tired, baby asleep in the back and Cammie sitting up on the front seat looking about with interest.

Jack said, "Darling, we are here. This is our turnoff, and you can see the house just up the road."

"It's not that dwelling on top of that rise?" asked Helen, "with no trees around, just sticking up like a melon on top of a white ants' nest?"

"Um, first impressions aren't always the best. Just think, you have a complete empty canvas to start a garden of your own design and there is a gas stove and oven."

Even tired from the long trip, she could see Jack was a bit worried about her first impressions. With a hint of a smile, she said, "Most houses have gas stoves, darling, but don't worry, until we get a closer look at the place you have chosen for your family, then I may have something to say. So, let's drive up, get Damon out of the car and have a nice cup of tea."

Jack was in a slight panic but that was forgotten when, just 100 metres from the house, the old truck let out a huge bang and came to a sudden stop with smoke coming out of the bonnet. There was a burning smell and Jack knew the dear old truck had gotten them to their destination, overdid it and died. No resuscitation was necessary.

Jack lifted the bonnet and saw lots of oil from the gasket cover, dripping on the ground. There was no sign of fire but Jack thought, *Better unload our stuff sooner than later.* Helen pulled up.

"What's wrong?"

"The dear old truck that managed to get us here, has just blown its engine and I guess it is passed fixing," said Jack.

"Let's go inside and have a cup of tea."

Cammie and Sparkle had already jumped out of their respective vehicles and were busy exploring their new home. Sparkle, giving the diarrhoea ducks a run for their money, while Cammie joined in for the fun. The poor dogs had been restrained for so long, they needed a good run. The resident old dog, Biddy, didn't even move when the newcomers came. Maybe one eyelid but that was all.

Helen lifted a cranky baby out of his seat. Guess he didn't like to be rudely woken up and the three of them went into the kitchen. What a surprise. There was a big welcome to Jack and Helen with a card attached to a bunch of colourful flowers and a note that a casserole was in the oven. The fridges had had plenty of food placed in them the day before.

Whew, thought Jack, *that might mellow Helen about her new home, better than getting the shoulder out of the butcher shop, light the wood stove and cook for five men.* That was the greeting at the last place.

After their cup of tea, Helen explored the house, finding a safe place for the baby, while Jack went out and started to bring in the baby food and all the gear from the Ford Escort. He dumped it all in the dining room and then proceeded to unload the truck, in case it caught fire.

Helen asked Jack, as he was too and froing, bringing their possessions inside, "I want to ring Mrs Frazer to thank her very much. Not only for the casserole and filling the fridges but she has also filled the storeroom as well. And the house is so clean, she must have spent a good day just to get it ready for us."

Jack gave her the number and was feeling a bit better there were no real recriminations, as yet, about their new place of work. Jack was unpacking and setting up essential items, such as building their bed and making it, organising the cot and changing table, bouncinette, nappies, bottles etc, etc. He wanted to make the home liveable, as soon as possible, until they had sorted themselves out properly.

He heard Helen chattering away to Mrs Frazer, thanking her, discussing the trip and, of course, the baby. Not realising the whole district now knew about the Alexanders at Jireena, as she was talking on the party line.

Dogs, baby and parents fed. It had been a big day for all and they were off to sleep for a new start in the morning.

Jack was up early, anxious to check out the whole property. After a quick breakfast and taking the baby to Helen, who wasn't quite awake yet, he let Sparkle off the chain, then went to see if the VW Buggy was drivable. It had fuel and oil, which were both full. Jack couldn't find the radiator to check for water, then noticed it was air-cooled with a big fan, to keep the motor cool, and two large air cleaners. Jack thought it was not the sort of vehicle for outback dusty conditions, however, it started and Sparkle immediately jumped into the spare front seat.

Crossing the dry Tower Hill creek, he drove to the sheep yards and shed, hoping to meet Max and get the low down on the property. Max had heard the buggy coming and was waiting beside the shed to see who it was. Jack stopped the buggy, jumped out and, with hand outstretched for a handshake, introduced himself as Jack the new manager. They both squatted down, rolled a smoke then Jack started the conversation.

"What's the go here? Are you employed by Mr Frazer and, if so, what do you do? And, if it's convenient for you, would you like to show me around the property?"

"No, Dick lets me and my partner stay here but we both have casual jobs on nearby properties and, until you came," said Max. "He paid us to caretake the place. If we are available, we can give you a hand but we are both busy for the next three weeks, so after this week you are on your own. But have a walk around here while I have a bit of breakfast and I will show you around."

Meanwhile, Helen could not get back to sleep with Damon wriggling around, needing a change, his milk and Farex. *So, she thought, let's see what the day brings, after fixing Damon and Cammie up and settling them both down.* She decided to have a leisurely breakfast. Cereal was okay, kettle for a cuppa boiling on the gas stove, but no toaster or wood stove to toast anything. She tried the grill. It was not perfect but a little practice might make a successful piece of toast.

She looked around at her surroundings: the newly painted cream walls, the cupboards and stove, all new. It was all better than Ardglen. But the bare landscape outside was a shock. *Jack will have to get me into Hughenden or to a nursery as soon as he can,* she thought, *I must have a garden and trees surrounding the house.* The phone rang. *What did Jack say? One long ring and three short ones was our party number, but I will pick it up anyway and see who it is.*

"Hello, this is Helen. We have just come here yesterday to take over the management of Jireena. Were you calling us?"

"Yes dear, its Mrs Archer, your next-door neighbour. You may call me Beryl. Just wondering how you're settling in and if you need anything. I may call in on Friday, if it's alright dear?"

"That would be lovely, any time that suits. I won't be going anywhere for a few days."

Helen had another three calls that morning with the same message. So much for her ringing Mrs Frazer yesterday to thank her. The word spreads fast and wide in the outback.

Jack, meanwhile, was checking out the four-stand shearing shed, equipment, and the condition of the buildings and yards and gate. He was quite pleased to see them well maintained and in good working condition. A 'hoy' from Max, who was ready to go. They both got themselves into the buggy, with Sparkle now residing in the back. They drove out of the sheep paddock into a much larger one, where a lot of cream, very large Brahman cattle were grazing. But what took Jack's eye was a very large-proportioned bull, which was not Braham. It was not cream but a dull, red and ginger colour. Max said it was an Africana bull that Dick had imported. Jack thought, *This is the breed*, just looking at the bull.

Max said, "Turn here, let's go back. I have never been down there and I don't want to go any further."

They had come to a cliff edge and the country just fell away. It looked like there was very thick bush down the slope and seemed to have a dark interior.

"But the boundary of the property must be down there," said Jack.

"I suppose it is but as far as I know, cattle won't venture down there," said Max.

Jack was excited. He didn't say anything but as soon as he could, he was going to explore that area. He found out later, it was the watershed for the great Thompson River that ran into the Cooper and continued to Lake Eyre.

On the way back to the shearing shed, a group of horses were startled by the buggy and started to run. Jack spied a beautiful mare, a dark bay with a black, flaxen mane and tail.

"What and whose horse is that?" asked Jack as he pointed it out to Max.

"Oh, that belongs to the station. You can't ride it. It's only half broken in because no one could ride it."

"What a shame, such a beautiful horse. Max, could you please run those horses into the yard tomorrow? I would like to look them over."

"I don't know you yet but if you have a mind to get on that horse, you're crazy but I'll get them in for you."

Ah now, two challenges for the new manager.

Dropping Max off at the shed, Jack continued the inspection of the whole property, noting things that needed to be done. He also noticed something he had never seen before, lots of feeding troughs with cattle standing around. They were not normal feeding troughs Jack had known. They were a square frame with a 44-metal drum attached to the metal frame by a steel rod which was through the middle of the drum, enabling the drum to roll within the frame.

"Where have you been? You're in trouble," said Helen, as Jack arrived rather late for lunch.

"What have I done now?"

"You haven't told me where you have been and what time you will be home. You have left me and the baby in this isolated place, not knowing your whereabouts. What if you'd had an accident? And furthermore, you left a poor cow with a hungry calf locked up. Constant bellowing for hours. I had to see what was wrong with the animal, checked it out and it was the station's milking cow waiting to be milked and the calf to have her bit too."

"Gee, I'm sorry love. I didn't know we had a house cow, what did you do?"

"I stripped some milk out of the cow and gave the rest to the calf and let them go in their paddock."

"You're a wonder," and Jack gave Helen a loving kiss and hug.

"That's not getting you out of anything," she said with a smile, "you better come and have your lunch. I have lots to tell you."

She told him about the phone calls she had received from the neighbours and that they were invited to a waterskiing party at Lammermore station this Sunday.

"And we are going," she said.

Jack just nodded as he listened to all Helen had to say, trying to remember it all as he munched on his sandwiches. She seemed excited and, looking around, he could see she had the place looking like their home now.

"Oh and, by the way, Mr Frazer rang and said he would be here tomorrow," Helen added.

After lunch, Jack went and had an afternoon camp (nap) while the missus busied herself trying to unpack and find places to put their few personal items.

After his nap, Jack checked all the sheds and quarters out and went through the tool shed to find out what tools and equipment were there. He was pleased to see a tractor-driven welder and that the shed was well equipped. He got all his working gear out of the truck and placed them in the tool shed, thoroughly inspected all his riding gear, giving his saddle a good clean and rubbing it with his special saddle oil to make the leather supple.

He went to find the milking cow, a cross-bred jersey, who seemed very quiet, and her little three-month old heifer calf, which he locked up for the next morning. Feed was in a little shed near the milking bale.

"That will do me for the day, but I must get rid of those blasted ducks squirting shit on the concrete apron and path," he said. "Thank goodness Helen managed the cow and I see she has her chooks as well."

Mr Frazer arrived just as they were finishing breakfast, the next day. Jack introduced Helen and Damon. He picked up the baby and commented on what a beautiful child he was. Then he gave Helen a tiny kiss on the cheek saying, "I was hoping Jack would have a delightful wife."

And, of course, the relationship was sealed. Now, after a cup of tea and some toast, Dick said, "Here are some papers for you to sign, bank account, ledger and diary, and here is your company cheque book to pay for supplies or if you need some labour. All I require is for you to maintain an expense account and a diary for a day-to-day entry.

"Now, Max has already been paid for caretaking, so he is not owed any money. He and Madge are not very reliable. Only pay him a day's wage if you're desperate for a hand. I have explained to them, they can stay at the shearers quarters as long as they keep them maintained and clean. If we ever need the quarters, they will have to go.

"Now, I expect you to run the place as if it is yours but come with me, as I have to show you about feed and water."

They both walked outside after Dick thanked Helen for the cup of tea and toast. Walking to the back of the large shed, Jack noticed 20 44-gallon drums on a rack, side-by-side, about a metre high so they could be rolled along the frame. Also at the shed's back door was a stack of 20-litre drums and about 100 bags of stuff.

Dick explained the drums held molasses as he had shares in cane farms in Ingham in northern Queensland. The other drums held phosphate and the bags contained urea.

"Now, the mixing chart is there on the wall," said Dick.

"Yes, I see it," Jack replied.

"Now, mix it all in that 800-litre tank on the trailer there, hitch it up to the tractor and pour the mixture into the roller feed containers for the cattle. I suggest, start putting it out next week and continue until you think there is enough feed for the stock. Make sure the horses don't get to the urea; it will kill them.

"What about those large concrete cylinders?" asked Jack.

They were about one metre 20 centimetres high and a metre in diameter.

"Yes, that is the next thing I wanted to explain to you," said Dick. "Put one cylinder on the dry creek bed, get in and then dig all the sand out of the interior till it sinks, then put another cylinder on top and continue till you hit water. They become permanent wells.

"With the papers I have left you, there are instructions and diagrams on the feeds and wells. Now have you got all that Jack? If you haven't, give me a call.

"Sorry, I'm rushing you a bit but I am on my way to Rockhampton to our stud depot at Raglan." As they walked back towards the car, Dick said, "I have every confidence in you, Jack, to handle whatever needs to be done and congratulations on a lovely family you have."

And with a wave, he took off, leaving a trail of dust behind him. Jack thought, *What a nice grandfatherly-type man, pleasantly explaining what to do.*

Jack then went back to the house.

"What do you think of our new boss?" Jack asked Helen.

"I think he is a lovely man but I was taken back a bit when he gave me a peck on the cheek."

"I think that sort of thing for him was just a natural response," laughed Jack. "How about a cuppa? I just want to have a look at the papers and instructions he left for me. Come to think of it, could you make a sandwich for me with the cuppa? I better have an early lunch as I had asked Max to run the horses in and there is one that's taken my heart."

"Jack, you just gave me a shiver up my spine. I feel you may be riding something that might be too good for you. You have just started this job and may I remind you; you have a loving family."

"Don't worry, my sweet, it's just one of the station horses."

"I do remember the pummelling you got from the Ardglen horses when you tried them out."

Ah well, Jack thought as he finished his bite of lunch and put his riding boots on, *I wish she had not said anything, it might be a bad omen.* He picked up his saddle, hoisted it up on his right shoulder and turned around.

"See you love," as he walked to the buggy, then took off to the shearing shed.

The horses were in the yard and Max was waiting. He must have heard the buggy coming.

"Are you sure you're going to try the mare out?" He had put it into a large separate yard away from the other six horses.

"One thing you have to learn about me, if I say I'll do something, I will." said Jack.

He put the saddle and blanket on the top rail and with bridle and reins in his left hand, leant against the yard rail. He rolled a Log Cabin smoke and just watched his horse. The horse ignored him. After his second smoke, the horse slightly turned her head and looked at Jack.

"Oh, you know I'm here. That's good," he said as he slowly walked to the horse, saying how beautiful she was and how he was enchanted by her.

The horse pricked her ears. No one had talked to her before in this slow sing song voice. He held her attention with a hypnotic look into her eyes. She didn't move. He was still wooing her as he came up beside her, slowly putting the reins around her neck then the bridle. He gave her a rub down all over, never stopping his soothing, loving voice. He led her to the saddle. It was then she showed a bit of white eye. Jack slowly lifted the saddle blanket off the rail, letting her sniff it. He then rubbed her back with it and took his time to place it in the right position. The horse did not move except for a slight quiver in her flank. He then slowly and gently put the saddle on her back. She quivered more but still did not move. He leant down and reached for the surcingle and firmly, but not tight, fastened it to the saddle.

Max said, "We have all managed that, let's see you ride her."

Jack ignored him and slowly walked the mare round the yard, still praising her with his voice. He stopped and tightened the girth, walked her around again and made sure the saddle was firmly on her back.

Max said, coming into the yard with a hopple strap, 'I'll tie her nearside leg up, that will help you get on."

"Out of the yard now, Max, I don't need assistance to get on."

Then, on the left or near side of the horse, Jack pulled the left rein tightly, so the horse's head was close to his buttocks, leaving the right rein slightly loose. He took a deep breath and started to put his left foot in the stirrup.

Then all hell broke loose.

Because Jack had the horse's head turned so tight, when the horse started to buck it actually threw Jack into the saddle as she turned quickly. Now, all Jack had to do was find the other stirrup, which he did. God, she bucked. Head between her front legs, her hind feet to the sun. The reins were slightly loose in his left hand and his right hand held tightly to the monkey strap. A monkey strap was tied through two Ds near the saddle pommel, a great little handle to help mount and it's something to hold on to for dear life, especially when your family loves you.

She bucked, she twisted, she reared, until she was near spent.

"Max, could you open the gate for me now," said a puffed and worn-out Jack, "and follow me with the buggy back to the homestead."

The gate was opened and the very tired man and horse trotted out and headed for home. Jack was worried the horse may get its second wind and start to misbehave again because he had not a second or third wind left. They both started to relax.

He was surprised at the smooth-gaited rhythm of the horse and she maybe thought, *Perhaps it wouldn't be too bad with this human on my back.*

Two very tired and exhausted beings arrived at the house yard gates. Jack dismounted quickly and the horse didn't move. By the way, Jack named the horse on the way home, calling her Buffy. He spent some time unsaddling and rubbing and brushing the horse down, still talking to her in his soft, sing-song voice and let her go in the newly confirmed horse paddock.

"Well, I got to hand it to you," said Max as he pulled up in the buggy, "I never thought you would stick her. A few times I thought you were a goner but somehow you held on."

"Truth to tell Max, I thought I had lost her a few times myself. I think I have earned the right to keep her as my horse now. Let's get you back to the shed. Max, could you do me a favour before you leave? Run the horses down here, as I will be putting out that molasses lick next week and I'm told the urea is deadly to horses, so let's get them away to this side of the creek, out of harm's way."

"No worries, boss. I'll have them down here some time tomorrow and that was a good ride today."

"Thanks Max" Jack noticed the change of title from Jack to boss.

Jack arrived back home with a wife, baby and two dogs to welcome him. A great welcome, a great hug and whirl to his two loves and a great pat and rub for his two best mates, Cammie and Sparkle. *Gosh*, thought Jack, *it's great to be alive and in love.* He was pleased Helen hadn't seen the ride.

"I am having a visitor," Helen exclaimed excitedly. "A Mrs Archer from next door, it will be nice to know someone here."

"Darling, you know from your experience at Ardglen, that you will always have lots of friends in the bush, because you are one of them."

After a great dinner, Helen said, "Damon is starting to crawl and I'm a bit worried that he is missing you after you were so close together at Sandgate. He seems to be looking for you, as I can't keep him in his play pen."

"Bit early trying to get out of his play pen but I guess he is more a boy than baby."

"Yes darling, thanks to your feeds and play times. Do you have a big day tomorrow?"

"Yes, I think I'll start to make a new flood fence on the northern boundary. I will be working in the shed here as I have to make up some parts and scrounge for all the gear I need. What are you going to do?"

"I have to do some baking, as well as tidying up, as I'm having my first visitor, and, of course, keeping an eye out for Damon. I don't know how I will keep him entertained when he starts walking. He has so much energy."

Jack found some 5/8 steel rod, a coil of number eight wire, netting, strong tie wire and bits and pieces. He cut the rod into metre lengths, threaded them, cut a couple of links from a chain, welded those on to a large nut for each rod, gathered a few more nuts and washers, brace and bit, small sledgehammer, axe and fencing pliers and they all went into the buggy to make a new flood fence. Why did you have to know all this? You must be patient as you will find out soon enough.

At the flood fence, Jack soon had the old, wrecked wire down. The creek was dry but that is why he wanted to renew the fence as soon as possible. He found two suitable trees opposite each other on each side of the dry creek. He drilled a hole with the brace and fencing bit, right through the large spotted gum tree, about two metres from the ground. A very difficult job to do.

Once the rod was hammered through a nut and a washer was screwed on to it, the piece of rod pointing to the creek also had a washer and nut on and tightened. Then the large nut with the link was slid on, then a washer and another nut that was riveted on. There was his swivel. Then, threaded through the swivel were the three lengths of number eight wire, previously cut to length. Then, as Jack walked back with the three strands of wire, he twisted them into a cable and that was enough for the morning. He went home for lunch.

After lunch and a quick nap, Jack went back to the flood fence and started drilling the opposite tree to place the rod in. He did the same as he had done with the other rod, then threaded the newly made cable through the link and, with a large wire strainer, he strained the cable up as tight as he could, then tied it and knotted the cable. So, by the end of the day, he had a cable stretched across the creek that was attached to two swivels. And that was enough for today.

Helen was enthused about her visitor, Mrs Archer, who was perhaps 25 years older than her. Old enough to be her mother but she said they got on so well together.

"And guess what," Helen said, "she has invited me down to her place, because it appears she has a great garden and said she could give me lots of plants and shrubs to plant around our bare house."

Jack was pleased, gave her a hug, then he heard galloping horses. He looked out and there was Max bringing the horses from the shearing shed down to the yards. He went to meet him, knowing he had to drive him back.

"Any trouble, Max?" asked Jack.

"No, they couldn't wait to get back here to their own paddock. You giving me a lift back home?" asked Max.

"Sure am, when you're ready."

Buffy, now Jack's horse, galloped up to see her equine friends.

"Did you ride her this morning?" asked Max.

"No, but I must give her a ride in the morning," said Jack.

The next morning, Jack was getting ready to head out the door.

"Jack, where are you going? It's Saturday," said Helen.

"I am just going to give my new horse a ride, I won't be long," he replied.

"Well, I have a surprise for you. We are going to the Archers next door and you are coming with me to help with the pot plants and Damon."

"Oh, that is a surprise. I had no idea you were going there today. No, it will be good to check out next door. I will try to be back by 10."

"And Jack, you do remember that we have a skiing party tomorrow at the Browns' property?"

"Of course, I do," said Jack opening the kitchen door and making his escape before any more commitments were made.

He caught Buffy, going through the same routine as before, getting the horse to know him and not to be frightened. It took the time it took but everything was ready for the mounting. Jack lifted his pants, tightened his belt, screwed on his hat and started to lift his left foot in the stirrup after having Buffy's head turned tight behind him. Same thing.

As soon as the foot touched the stirrup, it was on. Again, Jack managed to get on and put his other foot in his iron as Buffy did her best to get rid of him. She bucked hard, landed hard and did her twist. Jack was surprised how keen she was to get rid of him the second time but she was such a good horse with plenty of spirit, Jack just had to win the battle.

When he thought it was safe, he rode her out of the yard to the front paddock.

"I thought you said it was a quiet horse," said Helen, "I was watching that wild horse trying to get rid of you. It's time you stopped riding those horses, you can't afford to get hurt with a family."

Jack replied as he slowly rode on, "It is a quiet horse, darling. She didn't make a sound; I'll be back at 10."

As he started to trot along, Buffy seemed to relax slightly but he could still feel a tightness in her and was prepared for anything. Jack decided to ride around the eastern boundary to check the fence and get to know the paddock.

The main and only road ran through the front paddock, which needed to be crossed but with one or two cars or trucks a day, there was no problem. Jack was dying for a wee but he hung on, as he was not game to dismount or mount the horse in the scrubby paddock so far from home. The trotting wasn't helping the bladder. It was getting late, so he got Buffy moving into a canter. Well, she must have been waiting for that signal as she took off. Jack let her have her run for a kilometre or so, then had to rein her in a bit, so he could maintain a steady canter but, unfortunately, he lost his hat in the take-off. He wasn't going back and dismounting to get it. He made it back just in time but had to give the horse a good rub down and brush before getting himself ready to take Helen and Damon to the Archers' place.

They were not far down the road before they saw the sign on the right – Fairlea - and turned into the driveway, having to cross the Tower Hill dry creek bed. They finally saw the homestead with a lovely, cool garden. A medium-sized, pleasant grey-haired man greeted them with a smile, introducing himself as Fulbert Archer, at the front gate. After a handshake and introducing Helen and Damon, they were escorted into the pleasant backyard where a pot of tea, scones, jam and cream, were waiting with the Royal Doulton china set on a beautiful tablecloth.

The scones were delicious, washed down with lots of cups of tea. The china cups were so small, Jack couldn't put his large finger into the handle, so had to hold the whole handle with his little finger out, as Helen said later, "daintily".

They talked, whether it was about various types of country here and the people, the newcomers received badly needed information. And the Archers wanted to know all about the newcomers: where were they born, where are their families now, what schools and likes and dislikes. They wouldn't need to ever repeat their stories, because the interesting bits of information would surely, at some time, be told to all who were on the party telephone line.

Fulbert mentioned that Tower Hill Creek could flood dangerously and very quickly. He said it didn't need to rain here as the watershed was near Prairie. So, if it rained in the north it could flood very quickly without people knowing.

"Thanks for the information," said Jack. "I am in the middle of putting a new flood fence on our northern boundary. What is yours like this southern end?"

"You don't have to worry about that, Jack; it is well repaired."

The women retreated, not interested in men's talk, as they went into the garden chatting and picking out plants for Helen to take home.

Fulbert said, "I think you should have bought a truck instead of that little car, as I feel sure you will be taking a lot of plants home, which will be good. I might be able to save water a bit here now."

Jack noticed Fulbert had a dry sense of humour.

"Jack, I'm in charge of the party line from here to Prairie and it would be good if I can ask you to accompany me when I need to check it, or someone can't get through. Do you know anything about party lines?"

"Yes I do, I was in charge of the party line in Cunnamulla that ran along a lot of different country for miles. Yes, there is not much you can teach me about party lines."

Fulbert was pleased he had a knowledgeable companion running the party line. The women called; the men knew they had to obey. What Jack saw lined up beside his car, he realised Fulbert was not joking, it was a truck, not a car, needed.

"Darling, you cannot take all these plants from Mrs Archer. It doesn't seem right," said Jack.

"It's alright, Jack. I have too many and it will do my garden good to be thinned out a bit. I've told Helen there is more for her when she has planted what she has," said Mrs Archer.

Helen had a smile on her face the whole time, as if all her Christmases had come at once. Jack helped her load the boot and around Damon's chair in the back seat and whatever room near Helen in the front seat.

Putting Damon in his chair, he was so dirty from head to foot, one would think he had been chasing worms through their holes. No doubt, by the look at his mouth, he could have eaten one but he was happy.

"A big thank you for the tea scones and plants and you must come up and see how the garden is going when I have it established it a bit," said a still smiling Helen.

"Oh Jack, if you ever need a killer when the creek is in flood, I will have one ready, as we know you have to cross the creek to get to most of your property," said Fulbert.

"Thanks, Fulbert," he said with a smile and a second thank you. One more wave and they drove home.

"Darling, it's getting late so, if you like, I'll feed Damon and make the sandwiches, while you sort out your plants in the car. Or would you sooner feed the baby and make lunch while I empty the car my usual way?" asked Jack.

"No thank you, I'll let you make lunch and look after the baby whilst I sort out and arrange my plants." Helen replied.

And so, it was.

Sunday was a sleep in for all, a good breakfast, a game with Damon and finding suitable clothes for a skiing party. Helen had bathers, Jack said his shorts would do and for their little son, nappies and a pair of little shorts his mother had made, along with his favourite top, a t-shirt with a lassoing cowboy on it.

Helen was busy cooking and making a macaroni nut salad dish as she had found out everyone was bringing food to share. They organised cutlery, mugs, drinks and all the necessary baby gear and food. Not quite sure how far Lammermore was but Helen was told about 20 kilometres north from Jireena.

When they eventually got there, they were surprised at how many cars were there, parked beside a huge man-made lake that Doug Brown had built. As they were introduced around, Jack, as normal, forgot every one's names but Helen had the gift of remembering everyone, so Jack often had to nudge her and enquire who was who.

They had a lovely time and met a lot of people they were sure would be welcomed friends. Some had heard that Helen wanted some shade trees and a few kind people presented her with some, which she was delighted with. A tall, sunburnt chap, a little bit older than Jack, asked if he had ever played polocrosse. Jack said he had, years ago as a jackaroo but had no gear now. This chap, named Ron, said they were starting up a club next year and asked if he would be interested? Jack said he would and that that would give him time to get the gear and practice but the difficult part would be to find a lightweight horse float to tow behind his Ford Escort. Rod said he would put the word out; they had six months till May before they were ready to play.

Helen was called. It was her turn to have a go at waterskiing. She protested and said she had never done it before. The protest was put aside as a lady helped her put a life jacket on and she was led down to the boat where Doug was the instructor and driver. It took Helen quite a few goes to get up but when she did, she got so excited that she came straight off. Doug picked up a half drowned spluttering girl who said, "Thanks, for trying but I really have had enough."

"Okay, you did your best and that's good. Now, how about we go in, it must be lunch time."

Lunch was a variety of everyone's food. Women chatted, men yarned, then the weather started to turn and a few started to pack up.

"Hey Jack, before it rains, you better have a go. You're the last one," yelled Doug.

Life jacket on, skis strapped, one false start then Jack was up. He was skiing well, even crossed the wake a few times. He had skied a little on the Warrego River at Cunnamulla when he was an overseer there but was not that experienced.

They were at the back of the lake when the hail came down. Doug didn't want his boat damaged, so he opened the throttle wide and sped for cover on the shore. Jack was hanging on for dear life with the hail cutting into his face, arms and legs. He said after, it was so painful with the hail hitting him at that speed he thought he would be scarred for life. But he wasn't. It was a great day except the packing up of wet gear and families. Then there were rushed goodbyes to get home before the rain really set in.

Helen was pleased with the trees she got and the rain to water her new plants. A shower for all and Damon had a fun one with his dad. Dry clothes, a cup of tea and a nap for all.

Monday saw Jack checking the tractor, full of fuel water and oil. It started a second time. He then attached it to the trailer and started the mixing of feeds and molasses and pumping into the tanker. When everything was ready, he dropped in for breakfast and wondered if Damon would like to go with him on the tractor and that would give his darling time to start working in her garden, unhindered. She thought it a wonderful idea.

"But how long will you be and can you really handle him safely?" she asked.

"Don't worry, we will manage, wont we ol' chap." Jack

picked up a smiling baby boy, who was going on an adventure of a lifetime.

"Hang on, I will give you a small bag with some biscuits and water for Damon."

Once they got the goods, they waved goodbye to mummy and headed for the tractor. The seat was quite large and the two of them fitted comfortable together with Jack's knees and legs holding his son safely in. And now to feed the cattle.

It was a big, exciting day for the two of them. Hearing the tractor, the cattle knew feed was being delivered and ran to the feeders. As Jack was piping the mixed feed into the troughs, the cattle would mill around, pushing each other for their feed. Now these cattle were huge. Braham breeders are larger than most cattle but Damon was fascinated by them. Sitting on the tractor seat, holding the steering wheel, he should have been terrified at these huge monsters milling around but, in fact, he was right at home with them. This seemed silly as how would a little boy of six months, show such a feeling towards these huge beasts?

They had four paddocks with three and four feeders in each, so it was time for a rest, as they were near the shearing shed. Jack drove the tractor there so Damon and he could get off the tractor and have a biscuit, water and a rest. An inspection was made of the quarters to see if Max and Madge had left them in a clean and tidy condition before they left and they had, which was a bit of a surprise to Jack. They had their rest and there was one paddock to go before heading home.

"Your mother will be getting worried about us, as we have taken longer than we thought and it will be a late lunch for us when we get home," said dad to son.

And it was and mother was worried as she lifted a little, tired boy off the tractor and took him inside for a change, a drink and sleep.

"That was a long time, darling, to have him out there."

"He seemed to love it and was excited about it. He only fell asleep on the way home, which took some holding, driving the tractor on the station roads and making sure he was safe, but it all worked out extremely well." Jack changed the subject. "Give us a look at what you have done while we were away. My, you have been busy, you must have found a hoe and fork to break up the ground and I see you have planted quite a few. It looks great what you have done."

Jack started to walk to the kitchen and felt a tug on the back of his shirt.

"You are not getting away that easily, young man," she said. "I want a trellis to put up here and, if you could build up this section of the garden, and where do you think I should put the shade trees?"

"Where we need shade from the western sun, dear. I'm hungry. Let's have some lunch and discuss the garden more. Have you drawn out a plan yet?"

"Yes, of course, it's all here." Helen pointed to her head. "Is a salad and cold meat alright for lunch? We are getting short of bread and, dear, I'm nearly out of meat. We will need a killer for tomorrow."

"I think the mail truck comes Wednesday, so you better make an order for him to bring it out then. I think we should go to Hughenden later this week and start to have a few accounts at the shops. Write me out an order for the mail and I will see what I can do."

"Thanks, I'll do that after your nap, now eat up."

Jack looked up the Hughenden bakery and greengrocer in the local telephone directory, rang them, told them his name and that he was the new manager of Jireena. He asked if he could make an order to go on the mail run this Wednesday. He would be in on Friday to pay and start an account with them.

That was fine. They agreed and asked what he was wanting.

He read out the items on Helen's note and they said they would make sure the order would be on the mail truck. Jack said, "Thank you so much and we will see you Friday".

"Oh, you are a clever one," said Helen, "you make things so easy, I would have been nervous doing all that and probably made mistakes but you did it as if you do it every day."

"I'm going to tow our truck into the shed. Want to give us a hand?"

"Yes, if you promise not to yell at me like the last time we towed a vehicle together."

"Okay I promise. All I want you to do is steer the truck and get ready to break when needed."

Surprisingly, it all worked out well. The truck and tractor were in the shed and there was no shouting but Jack believed one needed to keep a very tight lip now and then.

Now the jobs started in earnest. The flood fence was finished, the trellis put up and the garden set out, Buffy was ridden and started to behave when Jack was mounting and dismounting and enjoyed their rides together. Shopping and accounts were settled and made. Mail truck Dennis was pleasant and always on time with their goods. Damon was getting stronger and more active and started to cause his parents some very worrying times.

C.9

Baby Troubles, Townsville

Often, they could not find Damon. They looked under his bed, they looked under their bed, they looked and searched the whole house. Panic ensued. Where in the devil was he? They searched outside. No, not in the buggy, not in the tool shed. Where was he? He could not crawl that far, could he?

"I found him," came a yell from the hay shed.

Jack raced over and, there he was, sound asleep on a bale of hay about a metre and a half off the ground. How could he crawl up there? They were astonished how far the little fella could go. Another search, he was found sleeping with the calf in the calf pen in the cattle yards. It was a constant worry. Would a snake get him? What if he fell? He was here one half second and disappeared the next.

Jack came in from servicing the buggy; a never-ending job. The two air cleaners could not handle the dust, so all parts of the engine would be clogged. As he walked into the house to say something to Helen, she looked out the window and with a very frightened and shaky voice, choked, "Jack look!"

What he saw made his blood run cold. Somehow or other, his son had found his way to the horse yard and was surrounded by the station horses. Here he was, pulling himself up on the nearside of a horse's back leg. The horse took one step forward and so did Damon. His first step.

"Jack, for God's sake, get him out of there before he is kicked to death or trampled. Pleeeease go now!" Helen was mad at Jack, because he slowly sauntered over to the yards, instead of running, as she wanted him to do.

Jack said, "Hey mate, you better get over here. Your mother wants you."

The boy let go of the horse's leg. The horse wasn't the slightest bit distressed about a little human hanging on his back leg. Damon crawled over to his dad, who lifted him up and gave him a big cuddle, saying, "Son, please don't go in the yard with the horses, it really upsets your mother."

Whether he understood what he was being told, was another matter. A very relieved mother now holding her baby safe and sound, scolded him for giving her a big fright.

It was only a few months later, he learnt to walk and that became a bigger problem, He was in the garden with his mother, then gone. It was a frightening affair. One day, Jack was driving home from the shearing shed when he spotted something white in the distance. There were no sheep in that paddock so what could it be? It needed further investigation.

Driving over, he saw his young son in his nappy, about one kilometre from the house. He stopped the buggy, walked over and said to his boy, "That is naughty, naughty, to leave your mother at home. Now, we walk back to see if she is alright."

And when they got home, he walked the tired Damon around the house yard fence twice and continued saying, "You must not go outside this fence, you must not go outside this fence." Then gave him over to his distressed wife.

Walking back to the buggy, Jack was really worried. His darling son could easily have been taken by wild dogs or pigs, which were prevalent in the area, or dangerous snakes and spiders. Then there was water. He could take a big walk, be thirsty, have a drink and drown. How many bush kids had that happened to?

The dog goes for a walk with the child following happily together. Maybe the dog is actually leading the child away from the home because of jealousy or just doesn't like the little human nuisance. Then, when the two are a long way from home, the dog decides it wants to go home and takes off, leaving the child stranded. That was Jack's theory anyway. Unfortunately, this thing happened now and then, with a fatal finish to an adventure. What could Jack do to contain his energetic young son?

It happened again a week later. Jack was home when, again he saw a bit of white, this time in the road paddock, where he knew there was a gully with some water holes in them. It was his wandering son again. He caught up to him, turned him around and, with his open hand, smacked his son on the nappy bottom. More push than smack but doing it constantly till they reached home. He repeated as they walked, "Naughty boy, naughty. I have told you not to go out of the yard."

Helen was at the house fence gate watching. When the two reached the gate, her little son was crying saying, "Daddy hit me," and his mother said, "You will get a bigger hit from me, if you do it next time." The boy was led around the yard again, showing him his boundaries.

Both parents were so upset as they'd smacked their darling boy, who didn't realise the danger he was in. In taking off, they could not lock the gates as he could climb over the fence. How high would you have to build it? They could not lock him inside or install a very mild electric fence. No, he must learn his lesson himself that there are rules and he must obey them.

A rule the parents made for themselves, before children came along, was, one wasn't to threaten a child with discipline from the other. I think it was then when Helen broke the rule. Damon had been particular naughty this day and his mother said, "Wait till your father gets home, I'll tell him how naughty you are and he will be cross with you."

Jack came home and his darling said, "Damon has been very naughty and I told him watch out when daddy comes home. He is now hiding under the house."

Jack crawled under the house to find him, then saw two big brown eyes looking at him behind a stump. Damon said, "Is she after you too, Dad?"

"Yea, I think we will sit here a while until she cools down."

So, they both huddled together for a time, then Jack said, "I think it's safe to come out now."

And they both scrambled out and went into the kitchen. When Helen was about to say something, Jack frowned and said, "Don't say a thing."

As they often did, son and father would go out together, checking waters and the cattle, getting a killer for meat and doing normal station inspections. On this day, as they crossed the creek, it had a puddle in it, which didn't register with Jack. They were away for about an hour and half. As they came back home for lunch, they were surprised and shocked. The puddle in the creek was now a raging torrent.

How to get across? No way could they drive through; they would be instantly swept away. Jack thought, *We could cross it on my new flood fence.*

Now, remember, Jack put two rods with swivels in opposite trees and ran a handmade cable across the creek. What he didn't tell you, later on, he ran strips of netting from the cable to the creek bed, joining the sides together and placing small logs tied to the bottom of the netting. So, when a flood came, it all lifted up. All the debris and rubbish would flow under it and, as the water decreased, it would become a good stock proof fence.

So, with the water raging, father said to son, "I am going to piggyback you across the creek. You must hold very tight around daddy's neck and wrap your legs tight against mine. Now show me."

He lifted Damon up on his back and he held tight around his dad's neck. A bit too tight as he was choking his dad.

"Not that tight, just a little bit tight," said Jack. Damon was a very big strong boy, even at 10 months.

His legs were tight around his father's waist.

"Okay, that's the way you must hang on to daddy." He lowered his son to the ground for a rest and to work out how he could safely cross that flooded boiling creek. "Let's give it a try, son," as he lifted his precious boy to his back "Now hang on tight and never, never let go."

The two of them started to cross. Jack, hand over hand, on his home-made cable, his feet on the raised netting for support. Damon, on his back, holding tight. The further they moved along the cable, the more it was stretched and started to sag. Jack's feet were now in the water. Halfway across, Jack started to feel very uneasy. He could feel his son's grip on him starting to loosen.

If Damon let go, there was no way his father would be able to save him, if he fell into the dirty, churning water, in this fast, raging creek, now river.

"Son, hang on as tight as you can, we are nearly across. You are doing a great job. I am so proud of you son, you are so strong," encouraged Jack in a choking voice.

His other concern was, he was no engineer, just a handy man. He didn't know about physics, strengths and weakness of materials. Would the weld hold on the homemade swivels? Would it all collapse and have them swept away, tangled in the netting, to be no more?

"Hang on mate and we will make it to the other side."

And they did. The flood fence held and was successful and two very tired hungry boys walked home for their lunch.

"I didn't hear the buggy arrive; did it break down again?" asked Helen.

"No love, it just got stuck and we walked home," Jack replied.

Damon had to say, "Mummy I was good, I hung on to daddy's back very tight and I didn't get wet."

"What's that all about?"

Jack put his finger to his lips, gave a wink to his son and said, "That's our secret," and gave his son a big hug.

That night, whilst trying to get to sleep, he thought about how stupid he had been. All he had to do was for them to sit and watch the flood, as it would only be a few hours before it had gone down and they could have driven the buggy through the remains of the water. Yes, Helen would have been worried, wondering where they were, but she would have driven the little Ford down and seen the creek was flooded and her boys on the other side. It would not have hurt them to go hungry or thirsty for a few hours. So, why did he do such a stupid thing, risking his son's life and his own for no real reason?

Jack, years later, still got butterflies in his stomach, thinking how he could have lost his little man. Again, Jack had jumped in without thinking of the circumstances but, most times, it would be his best move.

"Darling, I have been talking to some of the girls about where and who would be a good doctor and dentist," said Helen. "They have given me a few good names, but they are in Townsville. There is not a doctor in Hughenden and the ones in Charters Towers are booked out for months. I do think I need a doctor to know my history if something happens to my stoma and to know a specialist in case something goes pear-shaped."

"I think it's a wonderful idea," said Jack. "I should have

thought of it myself, and we need a bit of a break. We have feed and water for the stock, so I'll check with Mr Frazer if it's alright to leave for a week. We also need supplies and a bigger car seat for Damon."

"That is all good but don't you think I should make appointments now and find what dates are available?"

"Good thinking. Why don't you do it now? You have some names and numbers and Christmas is only seven weeks away."

"Alright, I will see what I can do but don't stand around while I'm doing it. It makes me nervous."

They had an agreement with the Archers when they were away. Jack or Helen would go down and check the kerosene fridge, which was notorious for breaking down when one was away, feed the dogs and chooks and water the garden, if necessary. And they would do the same for Jack and Helen when they went away. A very handy arrangement.

This day, Jack went down with Damon to check on the Archers place. He left his young son in the car whilst he checked the fridge and fed the chooks and dogs, the garden was good after a shower of rain. He was only away from Damon for five or six minutes. He was horrified to see Damon crouched down on the floor of the buggy covered in blood.

Jack quickly picked him up, checked him out thoroughly, to see where all the blood was coming from. It was from a small cut on his thumb. Why all the blood? In the buggy was Jack's .222 rifle and a skinning knife which lived there and was not to be touched. He had done quite a few demonstrations to his son, showing what happened if he played with guns and what sharp knives did after killing a 'roo for meat for the dogs.

But Damon had to play with the knife, while his dad was away and he had cut his thumb. He knew he was in trouble and tried to rub the blood away. The more he rubbed, the more he bled. He tried to wipe it off his nappy and tried to hide the dripping blood the best he could. But, of course, he made it worse.

His dad put a band aid on it. It had stopped bleeding by then and they drove back home. He carried his blood-covered son out of the car. His mother saw all the blood on her baby and she was horrified. Jack said he was fine as it was just a cut thumb. He was not believed until Mother stripped the clothes off her son and gave him a good wash down.

"Darling, appointments have been made," said Helen. "I can get the doctor and dentist on the same day but for the specialist I can't get in till the following week, but I did make the appointment. I hope it's all right because we will be away for eight days. We can always cancel it if we can't spend the time away."

"No, it will be right. We will keep the appointments and have a bit of a holiday," said Jack.

"How far is Townsville from here?"

"I think it's a good day's drive, about 400 kilometres, and what are the dates you have made, so I can have everything organised here before we go?"

"Its two weeks from tomorrow and I have made an appointment for you at the dentist too."

Jack rang up his boss and asked if they could have a week off to go to the doctors and get supplies.

"Jack, you don't have to ask me," said Mr Frazer, "if you think water and stock are fine, well, it's your call. You don't have to call me if you need to go somewhere but early in the new year, we will do a muster and branding. I'll give you fair warning before I come."

Gosh, thought Jack, *that was different from Griffo just arriving without warning.*

Jack raced around to make everything right for the week off. He had sold the diarrhoea ducks weeks ago as he told the buyer they were layers. He didn't explain it wasn't eggs they laid but something else. The goat had gone to greener pastures rather smartly, after he fell through the canvas roof of the buggy and then proceeded to eat all of Jack's lunch.

Biddy, the resident cattle dog, laid around asleep all day and looked forward to the occasional ride in the buggy. The waters were fine, the cows and calves were stable, the sheep didn't have to be shorn for a few months yet and the Archers would check the fridge and feed the animals and water Helen's garden, which had made a big difference, although the shade trees were taking time to create shade.

They were all ready for their trip to the big smoke: Townsville.

Townsville looked a nice clean town. It had a pretty garden island strip down the centre of the road and a large well-kept park, looking out to the sparkling Coral Sea. A few people were shopping and there were a handful of tourists or, more accurately, hippy backpackers trying to find themselves. There was plenty of 'Peace' man!

They found a nice caravan park near the Ross River and hired a stationary caravan for the week of their stay. One problem was their disappearing son. They would have to keep him beside them at all times. They could not trust him for a second. He was like a wound-up toy with a self-winding spring.

Another problem was, Helen had made an appointment for herself at the doctors and one for Jack at the same time, at the dentist. What were they going to do with Damon? The people at the caravan park suggested a child-minding place in the CBD, so they had a look at it. The toddlers playing there seemed happy enough and the place looked bright and clean. Yes, they could mind Damon the next morning, while they had their appointments.

"We do that a lot for country folk that come down for business," the lady informed them.

The parents were happy with the place but they hadn't consulted their son. He was not going into a strange place with strange people. And you couldn't blame him. For his short life, he had only his mum and dad and really had not adapted to the outside world, as city kids would have. This was all too strange for him. He clutched his dad and wouldn't let go when he tried to hand him to the kind lady, saying, "You will have a good time here with the other children and Mummy and Daddy will be back shortly."

They had to leave numbers of the doctor and dentist so they could be contacted if necessary. They guiltily left their baby screaming at the centre, which they were told, they were used to bush kids being unfamiliar with strangers and they were assured they were experienced to handle it.

Jack got the message at the dentist. "Come and pick up your son immediately."

"Is he hurt?"

"No, we just can't have him any longer."

It was lucky that Jack had just finished with the dentist. All he had was a check and clean. He raced out of the building and ran to the minding centre and picked up a very distressed son, who just clutched to him more tightly than when they had crossed the flooded creek. Jack paid what was owed and was told, very firmly, never to bring him back. Ever.

They had arranged to meet at the centre, so Jack and Damon waited outside till Helen arrived. She could see Damon was stressed and clutching his father.

"What happened?" a concern mother wanted to know.

Jack gave her the information he knew and suggested they find a café and have lunch and work out what to do next. They had six days to fill in. Lists were made, shopping done, a tourist day package to Magnetic Island booked and familiarising themselves with the city.

"Oh, love, you didn't tell me how you got on with the doctor," said Jack.

"He was great," said Helen, "He wanted to know the surgeon who had done my operation and kept saying how well I managed my appliance. All doctors seem to be fascinated with my surgery."

"No, they're not, my sweet. They are not interested in that; they are only interested in a very attractive lady with a happy personality and are extremely jealous of your husband."

"What nonsense. You do carry on a bit."

"Well, you might not accept it but it's true."

Jack knew full well, she was flattered with the compliment but wasn't going to let Jack know that.

The specialists, an obstetrician and a gastroenterologist were again amazed at Helen's health and wellbeing and again quizzed her about her operation and who done it. Both doctors suggested six monthly visits and those appointments were made.

Happy Helen with Damon at Ardglen Cunnamulla.

Helen in the cleaned out waterhole.

Helen learning to ride a motorcycle. Note the safety gear.

The old PMG truck on the way to Prairie. Sparkel, Cammie, Gt Ford Escort, Boss and Damon.

A proud Mum with Deborah the cyclone baby.

Jack and Damon celebrating Deborah's 1st birthday. Susie the Basset in the background.

L) Damon with Susie the Basset hound.
R) The Dodge leaving Bannockburn for Shipfield.

Susie and the Boss taking the granddaughter of the Condamine bell inventor for a ride.

C.10

Water & Dog Incidents

A brand new, short base Landrover was waiting for Jack, as the buggy had had its time with sand and dust and could take no more. The problem was, the Landrover was in Hughenden and Jack had to get the buggy there as the trade in. Problem. It was undrivable.

There were only two ways to get it there: one on a tray truck but there were none around, the second choice would be to tow it for 102 kilometres. Jack rang old Mr Arty Brunner. He had vehicles and, besides being a farmer, he was a trucker,

"Don't worry, son. I'll get you and that buggy thing into town. Next Tuesday be okay?"

"Yes, thank you, I really appreciate that."

Tuesday arrived and so did Mr Brunner with his tow vehicle, a bloody semi-trailer with cattle in it. He was going to tow Jack 200 kilometres? Mr Brunner pulled out a chain and tied it to the front of the VW Buggy and to the back of his truck. He was a no-nonsense man.

"Well, what are you hanging around for? You wanted a tow, you got one, so get in the buggy. I'm late enough as it is."

Jack's life was forfeited in just five minutes. As soon as they were on the road, the truck was put into top gear and the tow of all tows began. The dust and stones flew up from the dual back wheels from five meters away. It was a cyclonic 80-mile wind. The windscreen dissolved just after the start. Jack was now fully exposed to, not only stones and dust, but rocks and the occasional shit from the floor of the truck. He had to steer the buggy straight, as it was in danger of rolling over if it got out of sync with the truck, which of course was invisible, not only from the dust, but also the squinting. Jack's sight was severely hampered with all the contents of the road. Maybe there was a bit of fan belt or part of an oil filter or even a tyre tread. If it wasn't in his eyes, it was in his mouth, nostrils, ears, hair and penetrated his whole body, which was starting to bruise from the onslaught of stones and rocks.

Imagine sitting in that opened little jeep, behind a semi-trailer for 60 kilometres of rough, potholed dirt road with the occasional dead kangaroo to bounce over. Jack knew what it was like.

Mr Brunner pulled up at Prairie to check the cattle in his truck. He saw Jack and casually said, "Well we only got 40 kilometres to go and it's all tarred."

He then promptly walked back and drove off to Hughenden. Jack could say nothing, due to a mouth chock-a-bloc full of dust and God knows what. He was also in shock. He didn't even comprehend that he was still sitting in a chair, because all around him was a shattered metal, unrecognised body of a vehicle.

Mr Brunner kindly stopped at the dealers and unhooked the buggy, then just drove off with his cattle, not saying anything. Jack eased his bruised and aching body out of the seat and walked into the dealers. They were shocked at seeing this semblance of a human being walk in. They, of course, were used to customers walking in with dirty work clothes, but this?

Jack walked up to the cleanest of clean salesman.

"I have come to pick up a new Landrover for Jireena station."

"And what is your name?" asked the salesman.

"Jack Alexander and I have the trade-in outside."

The salesman walked outside, saw the metal in the gutter and enquired, with raised eyebrow, "And this is your trade-in on a brand new, never before driven Landrover?"

"I was informed by Mr Frazer that you would hand over the vehicle immediately, as he has fully paid for it, plus registration and insurance. So, where is my vehicle?"

Jack was in no mood to be mucked about with. He was tired, bruised, filthy, extremely thirsty and hungry. The salesman, who wanted to have as little as possible to do with this dirty angry man, said, "The car is in the laneway and I'll see you there. I will just get the keys and vehicle's papers."

Which he did rather quickly. He was disinclined to shake the hand of the new owner and, in fact, dropped the keys and papers on the seat and walked away. Customer relations, ha!

Christmas? While they were in Townsville, Jack noticed a sign on a rather nice-looking hotel. It read:

Join us for a lavish Christmas dinner, Christmas Day, Limited 20 Guests. Accommodation included. Book now

Jack thought, *That sounds great. What a surprise for Helen.* Better than the three of them alone on Christmas day and Helen working in the hot kitchen just for the two of them. Why not drive down early Christmas morning? It should take four and half hours, then have a camp and a surprisingly great time at a prepared Christmas dinner. He took note of the phone number and, when home, he booked and posted a cheque for the full cost.

"Time to get up. It's Christmas morning," yelled Jack.

He had already been up, getting as much as he could ready for the big day. Damon was awake, so Jack plonked him on the bed, along with a few Christmas presents. Helen wanted to know what the rush was and sleepily asked, "Jack get back into bed, it's Christmas. Give me a cuddle and lets just enjoy the day with the three of us."

Damon was excited about the parcels on the bed and started ripping paper everywhere, much to his delight.

"My darling, here is your pressy. Open it now and you will see what the rush is all about and a very merry Christmas, my sweet." He gave her a kiss, a bit longer than necessary.

With her sleepy eyes she had to read the colourful tickets. The Great Christmas Dinner and Accommodation in Townsville. She wasn't that excited but Helen never got excited about anything, except when she saw Jack and her baby.

"Darling, I haven't got any clothes to wear and we have got to get all the baby gear. It's all a bit of a shock." Helen realised she was being ungrateful. "But darling, thank you. I know you have put a lot of thought into this lovely surprise and thinking about it now, it's something different and a bit exciting."

"All you have to do is get yourself ready. The car is ready to go, all the baby gear and food is packed, so all you have to do is get yourself a few things together," said Jack. "We can shower and change into good clothes down there, as we do have the accommodation already booked and the Archers know we will be away for two days."

"Trust you, just the best organiser. Come on, let's help Damon get his presents. He seems to be getting a bit frustrated finding what's inside."

There was a lovely, yellow teddy bear, just the right size to cuddle, walkaround with and take to bed, from his grandfather and some beautifully illustrated baby books from his gran. There were more presents but it was decided to stretch them out over a few days.

The drive down was pleasant. They got there at 2.15pm, in

plenty of time for the Christmas dinner. When they arrived at the hotel, it was quiet, as no one was around. They banged the buzzer and, after a good long wait, a very dishevelled sleepy woman came down and said, "Yes?"

"We are the Alexanders."

Her eyes widened. "Oh, you're so late, we waited ages for you but then went ahead and now we are all sleeping it off."

Helen whispered to Jack, "It was a lunch, not a dinner."

(To save Jack's hide, this writer shall read from the Macquarie Essential Dictionary: *dinner/'dina/n 1.the main meal, taken either about noon or in the evening 2. A formal meal in honour of some person.* Poor Jack, he did his best.)

The lady kindly found a few scraps of chicken legs and other leftovers that were not filling at all. It wasn't the lavish Christmas dinner Jack had envisaged.

"Well, darling, that was a surprise, wasn't it? You did your best. Let's find our rooms, have a rest and we surely will find something this evening." Helen, as usual, wasn't upset about it all. She was used to Jack's surprises, that always come with a twist.

There were no meals at any hotels or cafés. All kitchens were closed for that night. Our hungry couple and babe trawled the streets of Townsville and managed to get a couple of bread rolls, one half cold chicken roll and three dim sims from a late closing, corner outlet.

A Christmas never to forget and will always be remembered.

The wet season was a fizzle. Water holes were drying up but Jack came to the rescue. First, he had to find wells and dig new ones. Jack loaded up the trailer with four big concrete cylinders, the hand winch crane, three opened four-gallon buckets, a short-handled spade and he was ready to go.

Helen called out, "Why don't you take Damon with you; you can take some toys and he can play in the sand under the trailer. That will give me free time in the garden."

"Good idea," Jack replied. "Could you rustle up a bit of feed and a drink for him and I'll get the toys, and some gear for him. We will be back for lunch."

"Don't forget, Mr Frazer is coming sometime this afternoon. Remember, he is bringing a couple of racehorses down? Did you know anything about that?"

"Only that he is bringing horses down. I don't know why."

Damon was happy playing under the shade of the trailer in the sand with his toy truck and his little bucket and spade with a few dinky toys thrown in. Jack winched a cylinder down in the centre of the creek and started digging it out. Time to put the second cylinder down, remembering to put the bottom groove into the tongue of the lower one for a seal.

Jack was filling buckets full of sand and the cylinders, with their weight, were slowly sinking into it, to eventually find a good source of water. He got two down and was ready to put the third one in, every now and then, looking over the rim to see if Damon was alright.

Jack had to stand on one of the buckets to see over the edge of the top cylinder. For less than a second, his heart froze. A huge, wild sow, with six suckers, was hiding beside the trailer wheel. Damon was playing inside beside the wheel. The pig was ready to get a nice feed for her babies. Jack sprang out of those cylinders like a jack-in-a-box, yelled and screamed and frightened the murderous hunter that was going to eat his baby away.

It was all too much. Jack unhooked the tractor, picked up his son, put him on his knee and headed straight home. Jack was in a bit of a state. If he had not looked up at that specific time...? He hadn't been checking on his baby for a while, being too busy finishing off the second cylinder.

Helen said, "You're early dear, lunch is not quite ready."

Jack could not keep the close call from her; he just had to tell her. She knew he'd had a big fright Putting her arms around him in a loving cuddle, she said, "It's alright, you're both safe and that's the main thing."

After his early lunch, Jack went back to putting the well in, without his son. He needed to use a lot of physical work to get over the near tragedy.

The third cylinder was quarter way down and there was some seepage coming through, when he heard a voice, "You down there, Jack?"

He had forgotten about his boss coming. He had to put the four-gallon drums on top of each other to get out of the now two and quarter metre deep well. He was nearly out when the buckets he was standing on, gave way. He didn't want to fall back in the well and crack his head on the edge of the cylinder so he grabbed what he could to save himself from falling.

His boss yelled out, "Let go of my dick!"

Jack had, inadvertently, grabbed his boss' trousers in the wrong place. The boss pulled back. Jack was not going to let go of his safety hold until, with his other hand, he managed to grab the rim of the cylinder, thus letting his boss free, to lift himself out of the well.

"Well, that has extended the life of the ol' fella," said Mr Frazer.

Jack apologised and said, "There was no damage, I hope?"

"I'll tell you if there is in the morning." He seemed more amused about what had happened than worried.

"Jack, there are a couple of racehorses we have put in the yard. Rob brought them in his horse float and I followed him down, just to see how you and Helen are getting along," Mr Frazer said. "I told her I would be staying for tea and overnight and she said she was pleased to have me. More than my wife would say. You don't mind Jack?"

"Not in the slightest. You're most welcome. What about Rob?"

"Oh, he left for home as soon as he delivered the horses. You finish what you're doing, and I'll just go for a drive around the property and see you tonight and, by the way, Jack, you are doing an excellent job and I am pleased."

"Thanks," said Jack, keen to get the third cylinder down before evening.

That evening over dinner, Mr Frazer explained that the horses he had brought down were racehorses. One was called Jireena, after the property, had won races in Townsville and the other also had had some minor placings. If Jack didn't mind, he said, could he ride them and give them some stock work? Jack informed his boss he did not know anything about racehorses, in fact, nothing about the racing game.

"Not to worry about that, Jack, I just need them ridden now and then," said Jack's boss.

Did Mr Frazer have something in mind other than a bit of stock work for those horses?

Helen was worried about Cammie. She tried washing her, shampooing her, giving her flea powder but she kept scratching holes in her hide. They were bleeding and looked awful, so Helen and Jack took her to the vet. He said, "She has a bad eczema, typical for corgis. Cortisone treatment will help for a while, but it is not a cure."

What to do with one of their family. She had been Helen's close mate for four years. They must try everything and they did but, eventually, they couldn't let her suffer any more. It took some time for Helen, Jack and Damon to get over Cammie's passing; she was such a good little dog.

A replacement had to be made. Helen wanted another corgi but Jack said, "No, not if it gets eczema and we have to go through all that trauma again."

It was decided they would get a beagle puppy; they didn't

know much about them except they were hunting dogs. It was a good size for a family, a nice multi-coloured tan and black and the few pictures they had seen of them, they looked a happy dog.

With some research, they found a stud in Sydney that had a bitch pup for sale. Would it be possible to send it by plane and train to Prairie train station and does it have all its needles? And so on. They were assured they were a very reputable stud and had all the medication needed for her age and, yes, they often sent pups interstate.

"That's not a problem," they said, "and with the pup we will send instructions on how to look after her, plus her stud certificate."

Jack sent the cheque and they excitedly awaited the new member of the family.

The day arrived. Jack and Damon went to the station to pick up their puppy beagle. The station porter brought the crate to them and said, "Don't know what sort of an animal you have bought but, if it's a dog, it's the funniest- looking dog I've ever seen."

Jack thought so too. It was not like the beagles he had seen. The pup was pleased to be let out of its travelling crate and licked them both, wagging its tail to show its excitement. Jack pulled out the very thick envelope and opened it up to see if they needed to buy anything for the puppy before they took her home. Then Jack saw his mistake in the registration papers. It wasn't a beagle he had bought but a basset hound. Good on ya Jack, you have done it again!

They all fell in love with each other. They called her Susie. She was just the best puppy, except for her long ears that dragged her food and everything else along the floor. Damon used her for a sleeping pillow and, while he was sleeping on her, she would refuse to move.

Helen, whether with textiles, art, gardening or cooking,

loved to create. She would sketch something out, make a patten and a beautifully designed dress or blouse would appear. Same with the garden. She would put a lot of thought into its design and create a lovely outside area. She just loved seeds and would collect them, putting them in her handbags, pockets, kitchen drawers, just about anywhere. She would propagate them and be thrilled when little plants grew.

Jack was so proud of her and her creations but especially her creative cooking. He felt he was the luckiest man alive. Like a lot of creative people, Helen enjoyed a quiet environment and was very secretive with her feelings. She was a fun person, that now and then would play tricks and be mischievous. She was a listener, not a talker, very opposite to Jack in that field. She loved jokes and would gaily laugh with everyone else even if sometimes, not really understanding the joke. She would often encourage Jack to tell one of his stories when out with people and, even though she had heard them a hundred times, she would laugh as if she had heard them for the first time.

Dear old Biddy, the old cattle dog that came with the place, who laid around asleep all day, got slightly excited when Jack asked her if she would like a ride with Sparkle in the vehicle when he went to check out the property.

This particular day, besides checking waters, feed and fences, Jack shot a few wild pigs. When they came to a large water hole, a huge wallaroo was sitting in the middle, cooling off.

Biddy flew out of the vehicle, swam out to the wallaroo and started to bite the back of its neck with her gummy mouth. The huge, muscular animal put his arm behind his back, grabbed poor Biddy and held her underwater till she drowned and then let her go so the dead dog floated down into the water hole.

Jack was upset and furious. He got his gun to shoot the

murderer but had no ammunition left. He threw stones and rocks at it but the animal kept getting closer to the edge of the water, trying to draw him into the water so it could get him too. There was nothing Jack could do but drive sadly home with Sparkle as company.

C.11

Happiness and Cyclone

It was smoko time when Helen casually said, "Jack, I'm pregnant. We are having another baby."

Well, Jack was not going to make the same mistake twice. He flew off his chair, knocking over his cup of tea and the chair and grabbed Helen, who was in shock by the suddenness of Jack's reaction. She was hugged and whirled around so fast, they both fell on the floor, then they laughed until the tears of joy came.

"When is the baby due?" he asked.

"By my calculations, the first week in January," she said.

"Well, that means a few trips to doctors in Townsville then and, I guess, we could have a break in that time and have a holiday and travel up to Cairns."

"That would be great, but now I have a lot of sewing and crocheting to do."

And they went to Cairns. They had a wonderful trip and even drove up as far as Mossman. There was little traffic and the road was not too bad. They had a day trip to Green Island National Park, which was a pretty rough ride. Helen got very queasy. Damon was very brave and did not get sick but Jack was fascinated with his green coloured cheeks.

They enjoyed the day tour and the trip back was not as rough. On their way up, they had gone off road and came to a lovely beach. The only building on the point was a little art shop, selling local art, drinks and sweets.

Helen said it was a beautiful place and Jack thought the same.

"We should buy a block here," suggested Helen but Jack thought it would not be a good investment so far north. He asked the shop person what the land was worth about the area but they were not sure. We don't think many people would be interested, he was told. A few years later, a Mr Christopher Skace was interested and built a resort there in that beautiful place, called Port Douglas.

Another place they called into, was a reptile park with lots of signs bagging the then Premier Joh Bjelke Petersen. Jack and Helen thought it was worth a look and a chance to have a bit of a rest from driving. They paid the man, who was named Alf and looked in his 50s, unshaven, not smartly dressed to welcome visitors, just a khaki bib and brace overalls that had been washed last month. But he was very informative, lifting snakes out of the tin tank pens, describing them, their poisons, what they ate and so on. He insisted they handle a couple of pythons that the three of them were not keen on, not even Damon.

When the man dropped a baby python on his shoulder that slithered around his neck, Damon quickly said, "I'm thirsty."

"We can't have the little fella thirsty," the man said as he led Jack and Helen to his old house.

At the entrance to the man's house were two very angry Dobermans, salivating and enjoying showing off their massive flesh-tearing teeth. They were chained up enough to allow the family to just pass through in a line behind their host.

They nearly died when they saw the filthy sink with the dishes to match. The man got a tea-towel out to wipe the slime off the glass, before filling it with water to give to their precious little son to drink. He then wanted to show the family the tiling he had done in the bathroom, pushing them forward.

That's when both Jack and Helen thought they were going to be murdered. The bath was full of frogs as they were feed for the snakes. There were cages full of rats and mice and bits of other animals. The sink was full of something green from a witch's cauldron and there were all kinds of spiders in fine netting holding containers.

Jack and Helen could not picture a more filthy, spooky, murderous place in the worst of horror movies. Yes, the young family was going to be butchered. Oh, the tiling he did, was just as dirty and haphazard as the rest of the room.

Jack had to save his family. He stretched himself as much as he could and said in his best no nonsense voice, "Thank you so much sir, showing us your place and being so informative. We are impressed with your tiling but now we will be on our way."

He grabbed Helen and Damon's hands and marched out between the two man-eating dogs, turned around gave a wave. They felt relief at having saved their lives.

"Wah-wah, my teddy, I want my teddy," wailed Damon.

"You didn't leave your teddy behind, did you?"

"I want my teddy."

They searched the car, no teddy.

"I'm not going back to that place ever again," said a very determined Helen, "we will buy you another Teddy."

"Pa gave me my teddy; I want my teddy," said a very upset and distraught little boy.

"Darling, we must go back or we will hear about it for years."

Jack turned the car around and proceeded to the snake farm.

"I'm staying with Damon in the car and you, being a big, brave man, can go and get the teddy," said Helen.

"Darling, you surprise me, I really thought you might get

it, seeing with your beauty and charm, he would just melt at the sight of you again," said Jack.

"Nice try dear, it won't work. Stop mucking about and just get the teddy and we can get on our way."

"Alright, my love but if I get slain, you won't forgive yourself for sending me in there."

"I'll have the band-aids ready, off you go."

Jack took a deep breath and walked towards the house calling out. He didn't want to go anywhere near those savage dogs. The man came out on the veranda.

"You forgotten anything?" he asked.

"Yes, my little boy left his teddy here."

The man disappeared and soon came out with the precious bear.

"This what you are looking for?"

"Yes thanks," as the man walked past the dogs, who took no notice of him and handed Jack the teddy. Jack walked slowly back to the car thinking up a story.

"You got the teddy," said Helen, as Jack handed a now very happy little boy his favourite toy.

"Yes dear but it was not that simple. I had to arm wrestle him for it and, whoever lost, there was a tarantula waiting to inject the losing contestant with fatal poison."

"Yes dear, now start the car and let's get going."

They arrived safely after a much-needed holiday. It was back to work for them until a couple of weeks later in the middle of the night.

"Jack, wake up, Jack." She shook a dead man awake. "My waters have broken."

"So what, I'll shift to another bed," said a sleepy man.

"Jack, you don't understand, the baby's coming. We have to get to Townsville as quick as possible."

"What? Drive 400 kilometres now? I have just got to sleep."

"Never mind that, we have to go," insisted Helen, "I'll get Damon and his things I have prepared and you dress yourself, get the suitcase under the bed with all my things in it and make sure the car is ready. We don't want to break down."

Jack was tired. He'd had a hard-working day that day and, anyway, what's the urgency? They had the gear in the glove box. If they had to do an emergency delivery, Helen, being a midwife, had coached him in the finer points of delivering a baby, even practicing with a doll. He had delivered quite a few calves and lambs, so what was the difference?

"C'mon darling, let's get going. It will take four hours or more to get there."

"Helen, my darling, don't you remember? A cyclone is predicted to hit the area we are heading to. It could be dangerous."

"Yes, I did hear about that but their predictions are hardly ever right. Have you got my case and everything?" said a very calm Helen, as she was buckling up a very sleepy baby in his car seat.

It was just before Charters Towers when Jack said, "I can't drive safely anymore, I'm all over the road and it's too dangerous to keep driving, I just have to sleep."

And that's what he did, laid down on the side of the road and slept, leaving his wife and son sleeping in the car.

Jack rose with the sun, 158kms away from Townsville. He felt refreshed and started on the last leg of their journey. Helen said she felt hungry, so did Damon and Jack, who mentioned their stomachs.

"How you feeling? Anything happening down there yet?" asked Jack.

"No, I'm fine," said Helen.

"If you are fine, then why don't we have a good feed at our usual Townsville service station before going on to the hospital, all agree?"

All agreed. After a good hot country breakfast, it was noticed the wind was getting much stronger to the point it was getting difficult to get into the car. It looked like Townsville was going to cop a visit from Cyclone Althea.

They pulled up at the Mater Hospital. They had been advised at breakfast, that we would be there in five. Two nuns raced out, with their habits tucked into their panties so they wouldn't be blown away. Even at this crucial time, Jack thought, *I never knew nuns wore knickers with them long habits. What was the point?*

They took Helen inside with her suitcase. There was nothing Jack could do. Helen was safe in the hospital. Nothing for it but to head for home with Damon. Jack didn't know anyone in the town, so with the cyclone about to hit, it was safer to go west.

Going up the range, the little car was severally buffeted by the wind. In fact, Jack had to concentrate on steering it, trying to keep it on the road. It started to rain; it started to rain heavily. Would they make it home? No, they got bogged 30kms from home and that's where they stayed Christmas Eve and Christmas Day, until someone came in a tractor, pulled the car out and helped them get home that Christmas night.

Helen told her story:

The nuns bundled me into the hospital quickly as the wind was making it difficult to walk. I desperately wanted Jack with me but with Damon and the cyclone, I guessed they were better out west. I was put in the obstetrics' suite; I was the only one there. I was shaved, then monitored for the rest of day, but mainly left alone. There was a lot of banging and crashing sounds as the cyclone started to intensify in the evening. Even the hospital shook every now and then when a strong gust hit. I felt safe but was worried about Jack and Damon if they got home safely. I wondered if I would get a phone call to say they were safe.

Labour started. I didn't care about the noise, the cyclone. I was having a baby and Jack should be beside me holding my hand and telling me to breathe. I was desperate to push. Not ready, they said but then the power went out. It was dark, feet running, sloshing water, a smash of glass as windows shattered, a terrifying loud roaring, things were crashing on the corrugated iron roof.

"You can push now. Push, the baby's head is showing."

Another push and, amongst the holocaust a little baby cried.

"Helen, you have a beautiful little girl."

Helen gave birth in a flooded delivery room, with broken windows. Her baby was delivered by the light of kerosene hurricane lamps.

Helen continued:

Everyone was talking about the damage Althea caused with power down, phones not working, houses damaged and only very limited staff on at the hospital. It was Christmas Day, 1971 and I was alone except for my perfect, little, baby girl. I was put in a ward with other mothers-to-be and mothers who had had babies a few days before. I was so lonely, put in a corner of the ward, everyone trying to be bright and wishing everyone a Merry Christmas but all I wanted was my Jack. Where was he? Is he alright? Why doesn't he ring? I wanted to show him our little girl. It was now visiting hours: the flowers and gifts, the hugs and kisses to all, except me. No one cared. I was just left alone feeling like a disgraced, unmarried mother. Evening time, visitors, more flowers, and gifts for the mothers in the ward. Oh, where are you, Jack? Please let me know where you are. I have never felt so alone.

Giving Damon and himself a good feed late on Christmas night at home, Jack managed to ring Fulbert next door and said he'd had to rush Helen down to Townsville, as the baby decided to come three weeks early. He wanted to get back as quickly as possible, as he didn't know if Helen had had the baby or been evacuated somewhere. The news from Townsville sounded terrible with the damage the cyclone had caused. The radio was full of it. Fulbert said the lines were down further up the road near Prairie, so Jack had no hope of contacting anyone.

He could help Jack get back into Prairie tomorrow, following him in his four-wheel drive international Scout jeep.

"That would be great if the road is passable, thanks," said Jack, "I am leaving Damon at the Pitts place. They had agreed to mind him, as previously arranged if we had an urgent trip to Townsville. Damon likes little Ruth Pitt as they are the same age and they get on well together."

"I will call about one in the afternoon tomorrow and we will see if we can get you to town," said Fulbert.

Jack was worried about Helen. He could not contact her and wondered if she had given birth and, if so, were they alright? Jack had a very restless night.

They managed to plough their way to Prairie the following afternoon. Jack went straight to the post office and telephone exchange and asked if he could ring Townsville.

"Sorry Jack, most lines are down and only emergency calls are to be made." Jack pleaded his case; said it was an emergency. He must get through to find out if his wife is alright or if she was still at the hospital.

"Alright, I will try but I couldn't get through this morning." Ten minutes later, "Jack, they have given you just 30 seconds."

"Hello, Jack here."

Silence, then Helen was on the phone and she was crying her eyes out. A nurse grabbed the phone saying, "You have a beautiful daughter and they are both fine." Click, and that was it, the 30 second phone call.

Helen again:

A nurse rushed in and said quickly, "Your husband is on the line."

I raced to the telephone. I wanted to tell him we had a baby girl; I wanted to say how much I loved him and missed him terribly and find out when would I see him. But all I could do, when I heard his voice, was cry with relief, knowing my little family was alright. The nurse took me back to my bed and comforted me saying, "I'm sure he will be down to see you as soon as he can."

I was getting worried about my body. Was it anxiety, the birth, worry? Maybe but my stoma was acting up and my bag was full of liquid and I was feeling a bit off. Not to worry, all will be fine when Jack arrives to see me.

Jack dropped Damon off at Buster and Joan Pitt's place. Ruth was delighted to see her playmate, Damon.

Joan said, "You must stay the night; you can't go now, not arriving in a badly damaged town with power lines down and the recorded devastation of Townsville."

"No, you're staying here. That's final. Now, come and have a good strong rum. You look as if you need it," said Buster.

Jack was pleased to stay the night. Joan made a great dinner of roast beef and all the vegetables, finishing off with homemade apple pie with cream. Buster kept the drinks up. That relaxed Jack and gave him a good night's sleep without worry.

He was feeling refreshed and ready to go after a hearty breakfast and a little play with the two kids. Jack told Damon he was going to bring mummy home and a brand-new sister for him. Whether he was more attuned to what his father was saying or playing with Ruth and her toy horses, was any one's guess.

The run down was good, except after Charters Towers. Then the cyclone started to show what its power had done. Huge trees were down, the railway line telephone posts were twisted like corkscrews, power poles were leaning in all directions, some dangerously so. The closer he came to the city, the damage was worse. Houses looked like dolls' houses, with the front of them blown to the wind, some without roofs which had gone the same way.

Amazingly, the Aboriginal corrugated huts they had built themselves, seemed to have survived. Jack excitedly pulled up outside the Mater Hospital and quickly walked in and made enquiries of where to find his wife.

There she was, sitting up, looking just beautiful and holding a tiny bundle. Her face broke into the biggest, most gorgeous smile when she saw Jack approaching. They hugged and kissed passionately, nearly forgetting the little bundle. Then Helen pulled down the little rug, so Jack could see his baby girl for the first time. She was a bit wrinkled and red, bald as a badger but Jack knew his baby girl would grow into a beautiful woman. She had to, just look at her parents; she didn't have an option.

Jack was told visiting time was over. He kissed Helen and then the baby on the forehead, asked her if there was anything she needed or he could buy her. Her answer was, "Just you, my love."

Jack walked away with mixed feelings. He was so pleased to see Helen and now he had a daughter; a play mate for his son. It was exciting but he knew his bride and she was not right. He could not put his finger on it but something was wrong. He wanted to buy her some flowers but not a hope in a cyclone-wrecked town. He did manage a couple of magazines and some KitKats to take back that afternoon.

She was feeding the baby when he got back. She had a blissful look on her face as the feeding was taking place. A smile and a discussion about what to call their little girl. Of course, they had gone through dozens of names but the final 10 were a problem. Jack was keen on Carran, Helen wasn't. She was keen on Deborah. Jack didn't know any horrible Deborahs and thought it a good name that could be shortened. This was important if your surname was Alexander. Beth was decided as her middle name, after Jack's mother. And so, Deborah Beth Alexander was welcomed to the world, after being born on Christmas Eve, 1971 in the middle of Cyclone Althea.

That evening, they both hid what was worrying each of them from the other. Helen was not well. She looked dehydrated; her eyes were glassy and sunk. Jack was really worried. He could not see anyone that night but, look out tomorrow morning, he was on the warpath for his one and only love.

The very next morning, after waiting to see the matron for 45 minutes, this imposing nun in full habit, firmly told Jack, "There is nothing wrong with your wife. She has just got the three-day blues, probably because you took so long to see your wife and new baby. You just go in there and boost her spirits up and, if you continue to bother me with your wife is sick, I won't let you visit, as I think you are not helping in this situation. Good morning to you." With that, she just whisked away.

What was he to do? Three days! Bullshit! His wife was sick, real sick. He decided to just wait there until he saw their specialist doctor passing. It took a few hours. As the doctor rushed past, Jack caught up to him and said, "Sir, something is wrong with my wife. She seems ill to me. Could you see what's wrong with her?"

"I don't care what's wrong with your wife," the doctor replied. "My job was to deliver the baby safely and that's all I had to do." He walked off, leaving Jack standing there bewildered at what he had said.

What was he to do? The doctor and matron were not bothered or going to do anything to help a sick patient, so what could he do in this cyclone-ravaged city, to help his wife and newborn baby? He didn't waste any time. He went straight to Helen's wardrobe, packed all her things in the suitcase and said, "Grab the baby, we are getting out of here."

All Helen said, as she got out of the bed to get ready, was, "Good."

It was a long drive, stopping at the Towers to buy some food supplies, bottled water and baby formula. Helen and the baby stayed in the car while Jack did the shopping, following Helen's list. They stopped at Prairie where a call was made to Joan Pitt, wondering if they could mind Damon a bit longer. She was happy to do so saying, "Buster, Damon and Ruth were having such a good time together, at last I have some time to myself."

The three of them were tired when they got home, so it was scrambled eggs on toast for tea. Little Debby had mother's milk and some formula. Helen was upset, saying her milk was drying up and she desperately wanted to feed her baby herself.

Salt tablets, plenty of bottled water and a freshly made chicken broth, enough for a couple of days, helped. Peanut butter sandwiches to help block some of the fluid going into her bag. She was so weak. He tried his best but what can one do? He managed his little family for two days. When some visitors, the Browns, arrived, they had heard it on the bush telegraph that Helen was home with a new baby.

Mrs Brown was shocked. "Jack what have you done? Helen looks terrible."

He explained the circumstances and found he had no alternative but to discharge her from the Mater Hospital and bring her home. Mrs Brown, to Jack's relief, took over.

"Doug, we are taking Helen and the new baby to Hughenden Hospital now. A new doctor has just arrived and Helen needs a hospital desperately."

Doug Brown had a brand-new Goddess Citroën car. It felt like its whole suspension was on air. It was a godsend for Helen and babe on the rough dirt road to Hughenden. A very young Dr Bruce Stringer took charge. (When he was a boy, he was badly bitten by a deadly Taipan snake, his life was saved by a

Ram Chandler who helped developed the antivenom vaccine. Dr Stringer was the first person saved by that vaccine).

Jack would never forget him. When Helen was presented to him, he said, "I do not have a history of the patient. What can you tell me and what do you think I should do?"

That comment made Jack feel assured that even though he was only very young to be a doctor, he was smart enough to ask the husband, instead of relying on just his medical experience.

Jack gave a brief history. He mentioned why he discharged her from the Mater Hospital and that she urgently needed fluids as she was badly dehydrated. He suggested some blood tests. Immediately after that information, the good doctor called for intravenous fluid and blood tests. A bed was provided for Helen and the baby and it was all to be done straight away.

Mrs Brown said, "Nothing you can do here, Jack. We might as well go to the pub for tea and you can probably stay at the hospital, seeing Helen is so sick."

Jack was so thankful for the help and comfort of the Browns. He was a tough man but sometimes situations like this, affecting his beautiful wife, was more than any man could handle.

Later the next day, Dr Stringer gave Jack the results.

"Helen seems slightly better on the fluids, which we are continuing to give her. But she has got quite a few different infections from gastro enteritis, which could have been fatal in her condition, but even moreso for the baby," he said. "Surprisingly, your baby hasn't caught it yet but you will have to take her home as Helen is isolated. It's best you don't see her either, as she is very contagious at the moment. I'm sorry but now she is in good hands and we do know how to treat her. She will get better but it could take three weeks or more."

"Could you please tell her, I love her and I will take care of our precious baby and to hurry up and get better, because I need one of her special cooked dinners."

Dr Bruce smiled and assured Jack that he would give her the whole message.

Slowly he drove to the Pitts place to pick up Damon and relay what happened to Helen. They fussed over the new baby, waking her up and asked if he could manage the two. He assured them he could, knowing they were off to the States the following week. Could he manage an 18-month-old and a week-old baby? He had to. He could and would. And Jack, think before you act.

Routine was the answer: make up formula, sterilise and fill baby bottles to wait in the fridge for delivery to baby Deborah, a good supply of nappies and Napisan with constant sniffing to smell if a change was to be made. A bath. Now that was a problem to be solved, as we all know babies can be very slippery, moreso when wet.

Jack rolled his baby in a towel and placed both in the elbow-checked water, washed and lifted her out with the wet towel so he wouldn't drop her. There was something he needed to invent, to make sure his baby was clean, which was a little hose placed on a tap. Little girls seemed to get poo spread into their privates, so Jack, knowing his baby's privates were her privates, found it better to squirt water and clean the area without touching anything, then drying, powdering, putting on a clean nappy, giving a cuddle and a warm bottle, easy. Except for the night feeds and nappy changes which interrupted a good sleep. But Deborah was a good baby and it was a pleasure and a privilege to be her dad.

What about Damon? How was he handling it all? Very well. His dad said to him, he needed a hand and could he help? Like, getting a bottle out of the fridge and a new nappy for his sister or, we have to make lunch or a dinner. He wasn't much help, if any at all, but Jack wanted him to be involved and feel important. He had to help his dad, because that's what men did, help each other. It worked but tired children can get a bit cranky and so do tired parents. During these difficult times, cranky had to be treated with deep breaths, singing silly songs and a few rapid walks around the outside of the house. How Jack managed, he didn't know but, somehow, he did for the next three and half weeks. The three of them were healthy with no accidents and they still could play together.

A daily ring to the hospital on the party line kept everyone informed of Helen's and Jack's progress. Helen wanted to know how Jack was getting on with the children. The answer was 'fine' and he was sure Deborah's eyes were blue but no hair yet. And Helen told him she was feeling much better and how great the staff were at the hospital, giving her great care. But she could not wait to get home to her family and, of course, the everyday "I love you," from both of them got them through.

The exciting day came. Jack cleaned the house spotless, clean sheets on the bed, dishes washed, children scrubbed and brushed, all packed into the little Ford to pick up their mum. What a reunion! Damon was all over his mum, Helen desperately holding and hugging her baby. Dad lifted his son up so they could all have a big group hug. A very loving family, back together again.

Jack thanked the nursing staff and Dr Stringer but had a request to the good doctor.

"I don't understand medical terms or really what Helen's illness was," said Jack. "For our records, could you kindly write out the condition Helen had when you first saw her and the treatment given. Do you mind writing me such a letter for my records?"

Doctor Stringer assured him, he would write a detailed letter to Jack, knowing full well that somehow a copy of that letter would go to that obstetrician in Townsville and the Mater Hospital. The letter was sent, no reply was received and no bill was sent from her slack doctor for all of Helen's pregnancy visits, nor the birthing charges. Jack wondered how that doctor must have felt. He hoped he had improved his practice by 100 percent. Jack and Helen also wondered how the other patients and babies survived infections during that time of the cyclone.

Everything was back to normal. Helen had a wonderful time with her baby and weeding her garden, which was going well after all the rain. Jack was back to checking the property, cattle and waters and got his specially cooked dinners, with love.

They had just finished dinner one night when they heard a banging on the door.

"Did you hear a car?"

"No, I wonder who that is."

Jack went to see who was banging at the back door. When he opened it, he looked at a chest, then he looked up towards the evening sky and saw shoulders and a face belonging to the chest. It was a very big man.

"I've broken down five miles back and I saw your lights," said the giant.

Jack wasn't sure if he was friend or foe but asked if he would like something to eat.

"Helen, we have a hungry man at the door who needs a feed."

Jacks' idea had always been to offer a feed and, while the person was eating, he could find out more about the stranger. Anyone with bad intentions is pretty safe after a full stomach. Anyway, that was Jack's theory.

His name was Bronco Johnston, a big man with arms the size of bullock legs, his legs slightly larger. He was big and fit but you honestly couldn't say he had a handsome face. He appeared as a tough man who'd had a tough life. His age, at a guess, was about fortyish.

He was a 'roo shooter for a freezer down at Birrcannia Station but was looking for work. Jack took a chance.

"I have a job here, if you want to help me build two miles of suspension fence. Normal station hand wages and we can feed you and have some quarters over there for you."

"You're on," said Bronco, "but could you give me a tow tonight? I don't like leaving all my gear on the road."

"Okay, after you have finished your meal."

Helen motioned Jack to another room.

"Are you sure he is alright?" said Helen, "He is a big man. We don't know really who he is. You could take him down the road and he could break your neck, then come back and get me."

"Gosh love, I didn't think you had such a good imagination," Jack said. "No, I feel he is a genuine sort of chap; it will be fine, you just wait and see."

And it was. Bronco was a great worker. He helped cut gidgee strainer posts and they both put up the two-mile suspension fence. To be honest, Bronco was a boon for Jack. He was so strong that he alone put up a lot of the fence, while Jack cleared the fence line, did the sighting and ran the wires. On his own, the fence would have taken months.

To give an idea of his strength, Jack was breaking in a young 15-hand horse, who was giving him some trouble.

"Step aside, little man," Bronco said to Jack.

He walked over to the horse, where Jack had a rope around its neck. Bronco put his arms around that same neck and held him, until the horse stopped putting on a bucking turn. The horse was a pleasure to train after that frightening experience. The man was stronger than the horse. He stayed with the family for about four months and then moved on, as bush workers usually do.

The creek was in flood, so Fulbert rang and said, "You won't be able to get a killer for a while. Come down to my place at the creek and I will have one for you." Which Jack proceeded to do.

He was slightly amused but also concerned when he saw

what was happening on the other side of the boiling torrent. Fulbert had made a canoe out of a large sheet of corrugated iron. Then bolted both ends with rubber tubing in between to stop leakage. He then proceeded to lift a sheep, with both hind legs and one front tied, into the makeshift canoe. He climbed in with a home-made paddle. Honestly, the craft was flat out holding one, let alone two. He launched the canoe into the edge of the flooded creek with slow professional strokes of the paddle.

The sheep started to struggle within its confines. Fulbert's slow strokes of the paddle turned into strokes a fully steamed paddle boat would not be able to manage, as he hit the raging current. Arms working furiously, the sheep kicking, the creek was the winner, as the canoe overturned and poor Fulbert and sheep went into the drink. It was fatal for the sheep but Jack saw Fulbert walking up his own side of the creek, looking very much like a drowned rat. As he came opposite Jack across the creek, he yelled out, "Sorry about the killer," then walked home.

A family, they don't remember how they met them, were Kenny and Sam Bogan. The story goes, they were managing one of their fathers' properties, but he didn't pay them, so they were struggling, they had a sick little girl who had a serious heart problem. Dinner at the Alexanders was a regular event and they often went together at social events. Helen and Sam got on well together; Jack felt sorry for Kenny but couldn't say they were great mates. Jack had an idea to help the family with some income.

There were a lot of wild goats living at Jireena. They were an environmental pest and had to be culled. The idea was to round them up with the help of Sparkles, shoot and skin them, then salt the hides and sell them at the Cape River Meatworks. Over 80 good skins were sent. Jack wanted to know how much money was made. Kenny informed him the skins were no good for the current market and had been discarded.

Jack, as always, took a man's word. Many years later, as you will find out, if you get through this autobiography, Kenny was a very dishonourable person, causing Jack and Helen an immense amount of pain, heartache and money.

Meanwhile, back with the happy family, little Deborah still only had a few wisps of hair. She, with her chubby cheeks and cheeky smile, even at such a young age, tried her father out. Susie the basset hound was everyone's favourite, especially the children. They could lie on her, go to sleep, roll on her, do anything, except pull her ears, which they learnt very early not to do. Jack found a dingo pup out in the paddock and gave it to Damon who was the only person that could do anything with it. Susie, Helen, Deborah, even Jack, had not much success if there was anything to do with the pup. It was called Yogi and lived under the couch, watching everyone. Damon could play with it; they both enjoyed each other's company. But history repeated itself. As Jack was coming home, all the dogs ran out to meet him, including Yogi and, yes, he ran over it. Damon saw it and many times later, the young boy would look up at his dad and say, "You killed my Yogi," which broke Jack's heart.

Koorinya was the social hub of the area, where dances, the races and all types of events were held. Remember Mr Frazer had brought a couple of racehorses down and asked Jack to do some stock work on them. Now he asked him to train the two horses for the Koorinya race meeting. Jack informed Dick he had no knowledge of training racehorses and, in fact, had never ridden in a race or used a jockey pad. He was assured a registered jockey would be riding the horses and all Jack had to do was give them plenty of trotting and cantering and only a bit of galloping every morning for an hour each. That was fine. Life was quiet at the station at this time. It would be good to go for early morning rides.

Three weeks before the races, all horses entered were put in a paddock together, so no horse got any special treatment or extra feed. A week before the races, Dick called in and said, "I have got you a racing pad to practice on."

Jack exclaimed, "I told you, I have never ridden in a pad, let alone a race. You said you were getting a registered jockey to ride the horses."

"Well yes but he has other engagements down south. Don't worry, I know you will do your best, I have managed to register you as a jockey, so you're legal to ride."

Jack practiced on the pad twice a day with Buffy, his horse. But he couldn't get his balance right, going a bit to the left then the right. It was altogether different from riding stock work and rodeoing. A different grip using only the inside of the knees.

The big day arrived. Jack was nervous as he put the owner's silk colours on. The borrowed helmet was a bit too loose and there was no way he could tighten the plastic racing goggles. Any instructions or help? No, it was every man for himself. Money was flowing at the bookies and there was a call to the mounting yard. Jack was helped to mount his horse, Racket. There were six horses in this race.

Jack will tell you about the first and last horse race he did:

We all warmed our horses up with a slow canter to the start line, which was just a line marked in the dirt. We started to line up and I noticed, all too late, the riders, except me, gave the starter a slight nod of respect. When he thought the lineup of horses was good enough, he dropped his handkerchief for the start. The other riders and horses saw it. I didn't but my horse did.

Racket did a huge bound, last off the start but he must have been catching up. The goggles fell into my mouth and the helmet slipped over my eyes, which was just as well, as the flint and stones were shooting from the hooves of the other horses, like shotgun pellets. They became embedded into my cheeks, arms and chest. I didn't see the furlough markers. I did not see anything. I held on to the horse's mane as tight as I could.

We came to a turn and the pace was horrific. I lost my legs as there was no feeling and there was the thunder of hooves in my ears. Then, suddenly, all was still. Someone said, "A good ride, Jack." It was over.

I had to get off before I fell off. Everyone was yelling but I didn't understand, until one of the other riders said, "You can't dismount here, you have to dismount in the dismount yard, or the punters will lose their money."

Thank God, Racket was not a big horse and somehow, I scrambled on and rode slowly to the dismount yard, where I was helped to dismount and had to go with my racing pad to be weighed. A bell rang. All correct weight, it signified.

"Jack you could have won that race if you rode your horse properly but second was not too bad for your first ride."

I came second? Well, the horse did, I don't think I had anything to do with it.

Then someone said, "You're riding in the next race."

"Find someone else to ride or scratch it. I'm so weak I couldn't stay on a rocking horse," I said.

Someone rode Jireena and won, so I must have trained them alright, but I will never be a jockey.

Years later, Jack, amongst other pursuits, managed a thoroughbred breeding and racing stable but you will find out about that, later on.

C.12

A Fright and a Proposition

Jireena was a good place for the family. It was more of a relaxed management style. Even though Jack worked hard, it was more of a slowdown sort of job. Like all men who labour for a living, Jack ended up, with a bad back and hernia. But they had a good social life and were very welcomed in the district and enjoyed their family life together.

In the season, Jack played polocrosse on Buffy, towing a single horse float in the little Ford Escort over 60kms of very rough and corrugated road. It was a good social occasion, where the men had fun battling each other on the polocrosse field, while the women enjoyed the rare occasion of socialising with the other women and, of course, the bush kids enjoyed playing with the other kids, despite the occasional mishap or misunderstanding that caused a child to run to their mother bawling. They were great days: dances at Koorinya, shows in Hughenden, life was good.

They made six-monthly visits to Townsville, for supplies and dentists and doctors' visits. They always hired a caravan at the caravan park near the Ross River and spent a few days there. On the way home, Helen reminded Jack that her younger brother was getting married in Wonthaggi, Victoria and she would like to go with Deborah, to show her off to her dad and Jack's family.

"Fine I will book the plane tickets. What's the date you want to leave?" Jack asked.

"Um, Jack you might like to come down a bit later with Damon, as the family would love to see you both." Helen hesitated then added, "I'm sorry Jack, I just have to tell you. I know you have been through so much with me."

"C'mon, out with it. I know something has been on your mind."

"Oh Jack, I have to have another operation in Melbourne with my surgeon Dr Hughes, who performed the ileostomy on me. They have found something in the bowel that was released from my tummy when I was pregnant with Damon. Now it's all got to be removed. The operation is called a proctocolectomy."

"That's a big word, it sounds a serious operation, but if it has to be done, then it has to be done."

That conversation between them was like a normal discussion, but Jack felt sick in the stomach. His poor, beautiful wife had gone through so much the last few years, but she was so remarkable the way she looked after her condition, without one hint of complaint. He loved her so much but always secretly, in the back of his mind, knew he could lose his love at any time.

Jack always remembered Helen's words, "Be thankful for this day and enjoy it."

So, a month later, Helen and daughter headed off to Melbourne for the wedding. Jack and Damon came two weeks later, staying with his grandmother and mother in their unit. Helen went into Epworth Private Hospital soon after.

She was in a ward with four other women and seemed very relaxed and confident in her doctor, assuring Jack and probably herself, it was not going to be a big deal and they would soon be back home in Queensland.

Jack was there with a kiss and an 'I love you'. She answered with a smile and said, "I love you too, Jack," with a lonely tear sliding down her cheek, as the wardsmen took her to theatre.

Sometime later, Jack received a telephone call.

"Jack, this is Dr Hughes. The operation that we did on Helen was a complete success. But she has not taken it at all well and we are concerned about her recovery. Could you come to the hospital as soon as you possibly can?"

"Thank you, Dr Hughes, I'm leaving now."

Without a car, Jack raced over the little wooden footbridge, crossing the Yarra River to Burnley, then a mad run to the hospital. Why not a taxi? He wasn't thinking straight. He arrived breathless and full of anxiety. *Would she be alright? My God, she must.*

He found his dear wife surrounded by privacy curtains. She looked awful and very pale. He sat beside her, holding her hand.

"Darling it's me, I'm here beside you."

She moaned and repeated over and over again, "They have cut me open again; they have cut me open again."

Jack wasn't sure if she really knew he was there. He kissed her on the forehead and, with a damp towel, he wiped her face and neck.

"It's all over now my sweet. You just hang in there and get better. We need you: me, Damon and Deborah."

But all Jack got was the moaning, "They have cut me open again."

Dr Hughes walked in. Jack stood up to meet him, his face covered in worry and concern.

"Jack, as I told you, the operation was successful. What has now happened is Helen's body as gone into shock, which sometimes happens after a big and complicated operation. There is not much we can do for her now. It's up to Helen and, with your support, she will eventually pull through. I will see you in the morning. Goodnight Jack." And the good doctor left them.

It was a long night with Jack holding her hand until the early hours of the morning. Then Helen went into a deep, peaceful sleep and so did Jack.

"Jack, they have cut me open again."

"I know my sweet."

It must have been the noisy breakfast trolley that woke them.

"I feel so tired and weak and my tummy hurts so much. Could you call a nurse for some painkillers?"

Even though she managed to communicate, her voice was very soft and she was hard to hear. The nurse came in and told Jack that his wife was getting pain drugs through her drip, as well as vitamins, as she wouldn't be able to eat normally for a couple of days until her body recovered.

"But, Jack, you can have breakfast in the dining room," said the nurse, "I suggest you leave her now, as she needs plenty of rest and sleep."

Eating a late breakfast, he felt relief as his wife was going to survive.

That day and part of the next, Helen was a very tired girl that slept a lot, except when she was disturbed for the usual drip changes, temperature and blood pressure checks and the quick looks at her large surgical scars: one that ran from her chest to her pelvis and the other really uncomfortable one in her bottom. The children wanted to know where their mummy was, which had to be explained quite a few times, with a promise that soon as mummy was getting a bit better, they could visit her with some flowers.

The hospital was home to Helen for the next two weeks. Her tenacity and resolve helped her recovery much quicker than Dr Hughes thought. Then to Jack's surprise, when he was visiting, a nurse brought in a six pack of Fosters beer.

"Drink as much as you can and that might get the bladder working again. Doctor's orders," she said to Helen.

"But, I don't like beer," Helen said.

"Helen, treat it as medicine." The nurse popped the top of a bottle and poured half a glass, handing it to the patient.

"Hey, Nurse, if she doesn't want it, we do. C'mon, pour us three ladies a glass," said the desperate patients in the ward.

After the nurse left the room, Helen said, "Come and get it, girls. I hate the stuff."

They did and, because the beer was all gone, another six pack was brought in, much to the joy of the ladies, despite being intended for Helen. Then it was suggested, Jack take her for a drive on the roughest roads to loosen the bladder but that did not work either. Then maybe, if she went home, things might work and they did. At last, her body was working normally and the family flew back to Queensland three days later.

It had been a hard time for the two of them, since their marriage in 1967, with babies, operations, cyclones and what have you. But it brought them closer together, with a mutual understanding of each other, that whatever the crisis, they knew their love would always keep them together. Yes, that five years was rough but the future was looking bright for our two, with no further large operations. Still, Helen had to look after her stoma and appliances for the rest of her life.

It was good to be back at Jireena. The children were glad to get out of their restrictive city clothes and be in the nuddy. Helen was happy in her garden and doing her sewing and Jack was doing what he liked: checking the place, being in the bush and using some muscle.

A letter arrived, amongst others. It was an invitation to meet a Mr and Mrs Dart at the Great Western Hotel for lunch at 12.30pm, 2nd November 1972. A stamped, self-address envelope was enclosed. It was a mystery. There were some Darts in the district but Jack and Helen didn't know them. It was suggested by Helen, to answer the letter and accept the invitation, as it would be a free lunch and a bit of fun. Jack wasn't quite sure; he was not keen on mystery. Everything for him was black or white but he did end up accepting the invitation.

The girl at the reception pointed out the old couple in the dining room as the Darts. They were a well-dressed couple, town clothes, late 60s to early 70s of age. They introduced themselves and Jack asked if they would like something from the bar. They both shook their heads but Helen wanted an orange drink, so an orange drink was ordered and Jack had a Bundy rum and coke.

Mr Dart, a kindly, grandfather type, started the conversation by saying, "I suppose you two want to know what this is all about. My wife and I own Bannockburn and Tankred Stations. We are too old to look after them and we have a Down syndrome daughter we look after in Townsville. We have two sons which, we are ashamed to say, we have spoilt and bought them a station each, which we have regretted.

"However, we have made some enquiries about you two and the results have been that you're the sort of people we would like to give the opportunity for you both to own your own station. We don't want them. If you come and manage them for us and make a profit within three years, you will own Bannockburn. If you can still make a profit in the following three years, you will own Tankred."

"That sounds great, Mr. Dart," said Jack, "but we don't have that sort of money to buy stations."

"Yes, you will. You will have three years of wool cheque. Jack, we are alright. We don't need the money and my sons definitely don't need it. Mrs Dart and I want to help someone get started, someone who loves the land. We have discussed this between ourselves for quite a while and this is what we want to do."

A waitress came by and interrupted their conversation.

"Are you four having lunch? Here are some menus. You can make your order at the bar," she said.

"Gee, Mr Dart, you have left me bewildered with your kind and most generous offer. I really don't know what to say," said Jack.

"Let's order lunch, dear. I think Jack and Helen need to digest the offer as well as some lunch," Mrs Dart said.

When the men had gone to order lunch, Mrs Dart leant over to Helen.

"Dear, we do hope you take up Mr Dart's offer," she said. "It is a very generous one and we know you two have had a tough time. It would give us the greatest pleasure for you both to take over Bannockburn. Oh, where are your children and how old are they?"

"We weren't sure what this was all about, so Joan and Buster Pitt are looking after them this afternoon," replied Helen. "Damon, our son, is two and a half and our daughter, Deborah, is 11 months old and they are just great kids."

"Here come the men with our lunch."

Meanwhile, at the bar, the men ordered the women's salad sandwiches. Mr Dart decided on a meat and pickle sandwich; Jack wanted the fish, salad and chips but decided it was better to order another meat and pickle sandwich instead. And a pot of tea for four please.

Mr Dart advised, "Don't make the mistake we did with our children. You love them so much, you end up spoiling them rotten. Don't do that with your young children. Love them, yes, but rules must be obeyed, be strict and don't let them get away with anything. You will then have them grow up to be children you are proud of."

"Thanks for the sound advice and I will remember it," said Jack. "Now let's get back to the women before they start worrying about us."

Helen knew Jack was ready to jump in and take up the offer, without any real details as he always talked about having a property of his own, so she thought she would get some information herself.

"Mr Dart, I have a few questions, if we are to take up your offer," she said.

"Yes dear, go ahead," he replied.

"Will we be getting a wage and found (all accommodation and provisions paid for), while Jack is hell bent on making a profit?"

Mr Dart gave a grandfatherly smile, saying, "Of course, my dear, and there are three boys besides yourselves to cook for. I'll leave it up to Jack about a wage and all the conditions required, as he has to make a profit. I don't think he will be over generous."

Mrs Dart enquired of Helen, "You don't mind cooking for men, do you?"

"Not at all. At our last place in Cunnamulla, sometimes I cooked for six. I enjoy cooking."

After lunch, before parting ways, Mr Dart said, "Here is my phone number. Please ring if you have any more questions and please let us know your decision within three weeks. If it's favourable, we would like you to start early in January. Please keep this offer strictly between yourselves as we have not discussed this with our sons until we have your firm decision."

Later on that night, Jack and Helen discussed the Darts offer.

"Well, what do you think about that? It sounds too good to be true," said Jack.

"Calm down, Jack. I agree, what an offer but it would be hard to make a profit in three years. Most farms don't make a profit in five years," said Helen.

"You doubt me darling; I know I can, I have special qualities about me."

"Yes Jack but this time the proof will be in the pudding."

"C'mon love, what do you really reckon?"

"I think we probably should but we have a couple of weeks to think it over."

"I think I have thought it over already." Jack was getting excited.

"I know that but I think we should make a few discreet enquiries about the Darts and the property." Helen was being level-headed.

And they did. They found Mr and Mrs Dart were an old respectable, honest couple of the district. Their discreet enquiries into their sons were not so favourable. The properties were large, over half a million acres, mostly spinifex country, and fair to good wool production. Helen mentioned it was a bit further south on the Torrens Creek Road than where they were but they knew everyone, so their social life would not be any different except for the drive into Hughenden.

Leaving Jireena was going to be hard to do. Dick was a great fun boss and a lovely family to work for. They had been so kind, no questions about their often-urgent times away and on full pay as well. They both enjoyed the property, inwardly, however, they both thought there was no future in staying there for the long term. So, the decision was made, advising Mr Dart they would take up his generous offer.

Jack always had the hard task of doing the difficult things and, this time, it was telling Mr Frazer that, with regret, he would like to give a month's notice.

Mr. Frazer replied, "I guessed it would come to this sometime. You are too good a man to stay here and I have nothing better to offer you. Where are you going?"

The secret would have been out by now, after Mr Dart had received Jack's acceptance.

"Mr Dart at Bannockburn offered me a position that was too hard to refuse," said Jack.

"The old rascal, pinching one of my men. It will be good for you Jack, so congratulations are in order."

"Thanks for that, I do feel a bit guilty in leaving, as you have been so kind to us but unfortunately, we must move on."

"I do have one question for you," said Jack. "I would love to buy Buffy the horse from you."

"Would you swap Helen for her?" said Mr Frazer.

"No way."

"Then that's your answer." Jack thought it was a good way to say no, though he was very disappointed as he loved that horse and it would be putting a stop to his, not so budding, polocrosse career.

A sale was made of their trailer, horse float and little Ford Escort, which was a great car. The only trouble with it, when pulling the horse float over rough roads, were the two rubber rings holding the end of the exhaust on. So, a handy supply of spare rings in the glovebox was the rectifier. Jack had been offered nearly what he paid for the car a few months ago, so he called the chap who raced out and picked it up the next day. Jack had not realised it was a rare model with the lotus engine. They eventually were as rare as hen's teeth and he could have asked for so much more. Good onya, Jack.

They were busy. Helen made sure the house was spotless. Her most precious plants were re-potted to take, and everything was packed. While Jack was cleaning and servicing the Landrover, checking all the waters, cattle and sheep and the property was left in good hands. Jack's replacement came to get a run-down of his responsibilities. *It didn't take long to replace me*, thought Jack. It was Billy Pitt the eldest son of Buster and Joan. Jack had met him briefly a few times, a nice young 19-year-old, single man, born to the bush. So, he would be good for the position.

Jack didn't say anything to Helen, but he knew her beautiful garden and shade, she had created, was not going to be watered and loved. He expected it would end up looking like when they arrived. He felt sad, as he knew the hard work and love she put into it would be wasted. And so, it was.

C.13

Bannockburn
January 1973

It was a big homestead, though the same in design as most station homes. There was a large central room, surrounded by gauzed-in verandas. In the three corners of the veranda were a gauzed-in office and two bedrooms. On the other side was a large storeroom, kitchen and bathroom. Nearby were the jackaroos' quarters, and the generator shed with its 32-volt battery lighting plant.

The kitchen was equipped well and with two stoves, a gas and a wood combustion, it was a blessing to Helen. The house was old but in good order and condition and was comfortable to live in. The office had a flying doctor radio and an old-fashioned low frequency radio, which, later on, would be a godsend. There was also a large tin trunk, which was the flying doctor medicine chest.

The only phone was a private one, which was the only contact to the next-door property, nine kilometres away. The flying doctor radio was their lifeline. If the writer remembers correctly, it was the men's sessions at 6am, then at 7am. The flying doctor came on and asked if anyone had any medical problems and usually there were two or three. It must be remembered that if a person had a medical complaint, the whole Gulf of Northern Queensland would hear about it.

After the doctor's session, it was opened to telegrams, where people sent their grocery orders and general shopping orders, which would be delivered by the mail run to the customer once a week. Telegrams were also sent to friends and relatives. Then after telegrams, it was the women's session till School of the Air started. The flying doctor radio was the only communication most outback people had and they had to be darn quick on the mic button if they wanted to place an order or send or receive a telegram.

Stock was 30,000 wether sheep on the two properties, 90 head of cattle, a half a dozen horses and thousands of feral goats. Paddocks were large, from 10- 20,000 acres. Mostly open spinifex but there were isolated scrubby and eucalypt patches dotted around the property. Paddocks were so large, all mustering was done on four stroke 100 cc Honda motorcycles, with a shed containing spare parts for them. This included but was not restricted to, broken brake and clutch handles, brake, and gear pedals. Helmets or safety gear for the riders were not worn, even though there were no real injuries. However, there were plenty of sprains and bruises, as there were hazards waiting for the rider between the spinifex that could not be seen, such as extremely hard white ants' nests and mounds which were easy to collide with, so there were a few falls.

The property was well watered by bores and windmills and the fences in fair repair. Jack was impressed with the property, equipment, sheds and the shearers' sheds and quarters. All had been very well looked after in years gone by but he could see where, in the last few years, repair and neglect were evident.

Around the homestead were green lawns, a few fruit trees and small gardens but they didn't give much shade or keep the dust out of the homestead.

There were three jackaroos: Ross, Terry and Main. Ross thought he was the man and knew it all. Terry was quiet, a good worker and reliable. They were both in their late teens. Main was the youngest and most inexperienced but was a good lad who tried hard. He got teased a bit by the other two boys but they were all good lads.

Mr Dart arrived a few days after Jack's family, probably giving them time to settle in. Half a day was spent on paperwork and signatures for bank and management rights. Not sure what it meant but there was a legal document giving Jack custodian rights of the property or, as Jack thought, he could tell the sons of Mr Dart to get lost if they were a bother.

Jack was informed that they wanted the sheep shorn twice a year: May and November. Jack thought this was unusual, but if that's what was wanted, that's what he would do.

They took a drive out to a couple of paddocks where they had discussions on how he wanted the place to be managed.

"You do it my way and, if you manage that successfully, then you can try your way," said Mr Dart.

Really, all Jack had to do was manage the property, keep it maintained and improve where necessary, shear twice a year and make a profit within three years. What could go wrong?

Mr Dart was worried about all the feral goats and told Jack to pay a bounty of 50 cents a pair of ears to the boys. Jack said he would do so and asked how many pairs of ears the boys had brought in so far? Mr Dart wasn't sure but said a lot. Jack stopped paying the bounty three weeks later, when he saw a mob of feral goats without any ears. The boys were running them down on the motor bikes and just cutting the ears off, instead of killing the goats.

Their daily lives started at Bannockburn. Helen busy with two young children, cooking, sewing and a bit of gardening. They were the jobs she was happy doing and she would whistle bright tunes most of the time.

Jack was always up early to cook breakfast for his men, then he would pull a wire that rang a bell in the jackaroos' quarters to signify that breakfast was ready. One morning, the boys managed to connect a couple of batteries to the wire attached to the bell and, when Jack rang it, he got a decent shock. When the boys came in for breakfast, they had expectant looks on their faces but Jack wasn't going to give them any satisfaction and said nothing.

Hughenden was much further for them to travel. One hundred and sixty kilometres of potholed, corrugated dirt road, plus 42 kilometres of bitumen. Jack was always relieved when Helen and the kids got home. An early start and a late home coming for some fresh fruit and vegetables, maybe the hairdresser, meet a couple of girls, have a quick sandwich, feed the kids and then the long drive home to get dinner ready for the boys. It was so important for any bush woman to go to town, if only for their sanity.

Excitement, as it was rodeo time and a show. The family were all excited, especially Helen, having a day out. She spent so much time dressing the children and wearing her new outfit she had made and this was its first showing.

The first puncture and ruined tyre happened at the boundary; Jack changed the tyre and put the spare wheel on. It punctured 12kms further up the road. Jack had to mend the tube and put a vulcanised patch on it, fit the tyre back on and, with the hand pump, pumped it up.

Meanwhile, the children and Helen were getting more upset with the delay, blaming Jack. It was all his fault but, how, he didn't know. Then, when the fixed tyre was on, poor Jack had to make a devastating decision.

"I'm so sorry love and you kids, but there is no chance we can go to town," he said. "We will be lucky to manage the drive home. Sorry, but there is no other way."

It cannot be fully explained the wretchedness of Jack and

how crestfallen Helen felt. She had been looking forward to this outing for weeks, busy with her outfit and children's clothes and now, it was a return to the kitchen. When would she get another day out to a special event? There were other times they went out but Helen doesn't remember them, only the day they had the three punctures and had to return home.

There were two vehicles at Bannockburn: a near new Hilux ute, as the work vehicle and a HD Holden station wagon, that the children called the pictures car. They would go next door to Tiree station once a month for picture night, which was a good night for everyone. Kids to play with kids, wives to talk with other wives and the men, to talk about the season and events happening in the area.

Then there were the flying doctor clinics, once every six weeks. Everyone in the area would go, where the nurse would check up on everyone's health.

"Jack, you're due for your tetanus needle, come and get it."

Anyone with medical problems could see the doctor. Ross had a bad tooth ache and asked the doctor to take it out, But the doctor was too busy and handed a black leather case to Jack.

"You should be able to take a tooth out," the doctor said.

Ross sat down on a kitchen chair, while Jack opened the black leather case. Inside was a variety of tooth-pulling pliers. As Jack was examining them, to see which one would be best for the job, Ross was also eyeing the surgical instruments. As Jack was making his selection, he decided his tooth ache was not that bad and he would keep the tooth, thank you.

It was the day the boys wanted to go to town and Jack needed some gear ready for the first shearing, so off they went in the Hilux ute. When on the bitumen, Ross saw something on the road in the distance and yelled, "Whatever it is, it's mine."

When they pulled up on the road, it was a brand-new Akubra hat that Ross scored. A bit further they travelled on and

Terry yelled out, "Whatever it is, is mine," as he spied something lying on the road and he scored a nice swag cover.

Poor Main. As they got back in the car, he said, "The next thing we see on the road is mine, I don't care what it is, it's mine." and sure enough only a couple of kilometres from town, he spied, in the distance, something on the side of the road. Again, he repeated, "I don't care what it is, it's mine and I'm going to keep it."

Unfortunately for Main, we saw, as we came closer to the object, an elderly Aboriginal woman sitting on the side of the road waiting for a lift. Jack pulled up and said, "I'm not keen on you keeping this find Main but you insisted."

Ross and Terry practically pulled Main out of the car and said, "She is yours."

Jack told Terry and Ross to get in the back of the ute, told Main to get in the front and he offered to take the woman to town. As she was very large and a bit smelly, she climbed in and practically squashed Main in the middle. When in town, he let the woman and Main out, to go on their separate ways.

Poor Main was always copping it, so Jack decided to give him a reward by letting him drive the Hilux to Torrens Creek, a 350 kilometres return trip on dirt roads, and pick up a new motor bike at the Torrens Creek Railway Station. He left straight after breakfast. Helen was worried about a young lad travelling all that way on his own.

"What if he has a breakdown or an accident?"

"He has to have a go sometime and it will do his confidence good and give him some prestige with Ross and Terry," said Jack.

The return trip would take about six hours, including loading the bike and having a meal at the Torrens Creek café. Jack was starting to get worried at about 3.30pm. By 5pm, he started to put together a tow rope, extra fuel and water, a toolbox and anything that could or might be needed. He went to tell Helen he was going to look for Main when he turned up.

"You're late. What happened, did you hit a 'roo or something?" said Jack casting an eye over the ute, to see if any damage had occurred.

"Yes, I did hit a 'roo but it didn't do any damage to the ute," replied Main.

"Did you kill it?"

"Yes but it took me a while."

"What do you mean it took a while to kill it?"

"Well, it was badly injured and I couldn't leave it like that, so I had to kill it but I could not find anything to dispatch it with, so I tried to choke it to death."

"You what?" Jack couldn't believe his ears.

"I tried to strangle it but it took ages. I managed to do it in the end."

It was then that Jack noticed, in the fading light, Main's ripped and bloody shirt.

"Your home safe now, go and have a shower and clean yourself up ready for dinner and I will put the ute away and unload your new bike," said Jack.

"Is the new bike for me?" Main smiled in surprise.

"Yes, now go."

Jack did a lot of driving and motorbike riding on Bannockburn. It was a huge property and he needed to check all waters, feed fences and stock. It could never be done in one day. It could take weeks. One way to save a bit of time and help, was to employ a 'roo shooter. Besides the 'roo shooting, they would leave notes, 'mill not working in Tankred out paddock', 'trough not working in south paddock' etc.

Jack got on to Bronco Johnston and asked him if he wanted to do the shooting on Bannockburn and he agreed. On one of Jack's tours of the property one Saturday, he noticed Ross' car near a large dam and wondered what the boys were up to. As he stopped and walked up to the jackeroo's car, he heard a shot and a yell, "We got it!"

To Jacks dismay, he saw they had shot a pelican. He was furious.

"Get that bird out of the dam and start plucking it," he yelled at the boys.

The boys were in a bit of shock as they had no idea their boss was in the area, let alone having seen them shooting the graceful bird.

"Why do we have to pluck it?" asked Main.

"Because you don't kill anything unless there is a good reason. Pigs and goats are vermin and must be culled, 'roos are for dog meat and to keep numbers down. Now you have killed the pelican for fun, you will pluck it and gut it here and now. Then give it to me and I will give it to the missus to cook for your blokes' dinner until its used."

"You are joking, we won't do that," said Ross.

"Yes, you will or I will report you to the wildlife officer, where you will get a heavy fine and probably jail time. So, the three of you get plucking."

They did. Helen cooked it the best she could in a slow cooker and made some nice sauce to go with it but it was still tough and gamey. It lasted two days, including as cold meat for their sandwiches. It was a good lesson for them.

The first shearing came around and it was a very busy time but all was ready. Mr Dart came up to see the start and check that Jack had all the resources he needed and to see that drenching, spraying and branding were going smoothly. He only stayed a day but Jack thought he was impressed at the way the shearing was coming along. But Helen gave Jack something to worry about.

"Jack, Mr Dart is looking very yellow. I think he might have liver cancer and if he does, I don't think he has long to live," she said. "I wish you wouldn't take things on face value. People are not always as honest and trusting as you. I wish you had asked Mr Dart to put everything in writing that he offered us, instead of taking Mr and Mrs Dart's word."

"She will be right love," said Jack. "If you can't take a man's word, as he looks you in the eye and shakes your hand, then it's a sad, sad world."

Everyone has a talent, sometimes it is hidden but is still there. Jack was not sure if he had any talent but one thing he was very good at, that hadn't been taught but came naturally to him was an uncanny way of finding stock. Whether it was sheep, cattle or horses, he could literally sniff them out, cleaning a whole paddock of stock, whether desert or thick scrub. He did not know how he did it, neither did anyone else. But in that muster, for that shearing, he found 3,000 triple-fleeced sheep. Sheep that had not been recorded on the books in three years. Jack had made his profit.

Jack had no idea he was being investigated by the police. He had made a mistake in telling Mr Dart over the flying doctor radio he had found 3,000 triple fleeced sheep. Mr Dart could not believe it and asked him several times to repeat the number. Now that radio broadcast went all over the gulf. It didn't make Mr Dart's sons too happy, with the suggestion they were not the best at mustering. A bit of a loss of face within the grazing fraternity.

Now, one of the sons had it in for Jack. He reported to police that Jack had sold Bannockburn's wool all to himself. A big investigation was implemented, only to find a grazier in the Muttaburra district was called Alexander and his wool was branded with his name. All Mr Dart's son saw was a wool shipment with Alexander stencilled on the bales of wool and assumed it was Bannockburn's. The boys in blue went around the district and Jack heard about the so-called police investigation on him, through gossip.

Sadly, Helen was right and poor Mr Dart passed away from liver cancer. Mrs Dart asked Jack to ring her when next in town, which he did and paid his condolences, saying how sorry he was at her husband's passing. Mrs Dart, in a strong voice, told Jack everything was the same as their agreement but would he kindly send a copy of his daily diary and all accounts paid to their solicitor every month?

Then she gave him the solicitor's name, address and phone number, and said kindly, "Don't worry, Jack, Mr Dart was very pleased at how you are managing the property and it's a blessing to me you are there. But I would like all business and discussions to go through the solicitor so as not to worry me or my sons."

Jack said, "Thank you and I will certainly do what you ask. Is there anything else I can do for you?"

"No, Jack. Bannockburn was very kind to us and it's important that all mine and Mr Dart's life work not be wasted. Thank you, Jack," and the call ended.

Life went on at Bannockburn, everything was running smoothly. Jack wished Helen would use the radio but she wasn't keen. He thought it would keep her in touch with the other women but Helen was not keen on just gossip for gossip's sake. They had their social outings; and became very good friends with George and Margaret Price, whose son, George, was the same age as Damon and their girl, Annette, the same age as Deborah.

It was late October when the telegram came from Mr Dart's son.

"Shearers booked for Monday, for the year's main shearing," it read.

Despite being told shearing took place in November, the man had moved the date forward with only a week's notice.

"Jack, what are you going to do," asked Helen. "It's impossible to get the shed ready in seven days, plus the necessary supplies, let alone find 26,000 sheep in half a million acres or so. You have been set up; you just can't do it. Jack, where are you going?"

"I'm going to bed and having a good sleep," said Jack. "I think I will be pretty busy in the next three weeks."

"But Jack, it's only two in the afternoon."

"As I said, I need a good long sleep. Goodnight darling." And off he went to bed.

He rang the breakfast bell early. He had only two men, Terry and Main, as Ross had left to go to Dart's son's place, as it was a more relaxing environment. They started mustering the back paddocks, bringing the sheep forward to the next paddock and continued in this way till all the paddocks near the shearing shed were full of sheep.

It was not good for worms or feed overcrowding the paddocks. Jack was hoping after shearing he could lighten all the paddocks and hopefully good rain would come. Every morning, Jack rang the breakfast bell at 4am, for breakfast at 4.30am. They were on the bikes and mustering sheep by 5.30am and finished about 10.30am. Sheep won't run or move after that time as it's too hot. The boys were told to rest but have their motor bikes in good order for the next day.

Jack gave Helen a list of all the gear required for shearing, asking her if she could take the kids with her to Tiree station and ask if she could use their phone to place the order. It all must arrive on the mail this Sunday. Maybe, Mr Tearden, the manager of Tiree, might help Helen get the order done.

It was 18 hours a day for Jack. After mustering, he checked his bike for the next day, serviced all the machinery in the shearing shed and got all the gear ready for the eight-stand shearing shed. He didn't stop. If he did, it was in the office going over what had been done and what had to be done. How he did it, he didn't know, neither did Helen. On Sunday afternoon, all the supplies had arrived by mail, sheep were drafted and put into the pens and another lot were underneath the shed. The shearers started to arrive and everything was in place. He had done the impossible.

C.14

Troubles, Big Wet, Flooded

It rained in Longreach and it rained in Muttaburra. It didn't rain at Bannockburn but the shearers voted the sheep were wet and wouldn't shear them. That was not a concern to Jack. Usually, after a long drive and a gut full of grog, it was convenient for shearers to vote the sheep wet, to have a day off. It was a concern to Jack when they did it on the Tuesday as well. Jack could not hold the sheep that long without food and water. They let the sheep out and shepherded them around to give them a pick and drink and put them back in their pens. They did the same on the Wednesday. Jack grabbed a sheep and shore it and another five before the shearers voted again for wet sheep.

"They're not wet," said Jack, "Feel the fleece and sheep."

They declined to do so, just voted them wet.

Jack saw the boss of the board and asked what he was going to do about it, as he couldn't hold the sheep any longer. The boss said he would go next door and ring the contractor. What did Jack want him to say?

"Tell him, they start shearing this afternoon or sack them and get another team."

The boss came back and said the contractor said to sack

them and he advised Jack not to go near the shed till all the shearers had gone as they would be very angry.

A tired and angry Jack went back to the homestead and had a sleep for a couple of hours, then went back to the shed, thinking all the shearers were gone and he wanted to check on all the rations and kero fridges. But, unfortunately, they were still there having a meeting and not in a friendly mood.

A shearer raced up to Jack, with a loaded handpiece, ready to strike him down the face with it. Jack stepped in as close as he could, so the fella was restricted in his swing. While this manoeuvre was going on, Jack could hear the hatred in his voice, as he called him every swear word and disgusting name he could think of, saying, "I'm going to rip your guts out, you little shit of a cocky."

The other shearers raced up and grabbed the man from Jack, saying, "He's not worth it, forget it. Let's get off this dump."

A week later, the young Muttaburra policeman came to see Jack and wanted to know what had happened with the shearers. Jack told him the story. He answered, "You are a very lucky man to be alive." Then he told the story, of what happened that afternoon at the Muttaburra Hotel.

Policeman's story:

The shearers spent the afternoon drinking at the Muttaburra pub. Three were playing darts. The one that had a go at you, Jack, said, "You bastards are cheating. The next time you cheat, I will shoot you."

The men took no notice of him and kept playing darts.

"I warned you," he said and threw his dart and walked out of the pub.

The barmaid suggested to the men clear out as she thought she could hear him loading a rifle. The men said he was alright, he was just upset over a little cocky that sacked the team. Next minute, one of the dart players fell to the ground, shot. The whole bar emptied out and ran out the back. The shooter followed them out and sighted one man, who yelled, "Don't shoot me, I'm the bank manager."

"Sorry mate, I'm just after that other cheating bastard."

He couldn't find him and went back into the bar, levelled the rifle on the injured man, who was lying on the barmaid's lap as she was wiping him down with the bar towel.

He said, "I can't find the other cheat but I will finish you off."

He pulled the trigger and shot him a second time, then walked out, threw the rifle on to the back seat of his car, where the rifle shot a bullet through the roof, then took off.

Hearing the shooting, the policeman said, "I got into the police vehicle and chased the vehicle down the road, believing he was the shooter. After a few kilometres the car stopped. Evidently, he had run out of fuel. I stepped out of the police car with my new police pistol, held it up in the air and said, 'Come out with your hands up or I will come in shooting'. As I said that, my finger must have pulled the trigger and gave me quite a shock as I did not know who was doing the shooting. I jumped back into the police car but the shooter came out of his car with his hands up, saying, 'It's alright, I was just shooting those cheating bastards.' I walked up to him, put the handcuffs on him and arrested him. My boss asked me to come an interview you for the record and for the case against him."

Jack found out later, the shooter was not charged for the murder, because he had a mental condition and alcohol triggered it, or whatever. Jack wasn't sure but knew the man had got away with murder.

Another story about a shearer happened at Tiree Station when, on a Sunday, a shearer was playing with his old .303 gun in his room. Usually, shearers' quarters were divided by corrugated iron walls, two shearers to a room. He made an outline of his head while lying down and thought, in his alcohol-twisted mind, *If I shoot this in the centre of my outline, how many men in the following rooms could I hit?*

He fired the gun. Luckily the corrugated wall deflected the bullet in an upward direction and, thankfully, no one was hit. The police were called but nothing further happened. It must be said that shearers are good hard-working people but alcohol and in a group of other shearers, they seemed to change to a different group of men.

The next team of shearers came and got to work immediately. The hum of the machinery, the donk, donk of the lister engine, the click, click, of the wool press, the baa-ing of sheep, the sound of a huge operation in full swing. It was a busy job for Jack and his two jackaroos, bringing in sheep, drafting them, taking the shorn ones away, then branding and dipping them.

Three weeks later, all was finished. The cheques had to be made out. It was surprising some of the names wives and children had. Surely it wasn't to dupe the taxation department of their income. A very tired Jack and two jackaroos slowly made their way to the homestead for lunch. Don't forget poor Helen. All alone, who only saw her tired, grumpy husband at teatime then he went off to the office and bed, no conversation with her man for three weeks. The children missed their daddy too. They all suffered in their own way. But now was the time to relax and look forward to a hard-earned rest.

What, or who, is turning up now? were the thoughts of all. It was the obnoxious son of Mr Dart, who jumped out of the car and informed all, "I thought I would come for lunch."

An inward groan came from everyone. It was the last person anyone wanted to see. Helen raced into the kitchen to make another lunch. Thank God she had fed the children beforehand as she wasn't sure the boys would finish at the shed. Then they all sat down and had a cold meat and salad lunch with some fresh bread the son had brought.

While they were all finishing lunch off with a cup of tea, the son spoke, "The family want you to finish up now, as I will be taking over the property."

Sixteen words.

Knowing how tired Jack was, the adrenalin, anger, and a murderous look in his eyes flourished deep down inside him, as he got up from his chair.

As he stood up and looked the son in the eye, he said with undisguised venom, "How dare you! How dare you come and sit down for lunch with us, after we have shorn 26,000 sheep and tell us to move on. Well, that's not going to happen."

Helen and the jackaroos were in shock. If Jack had physically attacked the spoilt brat, they would have gladly joined in.

Jack continued, "Are you sacking me? If so, what are the reasons? And I want them in writing."

"No, the family are very pleased with the way you have run Bannockburn but it is the family property and the family wants to run it," said the son.

"Well, that's not the deal that your father and mother made with me and Helen."

"We have no record of that."

"I bet you haven't," said Jack, still very angry. "The other thing I will say to you, what sort of a man are you, to throw a family out with no home to go to, three weeks before Christmas? How dare you!

"If the family is satisfied with us, any reasonable person would pay us two months in lieu of notice, plus all money due, wages and holiday pay. We will leave in the second week of January. Are you in agreement?"

"Yes, but at least I had the guts to front you, instead of a telegram."

"We would like you to leave now, before any more damage is done," said Jack.

He got up and left but before he did, he said the words, "Don't leave the property till I take over." Then he was gone.

In actual fact, legally the son could have kicked them out on the spot. As a manager and employee, Jack did not have any rights. Thanks to a good angry bluff, they had some room and money to move.

Jack said to the startled jackaroos, "I think you should start your holidays now, I can pay you and you will have to negotiate with that person if you still want to work for him."

When the jackeroos left, Helen asked, "What are you going to do?"

"I don't know love; our world has just crashed down on us," Jack said.

"I told you we should have had something in writing."

"I don't think it would do any good. The family would always win a court case, no matter what we had in writing or what witnesses. We just have to cop it. Dear, I'm tired and upset, I think I will go for a long drive, a long think and come home for a long sleep with a cuddle attached."

"Be careful love and I do want to see you at tea."

Next morning, while lying in bed, Jack rolled over and asked Helen what she thought of yesterday's event.

"We should have known but we were so keen to have a chance of owning a property. That's gone out of the window. You have worked so hard dear, for no reward, it's just not right. So, have you thought what you are going to do? And don't forget the New Years party at the Harringtons."

"Darling, I don't know anything about a party. All my mind is taken up with, what are we going to do next?"

"I've told you twice, either you haven't listened or forgotten, which is fair enough as you have been so busy."

"For the moment, let's forget about the Harringtons and decide what we will do next. I think we should go to town tomorrow, have a talk to George and Margaret Price. Also, I have heard there is an old Dodge truck for sale, which we should buy, as we haven't got a vehicle and we have got to pack and move from here in the next three weeks."

"Have you any plans?"

"Not at this moment, except I'd like a cuddle now."

Jack and Helen caught up with George and Margaret the next day.

"What a bastard thing to do, especially after finishing the year's shearing. I know he is not liked in the district but I never thought someone from the land would treat another bushy like that," said George.

They had gone to George and Margaret's place, Hillview, as Jack and Helen needed friends to talk to about the events that had happened to them yesterday.

Margaret was astounded and kept mumbling, "I just don't believe that he did that. Anyway, you're staying the night. The kids are having a good time together and I guess Jack and George have a lot to talk about. Why don't you and I leave them and go and check the garden out. I want to ask you whether it's too hot to start planting anything in pots now?"

"Yes, I know who has the Dodge truck for sale, I will give him a ring now," said George as he got on the phone.

Jack listened as George started speaking to someone.

"Yes, but is it still for sale? When can he let me know? Alright, I will wait for his call." George hung up the phone. "Jack, the chap is out. His wife will give the message and she said he will call back."

"Let's hope so, because we will need a vehicle to move our stuff and have something for travel," said Jack.

"You can leave your gear here."

"Thanks George but I talked to Doug Brown on the way up and he has a spare lock up shed for us to use as long as we like. He can't understand Mr Dart's son doing what he did. He reckoned he badgered his poor widow mother, who would be still in mourning for her loss, to take over the place."

"That sound's good for your storage. Now Jack, if you want some work, we have plenty of mustering and branding to do early next year and we will need help."

"Thanks George, we might take you up on that but at this time I really don't know what we are doing. It's all such a shock. We really hadn't had any plans for the future."

The man who owned the truck rang that night and said it was still for sale. We could have a look at it at his place just outside Hughenden. He gave the address and suggested about lunch time tomorrow to see the vehicle.

It was a 60s model Dodge, a very clean vehicle with just over 100,000 miles on the clock. It was grey, slightly bigger and much better than the old PMG truck that brought them from Cunnamulla. Tyres were good, oil was clean, six months rego on it, yes, they would take it. They paid $550 and it was theirs. Two obstacles were overcome: a vehicle and somewhere to store their gear.

It was just what the family needed: a couple of friends to talk things over with, a few drinks and laughs, some plans made and the kids had a great time with young George, Michael and Annette.

Jack drove the Dodge home while Helen drove the station car. Back at Bannockburn, the packing up and labelling started. Helen was keen to wash all the walls down, which was a big job, as it was all tongue and grove timber with high ceilings. Jack told Helen not to bother about it.

"Why do it for them?"

"Because they left it nice and clean when we moved in and we should do the same for them. Don't be so vicious, Jack, it's so unlike you."

"Well, I wouldn't do it."

"But I bet you go out most days and check the waters and stock, still keeping the place well maintained."

"That's different. We are still on the pay roll."

Helen rolled her eyes and changed the subject.

"Now, Jack, about the New Years party."

"What party is that?" answered Jack with tongue in cheek.

"You know darn well and it's a formal party with ball gowns and dinner suits."

"Oh, that's right, it's at the Harringtons. I'm surprised we are invited; they are an old, established grazing family and rather posh and it's only the top social people invited. I suppose as a humble manager, it is a great privilege to be asked but I'm not keen on these sort of dos."

"Well, we are going. You can't get out of it, so behave, be a good husband and escort me to the party on New Years Eve."

"If you say so, my love, but I don't have a dinner suit."

"Bad luck, Margaret is lending me George's. You are both the same size, so no more excuses from you, we are going."

Sometime later, Helen reminded Jack of further commitments.

"Jack, we have to go to Townsville," she said. "Remember, it was planned to go after shearing for Christmas shopping, to buy for the store and a few sewing things I need to get before we go to the Harringtons."

"I don't think we need to buy for the store, as we are leaving in just over three weeks."

"I think we should, what if it rains and we could be stuck for a few weeks."

"Perhaps you are right. Check what we have and we will get what's really needed."

They got busy, taking all their packed gear to the Browns' place for storage, back up to George and Margaret's place to do a few chores for George. While there, they did a good service and check of the Dodge for it to be ready for its big trip to… they didn't know where yet. they left Sparkle and the truck at the Prices' place. Helen wondered why. Jack couldn't give a good explanation but that's what they did.

Then the trip to Townsville and the Christmas shopping, which was hell.

The Alexanders didn't like lots of people around and dodging them. The kids were tired of being pulled around, constantly complaining to their parents. Leaving Helen and Deborah to do their own thing, Jack and Damon did some shopping for themselves, buying a good, heavy tarp for the truck to cover all their gear when on the move, plus ropes, tie downs, jerrycans for fuel and water and odds and ends. Jack bought Helen an expensive silver covered gold necklace with gold leaves covered in silver, that lay flat around her neck. It did look great on her and everyone at the party said so too.

They had a fun great Christmas. The kids were spoilt by their Victorian grandparents and parents. Helen, despite not being a material or jewellery girl, was delighted with her necklace. Jack did well, with a few excellent books and much needed good clothes. The walls and ceilings were cleaned at the homestead, thanks to Helens hard work, the waters and stock were looking good on the property. Everything was ready to leave Bannockburn at a minute's notice.

New Year's Eve, Helen and the kids were excited, going to the big party at the Harringtons. Helen was looking so beautiful and happy, the kids were in their best, with Deborah swirling around to see how her dress flew in a circle. Even Damon, who, like his father, didn't like to be restricted by good clothing, seemed to be excited as well.

The only one not excited, knew that something was going to happen. Jack didn't like the shape of the forming clouds or the heat of the evening. He could feel it, couldn't explain it but he felt something was going to happen. He would not say anything to Helen and spoil her excitement and, anyway, she would ignore him, saying,

"You're not going to get out of it; we are going to the Harringtons."

They went in the old Holden, the pictures car, 160 kilometres on dirt rough roads to Harringtons' property. There were lots of people there, all done up to the nines. The kids were put in a room with the other kids, with a governess to look after them, having their own party.

Helen looked outstanding in her gown that she made. She was asked where she bought it and who the designer was. She proudly said she made it herself. Jack wasn't sure all believed her. Jack surprised himself by enjoying the party. Everyone had heard, via the bush telegraph, what happened to Jack. They gave their consolations, asked what he was going to do now and he said he had no idea but doubted whether he would manager properties again. There were very kind offers of help and references. Jack showed his appreciation for their kind words but, really, he just wanted to enjoy himself with Helen at the party. It started to rain about 11pm.

Jack suggested it was time; they had a considerable way to go and the rain was getting heavy. Helen said a definite 'no'.

"We will not leave until midnight," and that was it.

After the kissing and whooping and pulling popper streamers and singing, *Auld Lang Syne*, everyone picked up their kids for the drive home. They got about 5km when they all got bogged in the black soil with the rain still falling. It was well known, only men can drive a bogged car out, so all the women were doing the pushing, as the wheels spun in the mud, spraying all the beautiful gowns in a shower of black wet mud.

It was hopeless. It was decided by all, to go back to the Harringtons in the only car not stuck in the mud and stay the night. They all lay on the large dining room floor with the kids and little covering. The girls tried to clean themselves up in the bathrooms but there was nothing anyone could do but try and get some shut eye.

Bless the Harringtons. They manage to make everyone a breakfast and, now with the rain still lightly falling, tractors and the few four-wheel drive vehicles available, helped the cars out that were bogged the night before. It was relayed to Jack that he could not go south, as the road was impassable but some of the party-goers had to get down the Torrens Creek Road, which was thought may be passable.

It was a convoy of three two-wheel drive cars and two four-wheel drive cars: one a Landrover Defender, the other a new Toyota. They managed to get to Prairie without trouble, then along the 47 kilometres of bitumen to Torrens Creek, and finally 166 kilometres to Bannockburn. A slow trip on very wet, muddy, dirt roads, the two wheel drive vehicles had to be towed or pulled out when bogged. Even the Toyota was bogged once.

After a four-hour slog through rain and mud and boggy road, they reached the flooded Torrens Creek, which was now joined by Bullock Creek. The manager from one of the stations nearby must have been contacted. And there, waiting for the Alexanders, was a large tray truck to get them across the creek. All the others lived north of the creek, while they lived on the other side.

It was women and children in the cab of the truck, while a chain was attached to the Holden for its seventh tow.

"Good luck, Jack, we hope not to lose you," said Barney, the driver of the truck as he hopped into the cab.

Jack was not feeling very comfortable, being in the driver's seat. He would have preferred to be in the cab with his wife and children. The truck pulled the car into the current. Jack tried to keep the wheels in a straight line with the truck's wake. The water was not that deep, just covering two-thirds of the truck's back wheels but the current was strong and the Holden started to be taken by the pull. The truck reached the other side and, as it did, pulled the car straight again. They were across.

The truck went back across the creek and everyone waved to Helen, Jack and the kids and wished them a safe drive home.

"Will we get home, now we are on our own?" asked Damon.

"Sure we will, son, but we might have to walk some of the way."

Luckily, the 10 kilometres on the spinifex red road was passable, helping them get safely home.

That was 1st January, 1974. They couldn't leave till 21st March as they were completely isolated. One man, one woman, a little boy of three and a half and one little girl of two years.

The rain just fell out of the sky, no slant, no, wind. It rained nonstop for 38 days and nights, two days less than Noah with his ark. The noise of a great variety of frogs, toads and other creatures, kept them awake. There were also sand flies and monstrous mosquitoes in their thousands.

Helen put her finger on the mosquito net one night and hundreds of mosquitoes fought to get some blood off her finger. She, very slowly, moved her finger down the net and the fight and scramble of the black mob followed in a mad frenzy. Thank the Lord the homestead was mostly gauzed in, however, the children and the parents always slept under the finest woven nets. Even though it was hot, it was better than being carried away.

The first two weeks in isolation was normal for the big wet in Queensland for most western people. They got on with life as a normal seasonal event. But after two weeks, with the rain still falling 24 hours a day, one had to assume there could be some concern.

Helen kept herself busy, teaching the kids to draw and do cut outs, having fun with big cardboard boxes, as well as teaching the alphabet and doing story times. She taught very basic reading words and loved playing with her children. She always wanted at least four children but Jack had put the brakes on after the last two worrying births.

And while Helen had the children fully occupied, Jack had to burst in now and then and excite the kids, chasing them, catching and throwing them up in the air, swinging them around in aeroplane rides, rolling on the ground and wrestling them. There were lots of giggles, screams and laughter and poor Helen's little art session was all forgotten.

Helen started to be very careful with the food. She made good but simple, healthy meals, studying her various cookbooks and recipes. Who knew when the rain would end or their supplies? She was pleased she had coaxed Jack into getting more supplies when in Townsville.

Jack, on the other hand, besides having fun with the children, stayed mostly in his special, completely gauzed office. No one could go outside, it was impossible. Even though they were 10 kilometres from the flooded creeks, the current of the water was lapping the floorboards of the metre-high veranda. Whether on purpose or a coincidence, the homestead was built on a slight rise.

So, what was Jack up to? He was busy on the flying doctor radio. trying to get news on what was happening out there. There was no ordinary radio reception and television was only part of someone's imagination. It was the men's session, early in the morning, Jack could find out what was going on. The whole of the gulf was flooded down past Longreach and all the western areas. There were people isolated everywhere.

Stories abounded and a lot were probably true, maybe some exaggerated, like crocs swimming in the town centre of Mt Isa. There was another story and Jack believed this one, with a confirmation. One little town, possibly Kynuna, had a full tourist bus stranded with no help for some time. The publican was running out of food fast, even though he was strictly rationing. So, the situation was getting desperate. He thought he had no other option and made a huge stew to feed the tourists, who congratulated him on finding enough food and, with his cooking skills, was able to satisfy everyone. He did miss his two Alsatian dogs but he just had to feed the people.

People had their chooks in their houses. One person had cut a hole in his roof, so with a chain pulley he had his pianola hanging from the ceiling beams. Jack also heard that one family had their killer sheep in the spare bedroom and a few bales of hay.

It was the end of the men's session and the flying doctor calls. Then there were the telegrams which, if you were very lucky, you could get on the air. People were ordering food drops; one idiot wanted his drycleaning dropped off. What for, only he would know but he nearly brought the plane down as the suit, wrapped in plastic, caught in the vertical tail of the plane when it was thrown out. If the pilot hadn't manoeuvred the aircraft to loosen the problem, pilot, plane and dry cleaning would have had an untimely ending.

Another good pilot wanted to get the food drop as close to the house as he could but, unfortunately, he got too close and the bundle went straight through the house, which caused rain damage to the inside of the homestead. This was at Jireena, where Jack and Helen had lived and managed for a few years. The pilots did not use parachutes for food drops. They were usually dropped from 300 feet at approximately 80 kilometres an hour.

It was 26th January, 1974 when Brisbane got flooded. Helen and Jack had been isolated for 26 days and there was more to come.

One by one, the flying doctor radios failed, as the huge amount of moisture received damaged the works. As each radio went out, Jack guessed the people were evacuated. Bannockburn's radio failed as well. But there was an old-fashioned, low frequency radio in the office that worked. It had two dials on it and if Jack spent some time turning the dials, he could match a frequency. So, they had communication. Evacuation was not possible as they were 160kms from Torrens Creek and 111kms from Aramac. With only one helicopter in the gulf at that time and all the help in the world for the population of Brisbane, their little family didn't have a chance.

There was a static phone call that came from Tiree Station on the private line between the two stations. It was Mr Tearden on the line.

"Jack, can you hear me?"

"Yes but it's difficult, can you hear me?"

"Jack, no details or dates, did you copy?"

"No details or dates, go ahead."

"Helen's father has passed away, message via police."

"Please repeat message. Understand Helen's father passed away, is this correct?"

"Yes, police notified us of Helen's father passing."

"Understood and thank you."

They hung up. It was very hard to hear the message with the buzzing and interference on the private line but the message was clear enough. And Jack had the difficult task of telling Helen that her good-looking, fit, 62-year-old father had died, but there were no details of when and how.

Helen was in the kitchen. Jack called her to the lounge as the children were having an afternoon sleep.

"Yes, what is it?" she asked.

"Love, just come and sit down with me. I've something to tell you."

She walked into the room and saw Jacks face.

"What's happened?"

"Just sit down, darling, let me put my arm around you."

As Helen sat down, Jack put his arm around her, pulling her gently beside him.

"Love, I just got a message from Mr Tearden, who was rung by the police. I have to tell you that your dad has passed away."

A very teary beautiful girl sniffed, "What happened?"

"I'm sorry darling, that's all the information that could be provided. No date or details or why. I don't know what to say or do but hold you."

They never did find out till March. Her dad was playing bowls, won the competition, then rang his sister and daughter, Wendy, from the local telephone box to help celebrate the occasion with lunch. He had a massive heart attack and died in the phone box. Poor Helen. Her beloved mother, Dorothy, died at 52 and her dad at 62. It was also hard for her to be isolated and unable to go to the funeral or be with her kin folk and relations. What more can this family go through?

In the office, as usual, Jack was playing with the radio, finding frequencies. Slowly twisting the two dials, he heard, "May Day, May Day, May Day."

Jack answered, "This is 8QTA, go ahead."

What happened next was this: A fella south of Richmond left his haemorrhaging wife to find help by horse. He carried a field phone and, when he found a party line, he clipped in. By coincidence, two women were talking on the line and he interrupted them and spoke, "Help, help, my wife is haemorrhaging."

The women heard the call but they only had a school of

the air radio, and one of them tried it to reach help. It was Jack that received the call by coincidence, twiddling his radio set and answering the call for help.

Now, it must be explained carefully, as the reader might get the wrong idea. When the base in Cairns was closed, a mayday caller had to use a little whistle. Now Cains was about 1,000 kilometres away. How could you whistle that far? This whistle was blown into the microphone for a couple of seconds then the user put a finger on the hole and the whistle would send a much higher note and this set the alarm off at the base.

"Who is calling the Cairns base?"

"This is 8QTA calling, we have received an urgent mayday call from frequency #########. Can you contact them?"

"QTA stand by. Thank you 8QTA, we are now in contact with the mayday caller, you may stand down."

"This is 8QTA over and out."

These calls for help were received by sheer chance, fate or, if you like, heavenly help. By coincidence also, the only helicopter in the gulf at that time happened to be at Kynuna, about 50 kilometres from the haemorrhaging woman. Jack never found out the conclusion of that story. Did the woman survive? Did her partner get back to her in time? Were other kids involved? He had no idea.

(Authors note. I may have some of the details wrong or incorrect so please forgive me. This event happened 50 years ago. The memory, in writing this now, may not be that accurate.)

Our dear basset hound, Susie, you may have forgotten her but she was part of the loving Alexander family, always providing a pillow for Damon, loved cuddles from Deborah, loved getting under Helen's feet when cooking and leaving trails of food from her ears on the floor. She was such a good, fun, sleepy dog and just had to go where the family went. She was especially good now in isolation. She kept everyone on the straight and narrow. She was always just there when a child was miserable or a grown-up was frustrated, tired and worried. And they were worried.

Helen was worried they were not getting enough vitamins, worried what to do if the children got sick or anyone for that matter. Worried about the thousands of biting insects with no insect sprays to protect her children and how long would the rain and food last.

Jack was worried about the long days in isolation for his family, how was Helen managing with her stoma? Did she have enough appliances and what would happen, if not? He wasn't allowed to ask.

"That's my business, not yours," Helen would say.

Jack also worried about when they got out, where would they live and what job or career moves would he need to do? Also, if there was a medical emergency or any other, at this time, how would he manage? The children must have been worried also. When could they go outside and play? But there were no fights or arguments. They all had patience and knew they would have to survive this situation.

"Jack, wake up. Jack, I hear a plane, quick get up, it must be a food drop," said Helen one morning.

It was the second week in February and the rain had stopped a few days previously. They raced outside and there was a plane flying exceptionally low with bags being dropped from it. They raced out to collect the much-needed food but alas, the packing was not good enough. They had put bread in with a half sack of potatoes. The hessian bag split on landing, with the bread mashed beyond use and bits of potatoes scatted everywhere. Pieces were bayoneted on barb wire, others you couldn't see under the still lying water. Smashed tubs of butter were useless. There were only two things that survived and they were vital:

a 10-kilo tin of plain flour, very battered but the lid had been brazed on, and the other item that survived, which Helen was not pleased about at all, were three tins of Log Cabin tobacco and papers to match, for Jack.

To say Helen was not pleased, was an understatement. She was furious that the tobacco survived and not much else, when insect spray, fruit and green vegetables were much more important. They grabbed what they could, as fast as they could, before the insects carried them away. The mosquitoes were biting badly but they had calamine lotion to help get rid of the itch.

There had been a telegram, a couple of days previously, to advise of a food drop, but the congestion on the radio during the telegram calls was so heavy that Jack could not get through.

There was still plenty of water around. Helen managed, somehow, to gather hibiscus leaves and pigweed and did a wonder with her skills, to be able to supply meals with greens to stave off a vitamin deficiency she was sure the family might have.

Jack was restless now. The rain had stopped but the mosquitoes, sand flies and biting flies bred in their millions and the only way possible to go outside for short times, was to cover any exposed skin with kerosene. Jack got some plastic skin from the flying doctor kit and sprayed the whole engine of the motorbike to protect it from the water; he was going to check out the Torrens Creek. No thought to safety or what could happen, he was going on a motorbike ride and that was it.

"Be careful, darling. You really shouldn't go; how long will you be?"

"Be back in hour or two. I'll be right, even if I have to walk back. Seeya."

Jack was surprised. There was a good 18 inches of water lying in the paddocks but the water was so clear and the red ground was hard. The constant rain had cleaned the road and water. The bike made a wake in the water as it moved and the plastic surgical skin was perfect to protect the engine. The exhaust was just under the seat so the engine could breathe.

Jack got to the creek crossing that was flowing fast but the water was just overlapping its banks. It showed how high it got from the surrounding 100 or so metres of flattened, covered ground, littered with debris of all kinds.

Was that a car engine? Impossible but there it was, driving up toward him. *I'm seeing things*, thought Jack, *No way could this be a car on this road*. But it was. It was filthy and so were the six unshaven men inside. There was a strong smell of alcohol emitted from the car and the men. It was overwhelming.

"Where have you come from fellas?" asked Jack.

"We left Aramac, (100 kilometres away) that was five days ago," said one of them, "to get to Torrens Creek but we have been bogged. We pushed the bloody car half the way and now, by the look at that creek, we aren't going anywhere. You must be from around here."

"Yes, but I've ridden miles to have a look at the creek to see if its crossable. As you can see it's not. Well, I got to be on my way fellas, good luck," and Jack headed for home. He didn't think they would follow his tracks but they did, arriving half an hour after Jack.

This was the situation. Isolated, 100 kilometres from anywhere, one small family of two adults and two small children and now six strange, alcoholic, rough men. Jack was worried, really worried. He had to be in complete charge.

"I wish you chaps hadn't followed me in," he said. "We are nearly out of food and we really can't help you but, seeing you're here, go over to the shearers quarters and I'll bring you some food, though it won't be much."

The men just nodded and headed for the quarters.

"Who are those men? Why did you bring them here? We can't help them or give them the little food we have," said an anxious Helen.

"Love, I had no intention of bringing them here. Keep well away and let's see if we can rummage a bit of food for them. I will send them packing in the morning."

Jack took over a full packet of out-of-date Kellogg's Corn Flakes, a small tin of powdered milk, two tins of camp pie, some tea and sugar and one of his new jerry cans of petrol, to make sure they had enough fuel to get off the property.

"Sorry fellas, this is all I can give you. We have hardly any for ourselves and I'm giving you this fuel as well. And I must ask you to leave first thing in the morning as we cannot help you any further."

"Is that all your giving us? It's not much."

"Mate, yes we are giving it to you and by doing it, we are depriving ourselves of food."

Another chap stepped forward. "Sorry governor for Frank. Thanks, we will manage what you have brought." Jack left and as he did so, he said, "Remember, we want you gone early tomorrow morning."

Jack stayed up all night with a couple of loaded rifles and a shot gun. He didn't know how much grog they had had or if they thought they could raid the place. It was a situation that could get out of control quickly, unless he kept his nerve, patience and experience in dealing with a dangerous event.

To everyone's relief, they did leave early next morning, without a goodbye, which suited Jack. A good outcome but it could have been a terrifying experience if things had worked out differently.

That afternoon, the rain started again. It wasn't heavy or constant and they even had an occasional day without rain. Jack, again, had to go exploring on the motorbike, covered again with sprayed medical skin. He did not go anywhere near the main road this time and he wasn't gone long. It was too distressing, seeing black rain clouds in the distance getting closer, finding small mobs of cattle or sheep on raised bits of ground, covered in a black cloud of flies, mosquitoes, or any other insect that was after blood. It was horrible, how they must be suffering.

He went home, sat in his office and tried to think of a way to help. If he could only get old tyres out there and burn them for the smoke to keep the insects away but that was, in those conditions, impossible. He asked on the radio, during the men's session, if there was anything he could do. One old-timer came on the line and in a rough, gravelly voice said in no uncertain terms, "Young fella, stay inside. There is nothing you can do. Let nature takes its course as cruel as it is. Fella, I'm tellin' you, don't go out."

Slowly, blue skies started to appear, water slowly receded and dried out. Frogs and toads never stopped their mating calls. They were at their loudest at night but even they were slowly losing voice. Helen, the kids and Susie were well covered up and, with fly nets on their faces, explored the puddles and found various colour in all sorts of little frogs. They praised the feeling of the sun on their bodies, the clean air and freedom to be outdoors. It was good, no, it was real life and to be enjoyed.

They got word that the road to Hughenden was just opened but only to local traffic. Jack told Helen they should try the road and pick up their truck and bring it back to load the last of their gear before Son Dart came and took over the place. She agreed but there was a problem. Two, in fact. The Holden would not start. Even charging the battery, the moisture had got into the electrics and distributor and it would take a lot of time to dry it out. Also, that could not guarantee the problem would be solved. In the Hilux ute, the battery had to be charged and a lot of WD40 spray used, along with patience that eventually got it going, so that was good. Secondly, poor Helen. Remember, she had washed all the walls of the homestead as she wanted it all nice and clean? She should not have done it, as mould was growing on the ceilings and walls from the previous washing and all the rain. So, she tried again to clean it all up. Did Jack help? He felt guilty but he had other important things to do.

They managed to squeeze into the Hilux; Damon wanted to ride in the back and was upset when his mother told him a firm 'no'. There was room for the three on the seats while Helen nursed Deborah on her lap. (Jack knew it was unsafe and against the law but it was 1974 and desperate times makes one do desperate things. Fair enough).

It was great to see the Prices and Sparkle the dog again, the first other humans they had seen in months. They stayed for lunch and it was decided, when they left Bannockburn, they would come back here and help the family muster and do a count of sheep and fix fences as, of course, they had a lot of damage and loss like everyone else.

So, back to Bannockburn they went. Helen was driving the Hilux with Deborah well strapped in and Jack and Damon followed in the Dodge to make sure the girls didn't get themselves into trouble. A short stop in Hughenden to get some fruit and vegetables but, unfortunately, there was not much there, if anything.

"Sorry love, the train has not come yet with our supplies, it's all we got," said Mrs Cooper, the greengrocer. It was late when they got home and everyone was very tired.

A telegram was received from Son Dart to say they would be arriving on Friday to take over. This gave them a few days to pack up, move the rest of the gear to the Browns and clean the homestead the best they could. There was nothing Jack could do to the property or the machinery, as the water had not cleared completely and the moisture in everything would take months to get in order. As a matter of fact, it was a blessing they were leaving. That left Son Dart with one hell of a clean-up, not only of the machinery but sheds, fences, starving, dying stock and everything else, to have the property in a producing capacity.

The Alexanders did all they could to leave the place at its very best for the new occupants but not as they would have liked. There were still showers of rain and lots of water and moisture about.

The family came and moved in. The Alexanders started to move out but a problem arose, Son Dart handed Jack a cheque but it was not the right amount of money, and he said so.

The son said, "I have paid you exactly what we agreed. Two months wages in lieu, plus wages and holiday pay."

"The cheque is right as far as that is concerned but you have forgotten that you told me, 'Do not leave the place till I get here to take over.'"

Jack informed Son Dart, he could have left a few times beforehand but he had kept his word and did not leave until the Dart family came today, so he would need another cheque for 12 weeks wages, as he was employed by the company until today.

"I'm not going to pay you anymore; you did not do anything."

"Look, you can make it very uncomfortable for both of us. I think you should do the right thing and we leave on good terms," said Jack.

Son Dart turned, went back into the house and came back a few minutes later with another cheque for the extra owing. They shook hand, wished each other well, without smiling. Wife, kids and dog got into the Dodge, did a wave goodbye and drove off, heading for another adventure somewhere else.

C.15

(2nd Interval)
Sandgate

They stopped at the Browns place to say, 'hi' and checked all their gear that was stored there. Miraculously, none of it was damaged, thanks to Helen's good packing and the Browns living on a rise and a long way from flooded creeks. After a quick cuppa, they were off to the Prices. They received a great welcome from all, including Sparkle. They took a day of settling in, then there were three weeks of hard work under notoriously hot and humid conditions.

George's brother and another worker also helped but the clearing of fences from debris was a hard, dirty, dangerous job. Why dangerous? Snakes, spiders and sharp objects had been caught up in the piles of rubbish jammed against the fence wire. Wearing gloves was essential but that still didn't stop the worker getting staked on the arms or ankles.

The kids had a great time at the Prices and Marge and Helen got on very well together, having fun sharing recipes, cooking, which benefited the men and recreating new gardens.

George told Jack and Helen they did not have to worry about transport to Brisbane as he had to drive down to a couple of important meetings. He was an important backroom person in Queensland politics.

Helen asked him. "Why not fly down?" and he replied that he wanted to see representatives of the party in their electorates on his return.

Margaret definitely would not accompany him, so there would be plenty of room for them all to fit in the car.

After a good three weeks of fun and hard work at the Prices' place, they prepared to leave for Brisbane. With the car seats in and Helen squashed in the back with them, Jack sat in the front with Susie the hush puppy, (Sparkle was left behind as she would have gone mad in the city) the boot was jammed with suitcases, soft bags and items in plastic bags, shoved into any gap available. It was a rather crowded but safe trip doing the 1,600-kilometre trip to Brisbane with three overnight stops.

Helen had the forethought of ringing the motel in Brisbane with the unit they stayed in last time. The unit they had stayed in was occupied but the other one was available. So, Helen booked it. They now had a temporary place to stay in the city.

George dropped them off at their unit. Both Helen and Jack thanked him so much for the lift and hospitality at Hillview station. As soon as they had a future and work, they would let him know and would come back to Hillview to pick up their gear at the Browns and the Dodge and Sparkle which were staying at his place. A wave goodbye and a thrown kiss by Helen, to a very nice kind man.

Helen put her foot down.

"No, I'm not going back to the nursing agency for a while and you Jack, are not looking for work," she said. "We have had a pretty tough few years with me being sick, babies and you always trying to do more than you should on other people's places. I have decided we are having three weeks holiday, enjoying the children and each other. We have the beach, nice walks and we can hire a car for some nice drives as we don't know the Brisbane area at all, so that's settled."

"Don't I have a say?" asked Jack.

"Not this time my love, there are no options for you." And so, it was.

They did have a much-needed rest. They did the walks, enjoyed Redcliffe, even hired a boat and some fishing gear. Their catch for the day was a little crab but it was fun. They hired a car and drove around a city that was starting to yawn and stretch to become a big city like Sydney and Melbourne. Helen and Jack liked the way it was. They did not like big polluting cities that created their own weather with big buildings.

They saw 10 acres for sale in Moggill, near the Brisbane River for $10,000, a nice country area that they thought might grow in the future. They had the money but Jack, as cautious as anything, thought they were out of work and without a home, so they shouldn't spend their savings. The thought of a small deposit, a loan would have been the way to go. But to most people then, like Jack, if you didn't have the cash, you didn't purchase. Loans and debts were something that probably happened in the future but not in Jack's world.

You may have guessed that Jack was a worrier. Helen would say, "Jack, you would worry about not worrying."

But he did worry about the future. What would he do? Buy a small business or be a housewife and let Helen earn their living? Nurses don't get paid much and they would need a home for their little family. He did not share his concerns with Helen. What was the point? She was never worried, that Jack knew, and she would have said, "Don't worry Jack, something will turn up."

Everything comes to an end. It was a good holiday and it has stayed in their memories ever since. Even the children remember their holiday at Margate and Redcliffe. Helen made an enquiry at the nursing agency for any casual or permanent positions available. There were some coming up next month so she put her name down.

Jack went to see a chap called Tom that he knew at Primary and Mactaggart's Stock and Station Agency, with the idea of becoming an auctioneer or working in the stock department of one of the agencies or he might know something that could be of interest to Jack. Tom was a contact and the few dealings Jack had had with him in the past showed he was a very helpful and friendly person to talk to.

So, he called in to see if Tom was available. Yes, he was and he had time to see Jack. Jack told him what had happened at Bannockburn but Tom already knew. It always amazed Jack what got around in the bush. There wasn't much in communication out there but the bush telegraph was always effective.

Jack put his ideas out to Tom. Were there any prospects and did he have any ideas? Jack got the impression he was not really listening. Then Tom said, "Jack, you are a bloody good property manager and there are not a lot about. I know you have had a gut full and who could blame you but I had an idea you eventually would come and see me. I am going to ask a chap upstairs to come down and talk to you, his name is Reg Evans. Would you like a coffee while you wait?"

"Thanks, I'll have a coffee," said Jack, then added, "and you let me go rattling off my ideas, when you had something up your sleeve."

Tom had a mischievous smile. "I'll get you that coffee and ask Reg to come down."

Jack got the coffee and a handshake from Mr Reg Evans, a well-dressed salesman type, with a bit of gold edging to some of his teeth. He had an open face and looked about late 50s, early 60s in age. We sat down and Tom introduced Reg as the

Australian Manager of an international company called Ishiyama Corporation based in New York and Tokyo. The company had interests in Utah Coal, Leslie Salt and Collier Carbon and Chemical Corp. However, Reg's main interest in Australia were his five cattle properties in Queensland: Moray Downs and Broadmeadows stations in Northern Queensland, West Linster, south of Mitchell, Ridgewood at Taroom and Shipfield at Giligulgul near Miles in Southern Queensland.

Now, as it so happened, they were looking for a manager of his company, Shipfield Pastoral Company, and Reg had asked Tom to find him a good manager to run it, as it was the lead station of the five. Reg asked Jack if he was interested. Jack told him he was not interested in managing any property where he would be doing all the work with no real reward.

Mr Evans asked, "Are you free this afternoon? If so, we can fly out to the property and have a good discussion about the position, which I hope you will take."

"But you don't know anything about me and my experience," said Jack.

"Yes, I do. Tom has filled me in, right to the time you were managing Ardglen. As I said, you're the manager we want. If you are ready, meet me here at 1.30 this afternoon and we will look at the property."

They shook hands and Reg got up and left.

Tom said, "There you are, have a good look at the property, don't be afraid to ask difficult questions and ask for a decent salary package. Now, off you go and I will probably see you later."

"Thanks Tom, I hope you haven't put me in deep water."

"No, it will be a good position for you. Now go and do some thinking and let me get on to some important work."

Jack rang Helen to say he would be late home but expected

to be back by teatime. She wanted to know what he was up to. He just said, "Trust me and I will tell you all about it tonight."

She replied, "The 'trust me' part is a bit of a concern."

Jack and Reg flew out in a Piper light plane and the flight was just under two hours. They landed on the property's airstrip and were met by the local Wandoan agent. It was a beautiful property, all planted with improved pastures, except for the 1500 acres of farming land that grew oats.

The house or homestead, positioned on top of the hill, looked down on the property and valley below. The kitchen was huge with full windows looking down at the views it afforded. It had gas and electric stoves and ovens and stacks of benches and cupboards. It was not modern but, then again, not old and in excellent condition. There was a lounge room, four bedrooms, two bathrooms and an office. It was a very comfortable house. It had 240-volt power, a black and white television and all mod cons. Helen would love this. No generators, just turn on the power, day or night, by just flicking a switch.

There were stacks of outbuildings, another house, men's quarters, a big shed full of machinery and a couple of hay and grain sheds. It all looked well-maintained and Jack was impressed. Miles, a large town, was 12 kilometres away and Wandoan a fair bit further.

The job was explained. The cattle up north were breeders, the steers were then sent down to West Linster to grow, then shipped to Ridgewood to finish, then to Shipfield for the final fattening. Finally, they were sent to Toowoomba to the Darling Downs meat factory to be made into special cuts then sent in special Shipfield containers direct to Japan. And Jack's job was to make sure shipment requirements were met.

Jack said he wanted to be fully found, have a decent car for his personal use and, as the house was not fully furnished, he wanted to purchase furniture at the company's expense.

Finally, he asked for a starting wage of $100 a week clear, with an understanding there would be a wage review each year. All was agreed to readily, which worried Jack. He thought he should have asked for more.

Jack was keen to take the job there and then but knowing, this time, he must discuss it with Helen, instead of rushing in without much thought. He told Reg he would have to discuss the position with his wife, Helen, and could he give an answer by the end of the week? This was accepted but Reg wanted to know when he could start. Jack informed him they would have to fly to Hughenden to pick up their gear and drive back. He estimated another two weeks, after he had decided on the position. Reg said he would have to accept that and was looking forward to hearing from him on Friday with a positive note.

"Well, what has kept you and what's this 'trust me' about?" asked Helen.

Details were wanted, so Jack explained all that had happened, even the flight out to the property. He said the 'trust me' statement was about not saying yes to anything till he informed her. He told her about the property, the 240 power, the large kitchen, the close proximity of towns and schools, also about the deal he made with Reg Evans regarding wages and the extras he had asked for and had to give his final decision by this Friday.

"You have made up your mind to take the job, haven't you?" asked Helen.

"Yes, even though I didn't want to manage again," said Jack. "This time it is working for a big company, instead of an individual boss. It's a lovely property near town, a good area to live and not that far from Brisbane. You will love it. What do you think?"

"Well, it does sound good, even with your slight exaggeration, and we do have to find a home as I don't like renting. A school for Damon and Deborah, yes, let's give it a go."

"Are you sure?"

"Yes, I'll trust you as I have always done. Somehow, things usually turn out for the better. It looks like another adventure starting for us."

They flew up to Hughenden, the four of them. Helen wanted to see Marge again and the kids wanted to see George, Michael and Annette and Jack wanted to tell George about the new job and ask if he had any knowledge of Ishiyama Corporation and Shipfield Pastoral Company. George said Shipfield was a large and well-known pastoral company and that Ishiyama Corporation was big with Utah Coal in Queensland and also a reputable company. George thought it was a good move for Jack.

After spending two days with the Prices, it was time to leave. There was a final goodbye with Sparkle. As there were no sheep where they would be going and she had settled in well where she was, a good sheep dog and mate for Jack, they were now to be parted. It always wrenched his heart to part with his dogs.

They loaded up the truck with all their gear stored at Browns place, covered it all with the new tarp and with a 'thank you and good wishes' they headed south on a long journey. Damon was worried about Susie the basset hound, left behind in some reputable kennels. Jack assured him, as soon as possible, they would pick her up and bring her to her new home.

After the long uneventful trip to Miles, they had a two-night stay in a motel, until they could move to Shipfield. While there, Deborah ran into the corner of a door and received a deep cut to the left eyebrow. There was plenty of blood, so they had to find a doctor. He was not at hospital, so they were given a home address. They raced there and met the infamous Dr Saulter. He stitched Deborah's cut up with five stitches. She was screaming in pain while Helen was holding her tight. He didn't believe in pain killers for such small sewing jobs. Poor mite. You will hear more about Dr Saulter later on.

C.16

Shipfield Pastoral Co.
1974

Helen loved the place. She unpacked all her electrical gear she hadn't used since leaving Melbourne: fry pans, toasters, kettles, hair blowers, etc. Real power fridges with freezers, washing machines and all the comforts of a good home were running on 240 power. She confessed to Jack much later, "I loved it out west, really, but I don't want to go back. This is so good."

There was a phone call from Reg to come down to Brisbane the following week to pick out furniture required and company paperwork to be done in the Brisbane office.

"Bring the whole family down so my wife, Maisie, and I can meet them," he said.

The personal car they provided was a green Valiant saloon, about two years old. There was a Holden work ute and a Fordson 500 tractor, amongst a good selection of welders and grinders in an excellent tool shed, which enabled all sorts of maintenance and repairs.

Brisbane was only 340 kilometres from Shipfield. They arrived at Reg's home in Mount Gravatt, met Maisie, Reg's wife, who was a nice, neat lady but tended to be slightly bossy. After they supplied lunch, Maisie took Helen and Jack to a couple of wholesale furniture places to pick out some beds, (two singles and a double), a large kitchen table and chairs, a large dining room table and chairs, some comfortable relaxing lounge chairs, a couple of cupboards and soft furniture and material for Helen to make up some curtains, plus linen and blankets for the new beds. All was to be transported up to Shipfield. There was furniture at Shipfield but it was old and in shabby condition so needed to be disposed of.

The shopping took longer than thought, so they stayed in a motel overnight (at company expense). The next morning, Maisie took Helen and the kids for more shopping while Jack spent some time in the company office, meeting the accountant, Gordon and secretary, Betty. They went over the company books and bank signings for cheques and employment records. Quite a heavy load to take in and absorb but Jack had a good insight of what was required. Then it was off to lunch with the two-staff office and Reg but first, Jack peeped around the corner of the downstairs office to say a quick 'G'day' to Tom who had a customer with him.

After lunch, Jack excused himself and did a quick trip to Redcliffe to pick up Susie. When he arrived back at Reg's house, to pick up Helen and the kids, Damon just about cried with joy on seeing Susie. The rest of the family were happy to see her too but Damon had a special inherent way with all animals he loved and understood more than most humans.

"How was the shopping with Maisie?" Jack asked Helen after they left.

"She decided what was best and I didn't have much chance to have my say, but her taste was similar to mine, so it was not a problem. It would have been nice to have asked my opinion," said Helen.

A tired family arrived back at Shipfield that night. Helen

managed to get a meal for the family before they tumbled into their squeaky beds for a good night's sleep.

Work started at Shipfield (be careful how you pronounce it). There were a few things Reg had not explained to Jack but he found out himself. While driving around the property, he noticed about 200 cross-bred Braham cattle in good condition, hanging about grain feeders that were nearly empty. Water was by windmills, troughs and a large dam. The only things not good were the cattle yards. They were just adequate for the job. New ones were needed so that went on Jack's list of things to do.

They had a visitor, Jeff Campbell, who was minding a small holding next door. He introduced himself and said Reg Evans had rung him to meet up with Jack and talk about employment at Shipfield. He had worked there before and knew the layout and what to do. Jack welcomed the slim, hardworking-looking man in his 30s and said, yes, he could do with some help and needed information about feed for the cattle feeders. Jeff showed him the big silo that Jack had seen on his inspection, that was full of milo grain. He showed him the big hopper that mixed the grain with minerals.

"Have you got time now to show me, so we can fill the feeders now?" asked Jack.

Jeff said that was why he was here. So, they hooked the hopper on to the tractor, went and filled it from the silo then put the mix in the machine which combined it all up as they travelled to the feeders to fill them. That was going to be a never-ending fortnightly job.

Jeff asked Jack what he knew about farming and Jack said, "Absolutely nothing," but Reg had told him it was all done by a contractor.

"Well, if he said that," said Jeff "you're looking at the contractor and I am not. I help when I can but it's mostly up to you and anyone else you can employ."

"Well, Jeff, what's the arrangement with you and Shipfield?"

"It's a casual one as I have other work as well. If you need a hand, give me a ring. I'm usually paid $25 a week. I have been helping out here casually for the last year so I can help you get your feet on the ground."

"Thanks, Jeff, much appreciated. I think we will be seeing a lot of each other."

"I'm sure we will. Remember, just give me a ring. I'm only four kilometres down the road."

Damon had been pestering his dad, even back at Jireena, that he wanted a horse.

"Son, you're too young. You are just four years old."

"Dad, pleeease."

"Well, if I can find one suitable for you, I will get you one, alright? Now, don't ask again but I will try and get you a horse if I can."

He noticed a three-year-old pony for sale in the Queensland Country Life classifieds. The ad looked alright, so the family travelled to Gatton to look at this pony. It was 12 hands, all white with no blemishes or marks. It looked a good type.

"What do you think of it, Damon?" asked Jack.

"Yes, it is just what I want."

"Well, if you want it, you have to ride it then."

"That's a bit hard," said Helen, "he has never sat on a horse and you are telling him to ride it, even without a lesson."

"It won't hurt him to sit on it bareback and see how he goes," said Jack, as he lifted him on to the pony that only had a bridle and reins attached.

Damon had a good balance on the pony and he was told to get it moving by squeezing his legs and leaning forward and saying, "Walk on, walk on." The pony started to walk.

"Now, pull the left reins gently and see if you can turn him," said Jack, as he guided his son.

Damon managed that, then Deborah was running around and tripped and fell into the pony's back leg. The pony ignored her and did not take any notice. He was a good pony.

Jack lifted Damon off the pony and said to the elderly gentleman, "We would like to buy him, what price are you asking?"

"Five hundred dollars and that's non-negotiable," said the owner.

Jack walked over to Damon and said, "It's very expensive and we don't have that sort of money. I could buy two television sets and one specially for your room. That's the cost of the pony."

Damon replied, "I will take the pony, Dad. I can always watch television at someone else's place."

Jack was stuck. He talked to the man and said, "I have not got the money you requested. All I can give you now is $300 and $100 a month for two months," hoping he would refuse.

Instead, the man agreed and said he would put the pony on the train to Giligulgul siding and rail cattle yards, which were at Shipfield's boundary. So, the purchase of Chester made a little boy very happy.

Another intake at Shipfield was Sterling. Reg had promised his mother that he would find a job for him and asked Jack to take him on, which he did. Sterling was a thin, tall, 19-year-old, straight out from England, greener than a raw prawn and every time he saw a spider or snake or something out of the ordinary, he would say, "Can we go back up to the house and have a cup of tea?"

Jack was tough on the lad but, knowing his own tender foot experience, had patience and taught him as much as he could. Sterling was with Shipfield for three years and became a valuable member of the staff.

Much later, other good workers joined the staff: Eric, Robert and Terry, all good workers in their own field of knowledge. And they were needed, as Jack soon learnt that Reg had decided Jack should get to know the other properties in the company and their managers. So, he spent some time travelling away from home.

Station work, maintenance, farming and the moving and feeding of cattle were the main priorities of the property. Cattle had to be weighed to reach the desired weight, to then be sent and drafted. K wagons, or railway stock-carrying carriages, had to be ordered. One hundred head a month were to be sent to the meat works. This was done by rail, loaded at the Giligulgul siding. Huge double decker trucks would arrive from the other properties, bringing cattle with very little handling. It was not uncommon for a beast to jump out of the top deck of the trailer when it was unloading. They were half wild Braham cross cattle. They had to be educated and large, dangerous horns were to be cut off.

This was an exciting adrenalin rush, a dangerous activity, which Jack and his team all secretly enjoyed. Once unloaded into the big yard, it was a very wary man who tried to move the cattle into the smaller yards to finally end up at the weighing scales, then the crush for horn removal. There was much running up rails, being chased by bullocks, who had been mustered and trucked, and were not in a good mood at all. One had to keep his wits about him at all times or he could be hurt. There was no place in the yard for beginners or the faint-hearted. Once they were weighed and drafted and horns cut off, they were taken to their individual paddocks to be quietened down and fattened up.

It was hard for Jack, getting the cattle quiet, well-conditioned, shiny and educated, then in their peak condition, see them sent off to the slaughterhouse. It didn't seem right, but that was farming.

Helen was busy, not only cooking for the men but she was taking Damon for home kindergarten. He had refused to go after the first day he went to the Wandoan kindergarten. She was also keeping an eye on Deborah, who would get up to all sorts of mischief, mainly because she thought she was missing out on something important. Helen started to get involved in the community by joining the local National Party and the CWA.

Not far from Shipfield, on a tiny piece of land, were the Horsewoods, an elderly couple. She was very large and he very thin. Both lived in a dirty, little hut with their pigs and chooks. Cleanliness for the hut and themselves was unknown. Even their drinking water, in open kerosene drums, was covered in slime. They must have been loaded with bacteria and had a high immunity as they were healthy and never sick. Nothing would attack them. One day, Jack and Sterling, while visiting to check if they were alright, were asked if they had some old grain suitable for their pigs. Jack told them he would send Sterling with a couple of bags, as long as they gave the young lad a cup of tea, which was agreed on. Sterling never forgave Jack for that request.

Now and then, Mrs Horsewood would catch the train at Giligulgul Siding. This day, nature was calling loudly so, while waiting for the train to move off, (Jack was loading 100 head of cattle into the K wagons) she stepped out of the train, stood on the running board, while hanging on to the two handles each side of the carriage door and proceeded to relieve herself. Unbeknownst to the guardsman, who was bent, double-tapping the iron wheels for cracks, ended up getting a golden shower. After that occurrence, the train never stopped at that siding to pick up passengers, only when Jack rang to be able to load his cattle.

Another family, living in the opposite direction across the road, were the Burnsides. Bill, the dad, was one of those very hairy chaps with thick hair all over his body. He thought he would teach his daughter a lesson as she always took off to the toilet when the dishes had to be done. So, for some strange reason, he covered the black toilet seat with treacle. During dinner time, Bill had a gastric attack and raced to the toilet. In his urgency, he forgot the treacle on the seat and sat down heavily. The aftermath was a very sticky, hairy bum that needed attention from his wife. While he laid on his tummy, his wife tried to shave his bum with a razor, which was not very successful due to the stickiness. So, one thought was to singe the hairs lightly then remove the remaining treacle. Eventually, all was cleared up.

Poor Sterling had heard about Jack's rodeo riding and thought he would give it a go when the rodeo came to town. He entered himself in for the coming Saturday. Jack gave him plenty of advice as he helped him mount his steed in the chutes. The gate opened, the horse bucked. Sterling came off in two seconds, so did two front teeth as he hit the ground. They were good, strong, white, English teeth, never to be found in the dusty, dirty arena.

Jack took him to the dentist, Bud Ford, who was putting rings into the noses of his bulls while in the crush, but told to wait till he finished the bulls. Then he put Sterling in the crush and locked the head bale on his neck. He proceeded to push the teethless gums back into place. Sterling's eyes fluttered and he slid down in the head bale. Jack and Bud released him. Bud said for them to make an appointment for next week at the surgery, as Jack helped his employee to the car and drove him home to his quarters.

Sterling was in agony all that week, till they got an appointment with Dr Ford on the following Friday. Why was Sterling so sick and in so much pain just losing two teeth? It was found that the horse had kicked him in the mouth and sent his back teeth into his cheek area. Sterling was not a happy boy and, not surprisingly, decided the rodeo was not a sport for him.

Another employee, Robert, told Jack his father had three horses for sale and would he be interested. Jack said he would be as he had to find a horse for Deborah and, later on, Damon would be growing out of that fine pony, Chester. Jack checked the horses out. They were a family: grandma Susie, mother

Queenie and daughter Tarkey. They were a good buy and were shipped to Shipfield. They cost $50 more than Chester, at $550. They were a bargain and were with the family for 18 years.

Something Robert's dad said had tweaked Jack's imagination.

"You might be interested to know that Susie can pull a sulky and she is very good at it."

So then, a search for a sulky and harness was in earnest. Helen was keen and asked around and so did Jack. At last, they found one tucked away in an old garage. It was an old military sulky and needed a lot of work. This included the wooden wheels needing attention. There were oddments of harness also in the shed that Jack thought he could revitalise. The project began with Helen stripping all the old paint off till she had it all down to the bare wood. Sounds easy but it was very old paint, likely a shellac and extremely difficult to get off. However, with time and patience, Helen did an excellent job.

Jack bought a good side of leather and proceeded to repair and oil the dried-out harness. The only retrievable parts were a horse collar and a nice pair of hames. So, in their spare time, they were busy putting it all together. Helen, with her art talent and, after the whole sulky was painted, she proceeded to paint gold scrolls around the wheel spokes and a very fancy bit of artwork on the kickboard. Helen also worked on the seat. After Jack did some extensive repairs to it, she then upholstered it in a royal blue cloth with buttons. When finished, it looked the real deal. The sulky looked a picture; the harness was also highly polished, after gallons of oil had been rubbed on.

Jack, on his searches, also found another sulky, fitted with hard iron wheels. It was a bit of a wreck but good enough for a trainer. They checked Susie out in it and she loved to pull it. Off they trotted, until Robert, as a passenger, asked Jack, "Is a wheel supposed to pass the horse?"

The wheel did indeed pass the horse. It had come off but, with the momentum, the sulky had stayed upright for a few metres until Jack slowly pulled Susie up, then one side of the sulky collapsed. Jack retrieved the wheel and Robert searched for the pin which, he managed to find. So, a heavy lift of the sulky to slide the wheel on, put the pin back in place with some wire around it, so it would not come loose again and no one, including Susie, were any worse for wear.

Helen, Jack and the kids had great fun with their sulky, giving rides at the local shows for twenty cents. It surprised them that the older people were the main customers, a few kids but hardly any teenagers or baby boomers. They even took the great-granddaughter of the chap that invented the Condamine Bell in the sulky, leading the procession of the 100-year celebration of the bell.

They did a few weddings until Jack thought it unsafe.

The last wedding they did, as the bride was stepping down from the sulky, a photographer rushed out from nowhere and startled poor Susie. However, with his voice and a good hold of the reins, Jack just managed to stop the horse from moving and running over the bridal train. Jack thought, *if Susie took off, it would be her that stripped the bride before the groom.*

Helen, Jack and the kids harnessed up Susie for a picnic, which they did on a few occasions, when not too busy. Helen would make a basket lunch, take a large travelling blanket and some toys for the kids, while Jack got the sulky ready and put Susie in the shafts, ready to go. It was always great fun; they trotted to the far end of the property where there was a small dam with a sandy section for the kids to play. It was interesting to notice, as they were trotting along the six kilometres, unlike a car, truck or tractor, the cattle didn't move as they went past. The kangaroos did not hop away in fright and the birds kept singing. It was all surreal and quiet. There was just the slight jingle of harness and the rhythmic noise on the gravel from the wheels. They all enjoyed the ride.

This day, while relaxing after a great lunch made by Helen, they all decided to have a camp or a nap. With hats over eyes and the sun beaming down, it was not hard to fall asleep, even for the children. As the day lengthened and the sun turned down its warmth, the kids yelled that Susie had gone. Yes, she must have got herself loose. Jack tried to blame someone for it but, unfortunately, he was at fault.

He knew Susie had decided to go home early when the family were sleeping. It ended up that Jack had to pull the sulky with the harness, kids, wife and picnic basket all riding in it. Of course, the kids cracked the whip and yelled, "Start trotting, Dad."

They were threatened with walking home if he received any more cheek. Helen took pity on Jack and helped him, pulling it up the two big hills to the house. When they got home, there was Susie, looking very pleased with herself. Jack was sure she had a slight smile and some mirth in her eyes. Jack didn't feed her that night as a lesson but Susie wasn't worried, it was worth seeing him struggling with the sulky.

Damon was getting very good at riding Chester but he wanted a saddle. Jack said he would have to save up and buy one himself. He said, "If you get the cow in at night, feed the chooks, make sure the dog bowls are clean and have plenty of clean water and that Chester has plenty of clean water to drink."

It was a big ask for a child just before his fifth birthday. Jack was a hard man sometimes but he wanted to teach his son that hard work gets rewards and lazy work gets you the sack. Jack paid him at the end of the week, after an inspection. He also went and saw Bill Scholler at Chinchilla Saddlery and asked him to keep an eye out for a good stock-style saddle for a child. He said Damon was saving his money.

"When you have found a saddle, we will come in and I will subsidise the balance," said Jack.

After three months of hard work and a phone call, Jack took Damon in to buy a saddle. Bill played the part.

"What brought you in here, young man?" he asked.

"I want to buy a saddle," said Damon.

"But you have to have lots of money to buy a saddle," said old Bill, keeping a straight face."

"I have the money but have you got a saddle for me?"

So, Bill did a lot of rummaging around, pretending to look for a saddle, until he found one and showed it to Damon.

"That's the type of saddle I want," said Damon with excitement in his voice, "How much?"

Bill rubbed his chin whiskers and said, "How much money have you got?"

Damon proudly emptied both pockets full of the silver coins, he had worked hard for, on the counter. Bill, very slowly and deliberately, counted all the coins, with Damon anxiously looking on. After a lot of counting and checking, he said, "Young fella, that's just the right amount of money. You have bought yourself a saddle."

The joy on Damon's face could not be described as Bill handed him the fully mounted saddle. As Damon felt and checked out his saddle, Jack paid Bill the balance owing and said, "Thank you."

Bill said it was his pleasure and that it was great to see Damon's face when he put all his money on the counter. It's a pity more young people didn't work for the things they really want or need. Damon treasured that saddle more than anything. It was always beside his bed, looked after and oiled. It is still one of his prize possessions 50 years later.

C.17

More Jobs & Travelling

It was getting busy at Shipfield, with more responsibilities and more work for Jack. Reg wanted him to visit all the other Shipfield stations, familiarise himself with them and do inspections of the properties to ensure they are being managed properly. And then there was the suggestion that Mr Ishiyama wanted a thoroughbred racing and breeding stables at Shipfield, as well as turning over cattle once a month. Good on ya, Jack. No more picnics for you.

It was a lot of travelling for Jack. One property, Moray Downs, between Charters Towers and Clermont, was one of the first properties to visit. Reg wanted a bang tail muster to be done. A bang tail muster was where all cattle were mustered to the yard, one paddock at a time. Then, with a sharp knife, the hairy part of the cattle tails were cut off. This would indicate the beast was counted. So, there was lots of mustering, counting, making sure paddocks were clean of cattle and finally, correcting the books to know the actual head on the property.

Now, it was clearly a setup. When Jack approached the yards, he noticed all the ringers were sitting on the top yard rail, with their already caught horses tied to surrounding trees.

There was only one horse left in the yard, snorting away, nostrils flared, ears back and prancing around the yard. This was Jack's horse for the muster. With some trouble, he managed to catch and saddle it. He could feel the excitement and expected show the ringers were waiting to see.

Jack walked the horse around, talking to it calmly a couple of times. He tightened the girth a bit more and gently mounted the steed, easing himself into the saddle, talking to him and rubbing his mane, waiting for the explosion. It did not happen. He walked the horse a bit then trotted him around and said to the disappointed ringers on the rail, "What are you waiting for? We have a muster to do."

It was a hard day: the cattle mustered, the tails were cut, then placed in a clean paddock. The ringers and their horses were tired. Jack's horse, called Bottle Top, had done a great job. Walking back home, his head was down and he needed a lot of encouragement to get him moving as he was that worn out.

Next morning, there was a tired Bottle Top to be ridden for that day's mustering. Jack thought he had such a hard day before, he wouldn't do anything. How wrong he was. As soon as he mounted, an explosion happened. Jack didn't know what happened. He was on the ground with Bottle Top fizzing all over the yard.

Jack was in pain, particularly in his right shoulder (later, it was diagnosed as a Rotator Cuff syndrome) but the job had to go on. Jack, in pain, caught his horse and needed help to mount it. Then they were off again, mustering. This was on for the next eight days. The pain was awful. How Jack managed, no one knows but, in the end, he finished the job he was sent to do.

Driving home, he passed the Emerald hospital and wanted to call in and get pain relief. But no, he continued on the extra 230 kilometres to family and home, driving all the way with his left hand while his right was across his upper chest. It was worth it. With Helen's soothing concern, a sling to keep the arm up and a drive to Chinchilla to see the doctors, he was dispensed pain relief and said to give it plenty of rest and time and it should heal itself.

Did he say rest? He did not know Jack that well. With only one arm, Jack, with the help of his two men, decided to build a new cattle yard. It was a must. For example, Sterling had been confronted with an angry bullock. He took off for the yard rails with the beast after him, then climbed the rails to get away but the beast started to climb the rails too. The rails splintered and broke.

Here was Sterling in the open paddock with the beast still after him. He managed to duck behind a tree and the beast trailed by all the other cattle who also went through the broken rails.

This sort of event was happening too much and they were all in danger due to the old, tired cattle yard. To give an idea of how wild the cattle were, there was a lonely beast in the yard as they couldn't get him out to join the others. He would charge everyone. Robert, sitting on the top rail, threw his hat to distract the beast. It caught the hat on its left horn then threw it in the air, did a 360 degree turn and caught the hat coming down on his right horn. Who was going to get in the yard with that beast?

Jeff Campbell was contracted to help cut the huge ironbark crush posts and the regular posts, as well as good solid rails. Jack rented a big hydraulic post digger that, with some engineering, managed to fit on to the back of the Ford tractor. It was a great tool and saved a lot of work. While Jack was recovering, he made the plans for the yard. They were circular yards containing the crush and scales, part facing the paddock the cattle came from. They ended up good, solid easy working yards that saved a lot of adrenalin and near heart attacks. Jack forced himself to work on the yards and do physical work on his injured shoulder. It was good for him and the shoulder slowly healed itself. Rest indeed!

A lot of things were happening at Shipfield. Jack learnt to spay - an operation removing the ovaries from cows and heifers to make them sterile - at a weekend school. This ended up having him travel up north to spay all the company's culled cattle. He also did it privately on weekends in the local area, charging a dollar a cow. He could do well over 100 with his assistant, Damon, who was handed the instruments after each cow was operated on, washed and disinfected, while the next cow was put in the crush.

Jack was doing a job for two old-timers, and one said to the other, "Why are you getting this young fella to spay your cattle and not the vet?"

The other replied, "This young fella charges a dollar a cow. The vet charged me $120 to spay me cat. I wasn't going to get the vet to do this job, I would be broke."

Helen was busy with her cooking for the men, her community work and driving Damon to school at Guluguba every day and return. She was also trying to keep mischievous Deborah amused as she couldn't understand why Damon was going to school and not her, even though it was explained a dozen times she was too young and would be going the following year.

Then it was decided by Mr Ishiyama, that Shipfield, as well as turning over cattle for the Japanese meat market, was to become a thoroughbred racing and breeding stable. Jack said he knew horses but nothing of thoroughbreds, breeding or racing.

He was asked the best place to go to learn all about thoroughbreds. He said England and was told to go there and learn, as Mr Ishiyama wanted the stables established by the end of the year. The company would pay return airfares for Jack at limited cost.

It was all Jack needed. Didn't he have enough to do with producing 100 head a month for the Darling Downs meat works at the correct weight? There was also the farming of oats and milo, dealing with feeding out of grain, plus maintenance, along with the spaying and inspection of the other four company properties and now bloody breeding and racing stables. How much can a fella do?

C.18

England & Thoroughbreds

Jack wanted Helen to come with him, but no, only if the children could come. That would not work, trailing kids around to different stables.

"They would be tired and grizzly and that would not be good for any of us," said Jack.

"Well, I won't go if they can't go," said a determined Helen.

Now, Jack was starting to learn a bit about the female mind. One must let a woman make her own decisions. Never, never suggest or tell her to do something. Because it just won't happen.

He left exciting brochures around the house and on her sewing table, not saying anything. He managed to get her a passport in secret, getting her to sign some forms he said were for his passport. Then he rang up their old friends, George and Margaret Price, to see if they would mind the children. They said they would love to as the children were no trouble, and they were good company for their own children.

This was all done in secret, as Jack expounded on the sites and history: Buckingham Palace, the changing of the guard, maybe seeing the queen. He never nagged, just casually made some comment on his travel itinerary every now and then. But there was no comment from Helen.

Eight days before Jack was leaving for London, out of the blue, Helen said, "If I was to come, what would we do with the kids?"

Jack informed her that George and Margret would look after them. There was silence for a bit, then, "In that case, I suppose I could come."

Oh, Jack you're cruel, "Love, I think it's a bit late; you have to have a passport and there are extra plane tickets needed for you to come."

"You get them Jack, 'cause I'm coming with you."

Oh, life should be much simpler. So, they both boarded the jumbo jet, flying to London via Dubai. The children were safely picked up by George and Margaret. They were excited to see their old friends, George, Michael and Annette.

London was a big disappointment for these first-time international visitors. They were expecting cold weather, even though it was early August. It was stifling hot. They expected green, lovely English gardens but saw only dry ones. Even Hyde Park was just a dusty, dry area.

Their hotel in Marble Bar was large but with narrow passageways, small rooms and also stifling hot. So much so, Jack thought the whole bloody lot would go up in spontaneous combustion.

Jack checked the exits, fire escape and hose and alarm stations. He was worried. It was the 1975/76 drought, one of the longest England had experienced. Even the Thames had gone down so low, artefacts from Roman times and the Middle Ages were found in the mud. People were swimming in the historic fountains and the changing of the guard at Buckingham Palace was every 20 minutes as it was too hot for the guards to stay any longer. All animals were moved to the north in Wales and Scotland. It was Queensland weather in England.

As Helen commented, "Why did we bother to come here?" Jack thought the same.

Jack had previously written to the British Bloodstock agency, enquiring about information on thoroughbreds and wanting to learn about the industry and the care of the horses. Jack had also written to his father's sister and husband who lived in Hampton Court and had never met. Outcomes of these innocent letters came as a surprise to both Jack and Helen.

Now the British Bloodstock Agency was one down from Royalty, in social circles, or very close to it. Remember the queen owned a stable of successful thoroughbred racehorses. Jack and Helen were contacted by the agency and informed they would be picked up at their hotel by 9.30am sharp the following morning to visit some stables.

Helen said, "I'm not getting dressed up to walk around dirty stables. Jeans, blouse and my walking shoes will do."

"That's fine," said Jack, "I'll dress the same."

A well-dressed, suited man walked into the lobby where Helen and Jack were waiting.

"Are you Mr and Mrs Jack Alexander?" said the suited man.

Jack and Helen stood up. Jack shook the man's hand and introduced himself and Helen to a Mr Rodgers of British Blood Stock. The first hint they knew something was wrong was when they were led outside to be met by a chauffeur, who had the back door of a very shiny Bentley waiting for the two Aussies to step in the vehicle. Mr Rodgers sat in the front.

Small talk took place as they left London on their way to St Ives, Newmarket, Huntington, Cambridge. Jack wasn't actually sure where they were going but it was all dry, hot farmland surrounded by dry stone walls. They drove through a magnificent front entrance of a stud. In fact, it belonged to some titled person, perhaps an earl or a lord, and the Bentley rolled up to the stables. Not ordinary stables but grand ones with thick, divided oak doors that were highly polished. The main structure that housed 12 stables seemed to be made of sandstone or rendered brick, but it all looked very smart and highly maintained with everything spotlessly clean, not a hair out of place.

Mr Rodgers opened the nearest stable door, and behold, a groom was standing like a statue in front of a fine thoroughbred stallion. It was believed, the groom had stood like that with the stallion for more than a half hour, as Jack and Helen were late. The groom led the horse out of the stable and paraded it around as Mr Rodgers was expounding the virtues of the horse and the success of its offspring, with Helen and Jack making a few admiring comments about the stallion, its performance and career. The inside of the stable had padded walls with wood shavings on the floor and, believe it or not, air conditioning. A few horses were paraded around for them from the same stable. There was a groom allocated to two horses that they groomed, fed and cleaned. It appeared they were the slave to two horses.

The same happened at other magnificent stables. Grooms would stand at attention with their stallions. Everything was pristine. Again, Jack and Helen mumbled their congratulations and commented on the spectacular horses that were paraded in front of them.

They were shown the famous sale ring for horses at Newmarket and the racetrack for the steeple chasers, then taken back to London where the Bentley pulled up at some great mansion where, it appeared they were having a luncheon. They were led into a huge dining room and before them was a 12-seated, set dining table under a large chandelier. A group of nine well suited men were standing behind their dining room chairs. Helen and Jack walked around the group shaking hands and introducing themselves. That done, they all sat down as six butlers pushed their chairs in. Then, after retiring to the kitchen, returned to wait with a fabulous lunch including white wine, starters and a selection of turkey and beef roasts, followed by a small dessert of strawberries and cream.

They tried to engage Helen and Jack with their conversation but gave up after a while as the guests from Australia did not seem to engage well. These people were speaking with what Helen said later, "Posh, very upper-class English, which did not seem to mix with the Queensland tongue."

They were glad to be dropped off at their hotel as much as Rodger was glad to get rid of these Australians.

"What a complete disaster, I think there has been some kind of mistake," said Helen when they finally got to their room, sitting on the bed and taking their shoes off.

"They thought we had come to buy horses. They must have done a check on me and found out I was the Manager of Shipfield Pastoral Company, a subsidiary of the large and wealthy Ishiyama Corporation," said Jack. "But in my letter to them, I said I wanted to learn about the thoroughbred industry and the management of the horses. I said nothing about buying."

"They thought it a ruse and you really were in the market to buy. That's why they paraded horses in front of us and showed the selling house at Newmarket and gave us a great lunch, with, I guess, all the other salesmen of the agency," suggested Helen.

"Well, we got a decent lunch out of them, and they got nothing from us," said Jack with a smile.

But he did learn a few things. They let their stallions run into their individual paddocks of an acre and it seemed Australians only imported stallions, which did not improve the stock. According to Jack, they should import females as well, to get better blood lines. And why do they race two-year-olds in Australia, instead of waiting for a horse to turn four years after they have matured. They believed New Zealand did the same, which is why there weren't strong stayers in Australia, Jack was told.

Jack also got a name of a groom at the National Stud, that could give him some help. So, it wasn't a complete waste of time for Jack. Maybe for Helen, who wanted to do some shopping and send her letters off to the kids. They were never out of her mind, and she wrote to them every day they were away.

Their next adventure was to visit Jack's aunty and uncle, who Jack had written to before they left home: Jim and Nancy Redgrove. They found the cottage and later found out it had been the gate-keeper's residence for Hampton House Trust. Jack knocked on the door and soon a gentleman answered, wearing a suit, looking as if he was going somewhere important.

Jack introduced himself as his nephew from Australia, then introduced Helen.

The reply was, "We can't have colonials stay here but we will shout you a luncheon."

Helen whispered to Jack, "Let's get out of here."

Jack whispered back, "No, we are going to have a big lunch at least."

They were invited in and met Nancy. She looked very similar to an older Jack's mother, then trooped up to a very narrow staircase to see David's room, Jack's cousin, who was in the Queen's Household Guards and died in an accident.

The room had hardly been touched since that fatal day. There was a monument to their son in the centre of the room in a large glass case: his guard's breast plate and helmet with the white plume hanging from it. Jack wished he could have had that but, of course, it was out of the question.

While Nancy was getting ready, Jack was talking about their day with the British Blood Stock agency. He said they were a bunch of uppercrust salesmen who dealt with the rich and famous of horse dealers. So, Jack could understand the mistake he had made, even after writing to them about what he needed from them. He should have looked up different racing and breeding organisations to get the information he wanted.

They were taken to a cosy restaurant, not far away, where they had a satisfying lunch, except Jack really felt like a four and twenty pie. They had a friendly conversation about relationships in Australia and England. They learnt their other cousin, Peter Redgrove, was in Cornwall and did not like visitors. He was a literary lecturer at Oxford, had written quite a few books but, unfortunately, he had schizophrenia and was a recluse.

It seemed the colonials were not that bad after all, because they were invited to their golden wedding anniversary party, to be held at their place the following week. Helen was not that keen to go but Jack thought it wouldn't be too bad and might get some contacts. So, they went.

It was a small gathering, Jack guessed, of upper middle-class people. Ladies were expensively dressed and adorned with jewellery that was worn to be seen. The men wore vests with their suits with silk handkerchiefs tucked into their top suit coat pockets. One had a rose bud in his top buttonhole. It was a great little party; Helen was popular with the ladies. Always relaxed with people and talking about her life in outback Queensland. Jack was asked a fair bit about Queensland politics and a few mentioned that, if they were younger, they would have immigrated. And, of course, Jack could not help himself telling a few exaggerated stories.

What do you bring as a present to a golden wedding anniversary? A box of Old Gold Chocolates, that's what and they ended up with dozens of them. They tried to give Jack and Helen half a dozen boxes, but they could only manage two, thank you.

Helen stayed in London to do a bit of shopping. Every day they were away, Helen wrote to Damon and Deborah, always separately and usually including a post card of what they had seen on their travels. Jack hired a small Morris car and drove to the National Stud in Newmarket, where he had managed to get an appointment with the manager there. He also visited other thoroughbred racing and breeding farms, gaining a wealth of knowledge from all. They seemed pleased to impart their knowledge and secrets on to this young Australian man who just kept asking so many questions and seemed so enthusiastic about their industry. Jack arrived back in London with a full notebook of what he had learnt about the industry. Maybe they were not concerned giving so much information, as Australia was not a threat but if Jack was starting up in the UK, it would have been a very closed shop.

After Jack had got what he wanted, they were both keen to get away from London and England. Yes, they did visit the Tower of London and Westminster Abbey, watched the changing of the guard and they went to Windsor Castle and Stonehenge.

There was a very old pub near Stonehenge that could not be forgotten. It was old, older than when Cook discovered Australia. The staircase up to their room was so narrow and rickety, they had to haul their suitcases up by rope, which was supplied, from the balcony. The room was tiny, the floor was slanting at least 35 degrees, the legs at the end of the bed had several blocks of wood underneath them to make it level. The wardrobe also had blocks of wood under it. *Will we survive*? thought Helen. Or would the whole building collapse under them during the night?

Helen also warned Jack there'd be no shenanigans on the bed that night as it could disintegrate on the floor.

They went down to dinner; the sitting was in booths, and they shared one with a local called Al. Al was intrigued by the Australians and their accent so shouted a bottle of Southern Comfort, which the three shared. Jack ordered a second bottle, which was a bit of a mistake as it seemed Al was not very good at holding his liquor. Even though all three had eaten a roast beef and vegetable meal, they seemed so small in England and Jack always had to order more food to satisfy his hunger. The meals were quite adequate for Helen.

Now Al was starting to get a little bit drunk and slurred, "You Aussies call us poms- Prisoners of Her Majesty."

"Yes, we do," said Jack, "but you call us Aussies, convicts, so that makes us even."

Helen thought things might be going too far and said in a quiet, smiling voice, "Al, were you born in this area? And what do you do for a living?"

He seemed to sober up a bit and instead of answering the two questions, they got an hour of the ups and downs of his life. That is, until they pleaded tiredness and left Al. They negotiated the narrow staircase and very steadily eased themselves into bed, after their ablutions, of course.

It was time to board a flight to Holland. Jack made a mistake as he hired a car at Schiphol airport. The Dutch drove on the right side of the road and the cars was left hand drive. So, at the airport car park, Jack and Helen picked up their hire car, a little Fiat. Jack sat in the car for a while teaching himself to look right in the rear vision mirror, working the gears and the pedals, as well as the light and blinker switches from the right side.

Helen was getting restless and finally spoke up at the time Jack was ready to drive off.

"Don't you know, there is a policeman standing at the back of our car and he has been watching your antics, and I think he might be assuming you are having a mental episode," she said.

"I have to be familiar with the car, don't I?" said Jack as he crunched the gears on the way to Haven Oost. That was the place they had to head for to get to Amsterdam, but they got lost and ended up on a highway that took them all the way to North Holland in Den Helder. They tried to turn back several times but, every time they took a turnoff, they seemed to be back on the highway from where they left it. They eventually got to Amsterdam, stopped and asked a taxi to lead them to their hotel, as they were tired after driving all the way to the tip of Holland.

They spent a few days in Amsterdam, but Helen was keen to see their friend Karla who introduced Helen to Jack at her 21st party in Melbourne. Karla and her husband Ian, a major in the British army, were station in Dusseldorf, Germany, near the Dutch border. They were glad to see old friends again and caught up on all the news. Karla, very fat in her second pregnancy, was ready to burst. Ian took Jack in hand and said he would give him a mud map of a quick tour of Europe they could do in their hire car, which they were keen to do as they might never get the opportunity again, but they were secretly missing their dear children immensely and thinking of them day and night.

They got to Paris, but it had to be at peak hour in the afternoon. Jack laughed and Helen was distressed and miserable. Why? In the car opposite were a couple just like them. She was holding a map and in tears. The driver was looking straight ahead with a cross, worried look on his face. It was a mirror image of themselves that made an anxious Jack laugh. From then on, Jack took over the navigation and map.

So, no more tears and "Which way do I go now?"

"I don't know, oh you should have turned off at the one we just passed."

It was hard to find somewhere to park the car but, after some time, they found an empty spot, parked it and walked till they found the nearest hotel. They were physically and mentally tired and didn't care where they laid their heads, as long as they could.

Helen was sick. She must have caught a tummy bug which, for a person with an ileostomy, is not good. They can dehydrate quickly and fill their bag constantly with water.

Helen always had some tablets for a mild case but, this time, it wasn't mild. It seemed, by her diagnosis, it was a bad case of gastroenteritis.

Jack was asked to get peanut butter, rhubarb, bananas and chicken pieces to make broth and some vegetables. So, he went shopping for those items. It was a long and arduous journey. This street was full of fashion; this street was full of hats. Where in the hell could he buy groceries in the city of Paris?

After a lot of trouble, he found a shop down a flight of stairs. Buying the vegetables was easy but finding peanut butter and other canned items was difficult. Alot did not have pictures on them and Jack couldn't read French, so he had to shake cans and tried to smell what was in them. His sense of smell was good but through tin, impossible.

Jack, being Jack, managed to get most of what was required and headed back to the hotel. Not quite. He got himself lost, struggling with his parcels he couldn't find his accommodation. He found it after many turns and many streets that he dragged himself through.

They had brought with them, a small but effective, spirit stove, a small pot and some mugs. Helen needed good clean water and could not tolerate anything less. So, Jack, for the next four days fed and treated Helen, cooking in the bathroom with what he managed to purchase. As always, for Jack nothing was easy but, somehow, he managed. Helen gradually came good, but she had lost a lot of weight. However, being Helen, even under difficult times, was always cheerful and never complaining.

The car, where was the bloody hire car? Had it been booked or towed away? Jack did another search and found it. There were two policemen standing behind it. Jack had mistakenly parked the car outside the Paris police station. Good one Jack. With Dutch number plates, they must have thought the car was being held for some sort of investigation. Jack nodded to the policemen said, "G'day," and quickly got in the car and drove away, much to the astonishment of the two policemen.

Helen was feeling slightly better and managed to see the main sights of Paris: the Eiffel Tower, the Louvre and other must-see sights before leaving. A drive along the Mosel River back into Germany, then to Basel, Lausanne, Milan, Munich, Frankfurt and back to Amsterdam where they handed back their little Fiat. The hire people could not understand the huge kilometres the little car had done. Jack said it was a faulty odometer but was charged another 50 guilders.

It was a great trip, but home was beckoning, so they took a Qantas flight from Amsterdam back to Sydney then to Brisbane. They had a pickup to Shipfield, where George Price had brought the children back from Hughenden after being notified when they would arrive home. Soon there was a joyful meeting of tears, hugs and kisses to their dearest possessions, Damon and Deborah. Of course, the children were so happy to see Mum and Dad back, but it was only seconds, then the paper was ripped apart from the stack of presents the guilty parents had brought them in the hope they were forgiven for leaving them. But, it seems, they had so much fun at George and Margaret's property, getting up to mischief with their two kids, George Michael and Annette that maybe they didn't miss their parents that much.

Back to work, Jack straight away had to check the other four properties before planning to sink a bore for the large amount of water required for the new breeding and racing stables. So much to do in so little time. Mr Ishayama suddenly arrived from the States and wanted to see the new horse facilities. There was trouble.

"Jack why is the bore not sunk and where are the stables?" asked Mr Ishayama.

"Mr Ishayama, all is planned to go ahead immediately, but

Reg told me not to until you gave him the money to start the new program."

Mr Ishayama turned to Reg and said in a very quiet and threatening voice, "Is that correct?"

Reg stumbled over his words, knowing dismissal could be imminent.

"I couldn't let Jack go ahead with the project as it was not in my budget," he said.

"I told you what I wanted. There is always money. You have delayed my personal program by six months, now are you going to tell Jack to go ahead with the program, or will I?"

A few seconds of silence, then Reg said in a husky voice, "Go ahead with the program immediately, Jack."

Jack was on the phone straight away, telling his people it was all go and could they start now or within a week? Jack was informed that they could start tomorrow. It was all local work and hundreds and thousands of dollars were involved.

From then on, Jack felt a coolness from Reg. Maybe he thought Jack might take his job, which was ridiculous as Jack could never work in a city office. But from that day on, things were not as happy as they had been from Reg. It was found out years later that Reg really did think he might lose his job to Jack.

C.19

Frights and a Bad Accident

Jack was coming out of the office for a mug of tea to the kitchen, when Helen said in a panicky voice, "Jack, look over at the tennis court."

And what Jack saw, put ice in the pit of his stomach. Damon and Deborah were swinging on their bellies, on the top of the very high five-metre tennis court fence with hands and feet swinging free, as they rocked back and forwards.

"Jack, quick, race out and get them down from there before they cripple or kill themselves."

Jack slowly walked out of the kitchen to the tennis court and said in his normal voice, as best as he could, "Children, come down from there and come and get some smoko."

The kids scrambled down safely, then Jack said in a completely different voice, "Don't you kids ever, ever, climb that fence again. You could have killed yourselves. Now go and get your smoko and while you're there, give your mother a big hug."

Off skipped the six and four and half year olds to the kitchen, while Jack just sat down where he was, filling his bent stem pipe with tobacco and lighting it up, puffing the pipe and thinking over the disaster that could have happened.

Another time and place in the evening, the children were with a babysitter. Jack and Helen had driven to Taroom to an important cattleman's meeting, to discuss some of the policies of the Whitlam Government which were causing a lot of grazing families financial trouble.

It was a hot night, the windows of the Valiant were open to let some cooling breeze in. Jack had put his sports jacket on the back seat and, with a loosened tie on his ironed, white shirt, was thinking about the meeting and what he should say, when there was an almighty crash. The car came to a sudden stop, which usually happens when a bullock races out of the long grass and hits the car.

Jack turned his head and asked Helen if she was alright. She said, "Yes."

There was a long pause as Jack was waiting for Helen to ask if he was alright. She didn't. He said to her, "I'm in trouble. I must have hit my head on something hard and I can feel blood and bits of bone oozing through my fingers. I'm holding the right side of my head firmly to try and stop the flow."

Helen fumbled with the interior light switch. She managed to switch it on, then looked at Jack's injury. Then she went into hysterics. Helen had never been known to react this way before and, being a registered nurse had seen a lot of serious injuries. Jack knew it was bad.

When Helen recovered, she said to Jack through her tears, "Darling, take your hand away from your head and look at it."

"No way," said Jack, "I got to keep my hand firmly on my head to save as much as I can."

"Jack, do as you're told and take your hand from your head now and stop being silly."

Jack took his hand slowly from his head and to his utter amazement, didn't see blood or bone but cattle shit all over his hand.

It seemed, as the car hit the bullock, the animal had defecated all its bowel contents straight onto the side of the car, through the driver's window and smacked poor Jack on the side of the head. The blood and bone were digested grasses and shit. After cleaning her poor husband with rags and water from the boot of the car, she tried to sponge some of the poo from his white shirt, which she was sure would be covered by his sports coat.

Jack found a useful stick to bend the damaged front mudguard from the front wheel and did some bushman's panel beating to get the car drivable again. Helen was worried that now, with one front light not working, they could collide with another beast and asked for Jack to drive more cautiously. But Jack was already late for his meeting and said, "Let's hope the shit hits the fan and not me again."

The meeting was successful; the drive home was uneventful and the children were fast asleep. They paid the babysitter and, after a long hard day, the two snuggled together in bed. As Jack was about to fall asleep, he heard Helen have a little giggle over her husband's terrible head injury.

Jack was at the silo, which was in the centre of the property, when he noticed the Valiant speeding towards him on the dirt station track. The car pulled up. Helen raced out, opening the back door and had Deborah, his beautiful daughter, lying unconscious on her arms. In her distress, Helen said to Jack, "Look what you have done to my daughter."

Those words would cut Jack for years to come.

What happened?

The children, as soon as they came home from school, caught their horses, Chester and Susie, and rode them in the work yard, which was well over an acre, but had sheds, equipment and paraphernalia scattered around, as well as a big pepperina tree.

They were told, because of the hazards, that they must only walk or trot, definitely not canter or gallop.

On this terrible day, this rule was disobeyed and they were chasing each other at a canter. Damon was riding Susie and went under a branch of the pepperina tree, which caused it to move, frightening Deborah's horse, Chester, which shied. Deborah fell off Chester's back and her foot was caught in the stirrup. She was dragged with her inadequate pony club helmet falling off and her unprotected, little head was bashed on the stony ground. Eventually, her riding boot fell off and she was released from the stirrup. Helen saw the whole accident and, in shock, blamed Jack for introducing the children to horses.

Miles was the nearest hospital at 35 kilometres distance but Helen had no faith in Dr Saulter, so Jack had to travel to Chinchilla, an extra 46 kilometres. Jack wanted to speed to get her to the Chinchilla Hospital as quick as possible but the car must have had an airlock or bad fuel. It would only reach 40 kilometres an hour. Any faster and the engine would die. Deborah was diagnosed with a fractured skull, bleeding on the brain, a badly fractured jaw and facial injuries. She was in a very serious condition.

Helen stayed by their daughter's side, worried if she would even recover to a normal life. She never left her side for two weeks, while Jack drove home to Damon, worried about his daughter and not being there beside her. But home he must go and, believe it or not, the Valiant never faulted on the trip home. Maybe there could have been some spiritual intervention that blocked the car from going fast and maybe preventing a speeding accident.

It was a very worrying time for the whole family.

I have jumped a bit in this story, if I may, I should go back a bit. Damon was born to ride horses; at five years of age, he went mustering with his dad and the men, when they dealt with the large crossbred brahman bullocks. Of course, when the bullocks didn't seem to understand what was required of them, the men would swear and, of course, Damon would swear as well. His dad said, "That's paddock talk and if you work with the men, that's maybe alright but if I catch you using paddock talk around the house or near your mother or sister, look out." And Damon never did.

For Deborah, what her older brother did, she wanted to do too but her father felt she was too small and delicate at nearly four to go mustering with the men. Jack taught them how to ride and they ended up very good horse riders. Jack thought he could not teach them much more, so they joined the Wandoan pony club and, for reasons not mentioned here, Jack ended up doing an instructor's course and became club president. He was reluctant to take the role on but there was no one else wanting the position.

After Deborah's accident, Jack did some study on the pony club helmet and found them completely inadequate, mainly because they were held on by just a chin strap. He managed to find an inexpensive harness to fit over the felted pony club helmet and offered to buy enough for the club. But the pony club organisation said they could not be used as it was not standard equipment. It was a few years later when they finally decided the original helmet was not suitable and changed for safer ones. In the meantime, parents were picking up their fallen children and then walking back to pick up the inefficient helmet.

Deborah, being a tough Alexander, recovered well with no side effects, except a small scar on her chin and some dentistry done. Thank the Lord, her second teeth had not arrived. Our children are so precious but it can be unhealthy for them to be spoilt.

C.20

Busy Times. New Horizons

A huge drilling rig was used to drill down 2,000 feet to reach good stock feed water. This was happening on the hill near the homestead so the water could flow through the whole property, saving windmills, pumps and dams. The water was piped straight into the water troughs, all over the property. Builders were working hard on the stables, while Jack and his men built the stallion yards. Each stallion had two acres plus a large shade shed for their wellbeing.

Now that the children were going to school, Helen wanted to go back to nursing. Jack wasn't sure about this, as the two of them were employed by the company and, even though the company paid all their living costs and they were looked after well, they were paid a small wage for the position Jack held. He didn't think it was right that she took another job as well.

Helen informed him that she could have a job at the Miles hospital for the Friday, Saturday and Sunday nights, which would not interfere with her cooking and entertaining job.

"Oh, and there is one day a week as the bush nurse at Wandoan," she said.

Jack replied, "Seems like you have been doing your homework. I know you love your career but I feel it's not the right thing to do as far as our employment goes."

Helen had done her homework well. "Darling, you know how much you want to learn to fly, well there is a flying school starting up in Miles and my nursing wages could pay for the lessons."

Jack, after a pause, answered, "I suppose it's important for you to keep your qualifications current. Where did you find the information about the flying school?"

"I thought you might ask. Dr Saulter's wife is taking the bookings. Here is her number."

Jack could not keep the smile off his face. He gave Helen a big hug and whispered in her ear, "You little conniving rat."

Helen went back to her nursing and Jack started getting up at 3.30 in the mornings to do all his flight study, so he was able to continue his normal day job. He also found time, an hour a week, to do his flying lessons. Everyone was happy, except Damon who hated school and wanted to stay home and work with the men. Both parents spent a lot of time trying to help him but he just wasn't interest. It worried Jack because leaving school in year eight, he found he had had to really study to understand a lot out of school and ask stupid questions to get the right answers. Schools taught a lot of unnecessary subjects, according to Jack, but they did teach how to retain information and be able to puzzle things out.

Damon loved to be with his dad, mustering the big bullocks to the railway yard. This day it was an urgent call from the meat works. They wanted 80 head as soon as possible. The rail trucks were ordered on an extremely humid afternoon. Storm clouds were building up and the hurriedly mustered animals were hot and sweaty as they were pushed into the railway iron-built yards.

They were jammed together when short, coloured flames shot out as the beast clashed. There was so much electricity in the air. Was it lightning coming from them or some sort of combustion? Jack didn't know. It was a frightening sight to see.

"Damon, get out of the yard now, the whole area is filled with electricity."

As Jack, himself, got out of the yard, they stood together at a safe distance and watched the flames shoot out as the beasts crashed together. Never before had Jack seen such a sight.

It was time for the thoroughbred horses to arrive: eight young fillies. It was better to get them used to their new home first and to grow, ready for their trials, later in the year. A few months later, a big, black stallion arrived, called Coldridge, the full brother of Think Big, that had won the Melbourne Cup twice. He had been spoilt and caused trouble and some injuries to stable hands. Some trainers in Brisbane refused to take him on, so he was sent to Shipfield for Jack, to get mares serviced but, most importantly, to quieten him, educate him and give him some manners.

Did Jack have enough to do, still having to check the other four properties, do spaying and try to learn to fly a plane, as well as be a good husband and dad? How do you do it Jack?

Another requirement, being an overseas company, they were sometimes visited by foreign students for work experience and to experience Queensland country life. One such student was Masaru from Japan. Now the big Ford 500 tractor had a flat battery. The shed, where it was housed, had a nice concrete floor but just outside the shed, the ground sloped well enough for the tractor to be jumped started.

Jack thought he had explained the procedure quite plainly, not once but three times. Masaru said he understood and that he could drive.

Again, Jack said, "This pedal is the clutch. Put your left food on it and push down hard." Jack had already turned the ignition on, put it into gear and set the throttle. "Then, when the tractor starts rolling, slowly lift your foot off the clutch. When you hear the engine start, put your right food on the brake pedal and also push down the clutch pedal," Jack explained again.

"I understand, I know, I understand," said Masaru.

Jack had attached a towrope from the tractor to his little Datsun ute and the idea was to just move the tractor to the sloping ground where it would start rolling and therefore be jumpstarted. Masaru learnt his lesson well. As soon as the tractor started rolling, he lifted his foot off the clutch and the engine started on the tractor.

Masaru got very excited and yelled, "I drive, I drive."

He passed the ute, still on the tow rope, which nearly tipped the little car as it was swung backwards. And now it was the vehicle being towed by the tractor. Jack didn't know whether to bail out or try and keep the ute in line with the tractor. Eventually, Masaru got over his excitement and put the break and clutch down and stopped the activity before a fatality happened. Jack stopped the Datsun and flew out to the tractor put it out of gear and put the handbrake on.

Masaru flush with excitement repeated, "I drive, I drive."

He had never driven anything in his 19 years. The outcome was, the tractor had started, Masaru had his first driving lesson and nothing was damaged except Jack's heart and adrenal glands.

Helen was happy to be back nursing but she wasn't too sure about the town and hospital or the kaftan-wearing Dr Saulter. The first problem was, patients had to take off their clothes completely, for him to examine them, regardless of their medical condition.

There was a joke doing the rounds. In the ladies changing

room, there were two women. One was dressing, while the other one was undressing.

One said, "I don't know why this doctor wants me to undress just to examine a sunspot on my neck."

"That's nothing," replied the other women, "I just came in to pay the bill!

The second problem was, anyone that came in with an anxiety or stress problem, he would suggest the best cure was to have an extramarital affair. The Miles town was starting to have, it seems, a lot of 'wife-swapping' going on. The third problem, that really concerned Helen, was some of his medical practices. Even though Dr Saulter was a very clever doctor and found a lot of serious problems with his patients that he relieved or cured, he also liked to experiment, which was dangerous, seeing he did his own post-mortems. That was the reason Helen wanted to take Deborah to Chinchilla when she had her accident. As she knew Dr Saulter was waiting for a good head injury to arrive so he could practice burr holes in the skull.

Jack was friendly with Dr Saulter's wife, who organised his flying lessons. Dr Saulter was also learning to fly with Jack. Jack asked him why he stripped all his patients.

He said, as an example, "If your car is not running well, you don't just check the carburettor, you check the fuel pump, the fuel line and the fuel tank. In other words, if a patient comes in because she or he feels unwell, you should by sight and feel, check the whole body out, to really find the cause. The patient does not always tell you the facts of her problem, hence why I ask them to take all their clothes off on the first visit."

That made sense to Jack and he now could see the logic.

Helen did not have a lot to do with the doctor, as she only worked weekend nights and he was usually away, which left her on her own to deal with drunks, accidents and sickness. She often had to ring the doctors for advice at Dalby or Chinchilla.

She enjoyed her job and also loved going to Wandoan as the district bush nurse.

Jack took another job on. He was asked to train a half cross draught horse to pull a cart for the Chinchilla century celebrations so he had to find a suitable cart.

The following is Jack's story on finding the cart:

Back in 1932, the spring cart was expensive, second hand and hand made. It wasn't a pretty thing but it did the job for the old Chinaman who sold vegetables around the town of Roma, Queensland.

It cost the buyer five pounds to buy it off the Chinaman. It was a heavy spring cart to which he harnessed his horse and plodded the 160 kilometres to his new forestry lease outside of Miles. I should remember his name but it was 44 years ago that I met this old forestry worker. A bush character with huge hands and arms from swinging an axe for most of his life. For this story, we will call him Bill.

I was managing a property nearby and was looking for a spring cart to add to my collection of horse drawn people movers. Collecting sulkies, wheels, old harness and bits and pieces to restore. Making several enquiries, it was mentioned that an old fella in the forestry might have one.

I got directions to find Bill's place but whether or not I had listened carefully or the directions were not accurate, I don't know but I got lost. Frustration as I spent time driving around, up and down on forestry roads which, in fact, were a maze of old fire breaks, looking for a clearing with a funny, corrugated iron shed.

At last I found Bill's house/shed and, as I pulled up, a couple of lazy kelpie dogs stood up and barked a few times, which was enough to alert the old fella, then laid down and just watched me, as I walked up to Bill, with hand outstretched and said, "G,day,

I'm Jack and Peter Bushel mentioned that you own a spring cart that I could be interested in buying."

We shook hands and he said, "Come in and share a brew with me and we can talk about it."

I cannot remember much about the lay out of the kitchen, except it had a dirt floor full of pock marks, around a bush made kitchen table with yellowing newspapers for a tablecloth, no serviettes, a collection of condiments of sauces, various jars, jams, salts, sugar and some mysterious things which I'm sure would be out of date and probably poison by now. He lifted a boiling black billy off the hot wood stove and made tea into two old, chipped, enamel mugs.

"I ain't got no milk, but 'elp yerself to the sugar."

As I did, the chair seemed to collapse. I just managed to stay upright and not spill my tea. I discovered that one of the chair legs had sunk down in the dirt floor, which solved the riddle of all the pock marks around the table. After moving the chair to a safer position, I mentioned the cart again.

"What ya want the cart for?" I told him I had a hobby of restoring old horse drawn farm vehicles and had been searching for some time, for a spring cart.

"I got a cart here." I couldn't see one or, indeed, anything outside his shed except the dogs and an old, rusted Thames truck. "I don't know about selling it. It has been me home for years. You see, when I drew this here lease, I wasn't going to build a proper house because I would have lost it if the lease ran out and the government would get it. So, I used the spring cart for me home."

"Sorry Bill, I don't understand, how can you use a spring cart for a house?"

"Ya see, young fella, I cut a couple of uprights for the shafts, so the cart is level. Then placed some sawn planks on top of the shafts for a table. I had all me gear in the cart, covered with canvas and I slept in me swag underneath. What more could a man need?"

What more indeed!

"Do you still have it?" I said, "I don't see it around anywhere."

"It's here behind this wall. I actually built this shed around it. You want more tea?"

"No thanks but that was a fine brew," I lied as I felt nauseated from the tea, so strong my sugar spoon was almost upright in my mug.

We left the kitchen and walked outside; the two lazy dogs just sat at the door. The only movement was their eyes following us as we walked around the back of the shed. Bill struggled to open the temporary/permanent door which, by all accounts, had not been opened for years but eventually did, with some muscle from me. There, it revealed a very dusty, large spring cart with the shafts disappearing into another tin wall.

"Is this what yer looking for?" asked Bill.

"It's just the thing," I said with some excitement. "What do you want for it?"

"'Ere, follow me." Bill left the door open and walked around to the kitchen with me following dutifully. "You want another brew?" he said.

My God, my stomach was still churning after the last one but I knew he was a lonely old man who wanted to yarn and I was a young man wanting his cart. I accepted with the proviso that he put a bit of water in it to weaken the tea. He gave me a sidelong glance as if to say, these young fellas don't seem to appreciate a good brew.

We yarned about the seasons, the rain that wasn't as reliable as years ago, the bloody government, Vietnam war and the lazy youth of today.

He said, "You know I don't live here much anymore, I come here now and then to get away from the missus."

"I didn't know you were married."

"Yep, had four kids and live in Miles now. That's what you do when arthritis kicks in and the body is wearing out. You know I'm in my 86th year."

"Gosh, I thought you would be much younger than that," I said, hoping to still get the cart. "Did your wife and kids ever stay here?"

"Yep, we had the kids here. I met the wife in town. A real lively filly was she and moved out in the bush, working beside me: barking logs, on the cross saw helping me, pretty useful, you know. But women change after marriage. You married?"

I nodded and said I had a couple of kids.

"Well fella, you know what I'm talking about. We had our first in the winter and the missus kept complaining about the cold westerly wind and could I put some shelter on the western side of the cart."

"You mean, you and your wife just lived in the cart?" said I, rather shocked.

"I told you boy that I wasn't going to build a house for the government to get it off me. Yeah, she complained till I put up a frame and nailed a couple of sheets of corrugated iron on the western side of the cart."

"Was she happy then?" I enquired.

"Yes, she was. The baby kept her amused and busy until the second child arrived and the complaining started again. You see, it was summer then and the north wind seemed to be upsetting her. To keep the peace, I had to put another frame up and iron on the northern side of the cart. Doesn't matter, you never seem to please 'em. When the next two came along, I thought I better close the eastern and southern side before the complaining started again. But it was a wasted effort 'cause as soon as the fourth was born, she upped and moved to town".

I reminisced with him for a while and finally said, "It seems the cart is very special to you, so I guess it's not for sale."

He stroked his whiskers and after a while, he said, "Well, it's not much use to me now so I'll sell it to you on a couple of conditions. I paid five pounds for it. That's $10 today, so I want me money back."

"That's fine by me," I said with a smile.

"Er, you're forgetting the other conditions." He led me to his bathroom, which was made of patches of corrugated iron. It had a hand-made wooden bench with a hole in it to hold a galvanised tub for a wash basin. A shower rose was attached to a canvas bag, all on a pulley system, so he could lower it to fill with water. Where the water came from or where it went, I had no idea.

Sticking through the wall were the two ends of the cart's shafts. Hanging from them could only be described as something to dry yourself with.

"Yer see them shafts there?" He pointed to the side wall. "If you take the cart, I want some towel hooks to replace them. And I want you to replace the back wall and anything else when you get the cart out, so it's all back as it was. That's the conditions of the sale."

I readily agreed and asked when it would be convenient for me to remove the cart and do the repairs. He suggested a couple of weeks from then.

I got my friend, Ray, to give me a hand and we drove back to Bill's place in the station truck, loaded with sawn timber, a few sheets of corrugated iron, hammer, nails and a few other tools, as well as two towels to go with the two shiny chrome hooks, a new $10 note and a jar of jam and treacle, as I noticed the ones on his table were covered with ants, and a fresh loaf of bread, that I handed him with a hand shake and a thank you.

After a reasonable amount of labour, we managed to get the cart out with minimum amount of damage to the residence, restored the back wall, as well as the old door. We filled the holes where the shafts had poked through. We put the shiny new towel hooks up and hung the towels. Bill did a thorough and exhaustive inspection of our labour. He must have approved as he offered another brew of his tea, which we politely declined.

There was a dirt loading ramp nearby, which we backed the truck into. Then, with a lot of effort, pulling and pushing the very heavy spring cart into the tray of the truck, we securely tied it for *the rough trip home. Another handshake and, "Thanks for the cart, I will look after it," as I hopped into the cab and we drove off with my treasure.*

Jack had his cart. Now he had to train a very large, young, cross-bred draught horse to pull it safely in a procession. He called the horse, Molly. He found a collar that fitted, with a few repairs done, a couple of hames to fit the collar and a couple of tracer chains connected to a swingle bar. Attached to that was a great big ironbark log. Attached to her heavy bridle with blinkers was a couple of long ropes used as reins. Jack drove that horse everywhere; she was strong and young and she needed plenty of work to get her tired enough to quieten and lead a procession.

When the children came home after school, Jack would get Damon to wheel the old, iron wheelbarrow in front of him, so Molly would get used to the sound of iron wheels crunching on the gravel. There was a job for Deborah too. She had to manage a radio playing loud music, ringing a cow bell, as well as squeezing an old fashion bulb hooter, so the horse would get used to all sorts of sounds. This parade would go on every time he could get the kids to be involved; Helen joined in when she could, doing a lot of clashing of saucepans. The horse got used to the noise and pulling the large log around. Now it was time for Molly to be hitched to the cart.

It went well; she was a good horse. They had put a fair bit of time in to get Molly quiet enough for the cart. Jack was giving her driving lessons and Eric, one of Jack's workers, was in the cart as well when they were trotting up a hill. Suddenly, the back band girth snapped and all hell broke loose. Eric was ejected from the cart, actually flying for a few metres. Jack, at the back of the cart, was thrown forward where Eric had stood and big, strong Molly, twisted and bucked to get out of the broken harness then took off down the paddock to get away from it all.

Eric survived with some small bruises and was unsure what had happened. Jack picked up some large splinters from the cart's timber floor. The cart, thank goodness, was not damaged. Molly was happy eating grass, now she was out of the contraption but the harness was ripped to pieces. Only the bridle, blinkers, the collar and hames survived. Looked like a purchase of new leather, rivets and a lot of hand sewing for Jack. Molly probably thought, "I'm not going looking smart in a procession with an old harness. I want a shiny new one." And that's what she got.

It was the big day of The Chinchilla Centenary Parade. They all assembled down a side street. Molly was looking smart, all washed with shampoo, brushed and combed with a new harness. The dignitaries were all sitting on the two cushioned planked seats. Jack was done up in Fletcher Jones trousers, white shirt and tie with his tweed sports coat, wearing a smart tweed cloth cap and smoking his bent stem Peterson pipe.

Jack and Molly were the first in the lineup. Second was the brass band and bag pipes, then the marching girls swinging their batons, then the floats and the line went on. The whistle was blown, the band started to play and the noise didn't worry Molly. They started the parade. All was well until they came to the main street and everyone was clapping enthusiastically.

Oh dear, that was the only noise they hadn't trained her for. The ears went back, the tail was jammed, she was getting the hell out of there, not interested in the important dignitaries nor the centenary celebrations. She was ready to bolt for the far blue yonder. What was Jack going to do? Pull on the reins hoping the bit would stop her fleeing. But there was a large crowd. Jack couldn't take the risk.

He did what he did best. He jumped out of the cart, got hold of the halter and calmly talked to the frightened horse, telling her how beautiful she was and that any young stallion would fall in love with her, how her sweet little ears sent shivers down Jack's spine. She relaxed and, with Jack whispering sweet nothings in her ear, the procession was completely successful. You see, someone told Jack if you sweet talk a female, they usually relax in your company. True or not, it worked that day.

Helen was starting to get into all sorts of clever arty things. She was always good at drawing. To Jack's eye, she was very good. Helen always had the skill of dress making but she started to dabble in tapestry, fine needle work, crochet and all kinds of art. She was talented and clever, according to Jack, and a lot of other people, who had seen her work, agreed but she didn't think she was good and kept honing her skills. You will find out later on, she did extremely well in all her needle work.

Like Jack, Helen was busy, busy, still cooking for men, nursing, making clothes for the children: cowboy outfits for Damon and little Dutch dresses for Deborah, as well as normal street clothes. Helen always liked to visit second hand shops for materials, which she turned into smart outfits for herself and Deborah. Patching Jack's or Damon's clothes, unfortunately, were not on top of her priority list.

Maybe, that's why they got on so well together. They were both very good at their individual skills and they complimented each other regularly, always admiring but never getting in each other's way. Work wise, they were so apart but when the day was done, they were very much together. It was not uncommon for people to say, "You can see the love they have for each other." To be honest, they were inseparable.

The study was completed. Flying lessons were coming along nicely and Jack was ready for his first solo. He told Helen, as he left the homestead, "This may be the day I go solo."

He drove to Miles, arriving at Bud Ford's private air strip. Bob Keogh, the instructor, was standing by his 150 Cessna acrobat aeroplane, waiting for Jack. Jack did his ground inspection of the plane then they both climbed into the tiny cockpit. Jack did all his checks and lowered his flaps ready for take-off. Bob pretended to be bored but was actually keeping a close eye on Jack, that he did all the take-off procedures correctly.

They flew to the Condamine airstrip, their training area. Jack, with his instructor, was doing touch and goes: landing the plane but not stopping and taking off again repeatedly. There was starting to be a bit of a conflict in the cockpit.

"Keep looking at your instruments and speed." Next circuit, "Keep your eyes out and watch where you aim to land." This went on for quite a few touch and goes.

Jack, frustrated, said, "Make up your mind. Do I keep my eye on the instruments or do I look to where I'm landing?"

Bob said, "Stop the aircraft on the next landing, it is getting a bit hot in the cockpit."

Jack landed and stopped next time round. Bob got out of the aircraft, saying, "You can bloody well take the plane up yourself."

Jack turned the aircraft around, to give himself enough room for the take-off. Not being in the best of moods, he checked his instruments, lowered the flaps, mixture rich and took off. He didn't realise what he had done. He was angry until he was 500 feet up in the air and realised he was by himself with no instructor. The aircraft felt different as it was so much lighter with only himself. The dual control column was moving like a ghost had taken over.

The anger left Jack quickly and taking its place was a nervous, frightened feeling.

"How in the hell am I going to get back down on the ground safely?" He started to swear and boosted himself up. "I can fly this #@%&* machine. I'm the best F)*&%^ pilot, I can do this *&^%* thing."

And then, when Jack was on short final, he thought, *I have been swearing and cursing; I think I need help from the Lord.* The only hymn he could think off was, *Away in a Manger*, which he sang as he did a perfect landing. His first solo flying. Now Jack noticed, as he turned the aircraft into the holding bay, a couple of cars with the next lot of students ready for their lessons, doubling up with laughter. Bob had switched the radio on in the aircraft and, with his portable one on the ground, they had all listened to Jack's swearing, then him singing his only hymn – a Christmas carol.

After the other students had their lessons, Jack flew back with Bob and the others drove back to the pub in Miles, where they had quite a few celebratory drinks for Jack's first solo flight. Jack was so excited he couldn't wait to tell Helen, when he got home.

Helen rushed out with tears in her eyes and crossly said, "Where have you been? I thought you had crashed. You have been gone for hours and usually you're home after an hour and a half after your lesson."

Jack tried to explain. It was no good, a cuddle and an 'I'm sorry you were upset' was all he could do. No congratulations, hugs and kisses for achieving his solo flight, just an upset girl who had been very worried about her darling husband.

The thoroughbred horses were doing well. Some had success at the Gold Coast and at Eagle Farm. Jack took Coldridge to a few shows to get his name known, as he was going to start him breeding with other horses for a good service fee for the company. They got a Grand Champion win at the Miles show, first place at Taroom and third place for the best breeding stallion in Queensland at the Royal Brisbane Show, also known as The Ekka.

The horses not suitable for racing, as advised by the trainer, Jack joined them with the stallion for breeding. He was upset with the racing industry. Some of the two-year-olds came back with bandages on their front legs. They had been bar and pin fired: a procedure where they scar the tendons with branding irons to make them stronger. Jack's international enquiries found it did not make any difference; it was just a cruel practice.

The horses were always trouble getting into the float to take them down to Brisbane but when Jack picked them up to take them home, they couldn't wait for him to open the tailgate of the float and jumped straight in without any coaching. When they came home, they were glassy-eyed and took a couple of weeks to settle down and eat their feed.

Horse training and racing may be different in the future but in the 70s, Jack was disgusted by the way Shipfield's horses were treated. He guessed, when there was huge money involved, there were many corrupt practices.

Yarramalong's entrance, background, our house and Mt Edwards.

Helen and her canoe class, Yarramalong.

Jack with his horse class at Yarramalong.

Jack taking some challenged children for a ride with Major and the cart.

The children Damon and Deborah on Sudden Boy and Misty.

Helen protesting the East Link. "It's a sin to spoil the Scenic Rim."

L) Helen caught the first piranha while in the Amazon.
R) My darling Helen at 45 years old.

Damon and Jack in the Sahara Desert.

C.21

Time to Move

Jack was getting restless, while Helen was very happy at Shipfield. She had a good, large kitchen overlooking the valley, with 240-volt power, phone, a radio and even a coloured TV that Jack bought the family for Christmas. She had her gardening, sewing, her loving family and, of course, her nursing.

But Jack was getting tired of the travelling, the constant ringing up from Reg, who had nothing of importance to say. Jack guessed it was a bit of harassment. Why? He didn't know. Then he was upset about the treatment of the thoroughbred horses in his care. The truth of the matter, Jack was just sick of managing proprieties. He thought the ultimate was being your own boss in your own business. But what business?

Of course, he discussed his feelings with Helen but her thoughts were, *He will get over it, this is just a good position we are in, why should we leave?* Then it all came to a head when he got instructions to dismiss one of the property managers as he had attained the age of 40. It seemed the company felt, anyone over the age of 40 was not capable of running or working a large property. Whether this was true or they were just not happy with his management, the point was, he was dismissed because of his age. And Jack was 36 going on for 37. He thought it was time to think about moving on.

Being a manager or even a pastoral manager, wages were low. Yes, all living expenses were covered, including electricity, cars, fuel, etc. They were living very well, while with the company but were never able to save enough money to improve financially. So, Jack did something he never thought he would do and frowned on some managers that did. It was not illegal but it was not being honest with the company. That is, he started running his own stock on the property without permission.

Jack knew the price of the cattle market with a bit of inside knowledge, so he bought 60 head of young steers when the market was at the bottom, with their savings. Once, when Reg visited the property, he asked what the strange cattle were doing on company property.

Jack said, "They must have got through the fence from next door. Looks like I have some mustering and fencing to do." And that was the end of the matter.

The next thing on Jack's mind was, what sort of business should they buy? Jack did a lot of thinking of this. What was he good at? What was his expertise? All he could think of was horses. Then his line of thinking was, *I want to create something and get the money for it without a middleman.* So, his thoughts turned to spelling stables for racehorses or something in line with a fairly new industry: tourism or outdoor recreation. But he needed some land to start any of those ideas, so the first priority was to find some acreage in a suitable area.

Jack was doing a fair bit of flying and he noticed an area that looked promising. It was in the mountains near Cunninghams Gap, only 90-odd kilometres from Brisbane and the Gold Coast. This had to be a growth area in the future. It had mountains and lakes and fertile farming ground. *This is the area to be,* he thought.

Showing Helen on the map where he thought they might look for some land, she said, "Remember Kenny and Sam Bogan, that we were friends with while we were at Jireena? Well, I know they shifted to Boonah. Look, there it is, not far from your Cunninghams Gap." She pointed to a tiny town on Jack's map.

Jack was straight away on the telephone to "Information". Jack moved when he got an idea, didn't think about it, just did it on the moment. You know this anyway.

"Yes, the number is..." the telephonist quoted the number and Jack dialled it.

After a few rings, it was answered, "Kenny Bogan AMP Insurance."

"Kenny, this is Jack Alexander. Do you remember me from Jireena station?"

"We wondered where you got to. How are Helen and the children?"

"We are fine; you and Sam and the children?"

The usual banter that went on when establishing old friendships. Jack asked him what land was going for and were there many opportunities. The outcome was, for Jack and Helen to come for a visit. They had plenty of room in their large house to stay and said Jack and Helen were welcome to stay as long as they liked, so they could have plenty of time to look around the district.

They waited till the school holidays, so they could take the kids and maybe squeeze a few days in at the Gold Coast. Jack rang Reg and said he was taking some holidays. Reg said, "No," but Jack said, "I'm taking them anyway. I need the break and so does the family, so we are off during the coming school holidays."

Reg countered, "I need you to go to Moray Downs."

"That can wait," said Jack, feeling a bit bold as he had his sights on leaving the company as soon as he could find a suitable place to live.

A few work words between the two, then, "If you must," said Reg, "but it's so inconvenient for me to check on things on my own."

"Thanks for your understanding," said Jack and then rang off.

"Helen dear, we are taking two weeks holidays to see Kenny and Sam and maybe the Gold Coast during the school holidays. Remember we talked about it and you were going to try for some time off at the hospital?" said Jack.

"We had discussed this before but you said Reg might not let you have the time off," she replied.

"Well, I've just got off the phone to tell him we are going, so it's on."

The family were excited. It was the first holiday since Jack and Helen went overseas and that was nearly three years ago. Jack gave his men their jobs for the next three weeks including the feeding and special care for the horses and to ring him if any trouble occurred. He gave Kenny's phone number. The men were used to seeing to their chores as Jack was away a lot on the other properties. He also organised Julie to cook their meals for them.

The drive down to Boonah took just over three hours, including the necessary rest stops for children and wife. They arrived at the quaint town tired but safe, as they renewed their friendship with Sam and Kenny who had a two-storey home just half a kilometre from the main shopping centre.

The women chatted, the children explored, Jack and Kenny got down to business about property, prices and the area. Kenny suggested that tomorrow they could drive around the district to give Jack a feel for the area. The women were asked but they declined. Sam wanted to show Helen the main street and the kids would have been bored sitting in a car for another day.

Kenny knew the area well as he travelled a lot as the AMP insurance representative. The area was just as interesting from the ground as from the air. Jack felt this was an ideal place to set up a tourism business. They looked in the two real estate agents' windows in town to see what prices were and what was for sale. Stock was limited and what there was, in farmland or acreage, seemed very expensive for the amount of money Jack thought he could scratch up, even for a deposit. Jack suggested to Helen, with Sam's permission, if Sam could mind the children while the two of them could do some exploring on their own.

Helen seemed enthused about the district, while Jack was excited. They saw Lake Moogerah, the mountain scenery and the rich farmland.

"If we ever had to shift from Shipfield, I suppose this could be a nice place to live," quietly said by Helen.

Jack purposely drove past the hospital, the state primary and high schools. They parked in the main street and they both took a stroll, checking the shops and cafes. Jack could feel Helen coming around positively to the Boonah district but he knew she was happy at Shipfield and wasn't not going to make any statements that would encourage Jack's dream, knowing the way he rushed into his ideas.

Jack actually went into the real-estate agent's office the next day and said he was looking for a property, about 40 acres to run a couple of horses. He was shown some very rough blocks, thick with lantana and prickly vines choking the few shrubs and trees. The ground was covered with rocks, all very unsuitable. The next agent showed him very similar blocks. Then the agent suggested a deceased estate of 350 acres, that could be going for a reasonable price if Jack was at all interested.

The property was very run down, with lots of old farm equipment and rubbish lying around the house. The weatherboard unpainted house was over 100 years old on a hill looking over the Fassifern Valley.

The agent said, "It's only a couple of kilometres from Lake Moogerah. Alot of tourists go there from Brisbane."

But Jack said, "I want to see the whole property and not stand on a hill and see a tiny portion of it." The property was much longer than its width.

The agent seemed a bit reluctant but, with Jacks prodding, agreed to drive him down on a very rough hilly farm track to the end of the property.

And there it was, a large clear paddock that was used for growing potatoes. At the end of that paddock was a large flat area, covered by lantana and vine and at the end of that, was a large clear water hole, constantly fed by the outlet of Moogerah Dam for irrigation for the farmers of the valley. It was known as Reynolds Creek. This was it. Jack visualised a camping area, kids swimming and canoes for hire. It was two kilometres from the ancient house but this was it. Jack was going to buy this property, no matter what obstacles were going to be put in his way.

He casually asked the agent what the asking price was. The agent said the property was not listed for sale as yet, the estate of the deceased owner was still underway but the firm price they expected to get was $70,000, which they needed, to finalise the money side of the estate.

"Are you interested in the property?"

Jack informed him there could be a slight interest and could he have first offer anyway and bring his wife the next day to have a look. The agent agreed and said to meet at his office at 10 the next morning.

Helen did like the property, "But where are we going to get the money needed, what is the deposit and how can we pay it off? Darling, I love you so but you have set yourself an impossible task. Forget it."

Jack answered in the positive. "My sweet you were an impossible task for me to catch and marry and I can assure you this challenge will be won like I won you, my love."

Now it was time for the children to have their holiday at

the Gold Coast. They rented a unit near the beach at Southport and the children were so excited, as they explored each room on the run, checked out all the drawers and cupboards and had a wonderful time. They took a trip to Sea World to see the professional water skiers and loved seeing the porpoises doing their tricks, Helen took them on a few rides while Jack abstained. The beach, the sand, jumping in and over the little waves getting wet, building sandcastles and digging a big hole in the sand with mother's help to bury their father, all fun and games. It was the first time these bush children had been to the beach, which was a real exciting adventure.

Back to Shipfield for work and school, the family went back to their normal routine. Jack had a lot of work to do, visiting the other properties, receiving cattle then, when conditioned and fattened, sent to the meat works. Don't forget transporting horses to the trainer and bringing them back, trying to normalise them again as well as joining the mares and promoting the Shipfield stud. Yes, Jack was a busy man but his mind was very active on how he was going to get the property. First was a visit to the local banks.

Jack had always banked with the Commonwealth Bank, so he made an appointment with the manager and told him he wanted to buy a property at Lake Moogerah and start a recreation and tourist centre there. The manager didn't ask Jack what cash and assets he had.

He just sat back in his swivel chair and said, "You're mad even thinking about leaving your important job as the manager of the Shipfield Pastoral Company. You must be set for life with that company."

Jack got up from his chair and said, "I feel sorry for you. You are a country branch bank manager and that's all you will ever be," and as he walked out. "I have much more exciting and better things to do."

The next bank manager he saw was at the Bank of New South Wales. He was interested in what Jack wanted to do.

"I notice you do not have a credit rating," he said to Jack. "You will not get a loan till you have established a credit rating, so buy yourself something and start paying it off. Secondly, you have no experience in the recreation, tourist business, so no bank would take a risk on you. However, if you presented me with a profitable paper on farming the property, we might look at helping you. That's if you have or can raise a $40,000 deposit."

Jack thanked him for his good advice and said, "I will be back."

The manager, noticing Jack's enthusiasm, replied, "I know you will."

There was a lot of homework for the boy. He noticed the country where he was buying was used for potato growing and he also noticed there was a good crop of soya beans as well. Lucerne could also be another crop. He went to the Department of Primary Industry (DPI) and asked for the yields and prices he could get for the crops growing in the Fassifern area, along with information on the costs of seeds, fertilisers and planting.

He crunched a lot of figures, research and talked to experienced farmers who grew potatoes and crops in the area. They were very helpful.

He also did a paper on what costs and income he could expect, if he ran a farm then compared it if he ran a tourist venture. What were Jack and Helen good at, to be a successful tourist operator? Helen was a good communicator, loved meeting people and, of course, was a registered nurse and midwife.

So, what was Jack going to bring? He was a successful manager, knew how to keep to a budget and handle financial difficulties. But that wasn't going to bring tourists in from Brisbane or anywhere. He knew horses, so what about an upmarket riding school? And he had done a fair bit of camping, so he knew what was needed in that line. Jack also had a fun personality. Could they make a living with those skills?

Now with enquiries to Boonah council and asking Kenny to find out other information, this is what he came up with. The council caravan park was popular but a bit run down. Next to it was the new outdoor recreation centre for the Brisbane Grammar school. There were other private grammar schools that had started their own recreation centres in the district and the Queensland Education Department had their Recreation Centre at Maroon Dam, only 20 kilometres away. Of course, the popular Lake Moogerah attracted people from Ipswich and Brisbane on the weekends to have their picnics and days out in the country. Kenny told Jack he believed there was great potential in the district for what he was thinking of doing.

Jack did some rough estimates on what money could be brought in, then cut down his total profit to 15%. That was a much better business proposition than the farming plan. Jack thought the farming plan was unrealistic, considering weather, market fluctuations and the size of the property to make it a viable proposition. But if the bank manager wanted the farming budget, that's what he would get.

Now to the money side. Hmmmm. The cattle Jack bought were doing well on the company grass and prices were starting to look promising. They had $10,000 in savings but they had to buy a car and get a credit rating. Neither Jack, nor Helen, had ever being in debt, so they both felt uncomfortable borrowing money but that's what was done now to buy a house or property or even a new car. Jack thought, even with a good deposit on a car and being able to pay it off with both Helen and Jack's wages, he could have $20,000 after selling their cattle. That would leave another $20,000 short. He asked everyone he knew, who might be able to help out with a loan, but was unsuccessful.

Helen put her arm around Jack, who was working on figures and plans late into the night, as he had been doing lately.

"Darling, its time you went to bed, you have been working tirelessly on getting this property, and it's a big ask, I don't want you to be too disappointed if it doesn't work out."

Jack, who could hardly keep his eyes opened, mumbled, "That's a negative attitude. It will work; it just takes time for things to come together."

"Jack, I don't know if I told you but the real estate agent rang today to say next week we have to finalise the deposit or the deal was off."

"Thanks a lot love, you could have told me in the morning. I'll never get to sleep now."

"I think you will sleep well tonight, as I will help you, my sweet," and she led him by the hand to the bedroom.

The deadline was the following Thursday and on Wednesday, the real estate chap rang up saying they won't be able to conclude the sale of the property as there has been a problem settling the estate and probate. Jack was thrilled but pretended it was a serious setback for him and agreed to wait another month. Then he thought of the old lady who wanted her mare in foal to Bill's stallion, the man Jack bought the cart from.

Jack can tell this story:

I saw Bill in the main street of Miles. We had a bit of a yarn and he wanted to know how the cart was going. Then he said, "Can you do me a favour?"

I said, "Yes if I can. What is it you want?"

"You have a horse float, could you pick up my stallion? It's in a paddock just out of town, take it up the highway to Shirley's farm. She has a stud mare she wants my stallion to join and you have the know how to help us old people with a couple of randy horses."

I agreed and asked him to let me know when the mare was in season and that I would pick up the stallion and help them get the mare in foal.

The day arrived. I picked up the stallion and Bill and drove the odd 20 kilometres to Shirley's farm. We unloaded the excited stallion into a small yard and in the next yard, was a very excited mare.

I met Shirley. She was short and plump, with a very weathered face. I guessed she was in her 70s. She had on an old blouse that had seen better days, done up with only three buttons. Her large breasts were half out of the arm holes and a fair bit of something bulging through the gaps in the front her blouse/ She was wearing shorts and bare feet. She had a no-nonsense air about her but the twinkle in her large blue eyes showed her true personality.

It was time for the event we came for, so Shirley held the mare and I managed the stallion. Both horses were ready for the engagement, as they were doing what comes naturally. I noticed old Bill watching and the way he was moving his body, it seemed the horses' excitement was passing on to him. The stallion finished his job and, as I was leading him into another yard, I heard excited Bill saying to Shirley, "I wouldn't mind a bit myself," and I heard Shirley say, "Well, I'm still holding the mare."

I had to laugh. I took the now very quiet stallion and its owner back to their place of abode. As I dropped Bill off, he said, "You know, that Shirley is a very clever woman and if you need help, go and see her."

"Thanks Bill. I just might do that."

And Jack did the very next day. She had not changed, except for a clean two button blouse that let a bit more skin and breasts show.

"Jack has something happened, for you to come back?" she asked.

"No, it's just that I have a bit of a problem and Bill said

to have a yarn with you because he said you are a very clever woman," Jack replied.

"I don't know about that but come inside and tell me what's going on in that young head of yours."

She led me into the old Queenslander homestead which looked if it had never seen a coat of paint in its 100-year history but inside the place was spotless. We sat down at a bare scrubbed kitchen table.

Shirly said, "Let's have it and, if it's worth the hearing, you can put that there kettle on for a cuppa."

"We want to buy this property down in the Boonah district to start a recreation and tourist complex near Lake Moogerah," Jack started. "We have to have the full deposit of $40,000 by next Thursday or we lose it. We have managed to put together $20,000 cash but we are short of the extra $20,000. Here is the problem, the property has 25 acres of soybean crop ready to be harvested shortly and the estimated value by a farmer is $12,000 and I estimate the cattle on the property to be at least $9,000, so if we had the property, we would have the $20,000 needed but we have to buy it first, which we can't, as the money is in the property."

"Jack," she said, looking him directly in the eyes, "I want you to go back home, doublecheck, no, triple check, all your figures. Come back Monday. I want to see all the paperwork, your workings out and reliable sources that indicate the price of the crop and cattle. I never lend money but I think I may be able to help you some other way. First, I want to see all your paperwork. Off you go, you haven't any time to waste."

Jack was worried as he left her property. She was his last hope and no money would be coming forthwith. He felt like he was in the lap of the gods. The next week would show if they were meant to have the property or not.

When Jack told Helen about the old woman and that she

would not lend money but maybe help in another way, Helen, in her quite uncommitted way, said, "Jack, whatever will be will be, so don't worry too much. Just get on with the paperwork she wants and, if somehow it happens, it happens."

Jack didn't stop. He redid his sums, time and time again. He rang and talked to people in the know. Jack knew the cattle market but still talked to agent auctioneers and buyers. He talked to a soya bean marketing agent and farmers who grew crops in the area. The information was as reliable as one could get; this went on the paper, as well as his plan for the property and the information gathered about the profitable chances of the business.

With his workings and ideas down on paper, it all looked pretty good. Jack still thought, *But what will the old lady think?!* He drove down to Shirley's farm first thing on Monday morning and caught the old lady feeding her chooks and ducks.

"I won't be long," she said, "sit on the veranda and wait till I'm finished my chores."

She took her time. Jack was impatient; he wanted it all over and done with but wait he had to do. Eventually, she finished what she was doing, walked up to Jack, who was sitting on the steps of the veranda.

"Well, you got the paperwork for me to digest?"

"Yes, here it is," said a nervous Jack as he handed in all his precious work in a brand-new brown envelope.

"Now, you stay here while I read and take in everything you have written; I could be quite a while."

And she was. Poor Jack, waiting in despair for his future to be told by this strange woman.

It was well over an hour when she came and said to Jack, "Come with me into my office."

Jack jumped up and followed her into the house, down a passageway into a room which was different to the rest of the house. It had books, manuscripts, papers and items all over the floor, on the chairs and on the desk. It could only be described as an unholy mess.

She swept papers off a chair, saying, "Sit down here Jack," as she sat at her desk and picked up Jack's paperwork. "You have gone to a lot of trouble with this report and I feel your enterprise could be a success. This is what I will do."

She opened the front drawer of her desk and pulled out a lot of original blank letterheads, belonging to companies, stock agents, doctors and solicitors. Then she proceeded to write with pen and ink in a beautiful copperplate writing style, which was surprising to see from the gnarled hand of the old lady. When she had finished and blotted the fine watermarked paper, she handed it to Jack.

"I think this will work for you," she said. "Take it to your bank and I would think he will approve your loan. Now, if you don't mind, I have appointments in town, so you better get going and good luck, Jack."

She had put the paper in the envelope with his papers, handed them to Jack and told him to see himself out.

Jack said, "Thanks for everything and I will let you know of the outcome."

But she had disappeared. A very strange lady that one.

As soon as Jack was away from the property, he stopped at the side of the road and pulled out the letter that the old woman had written. The letterhead had a few solicitors' names on it, with an address of some chambers in Sydney. It looked genuine. Where she got the letterhead from, no one should ask but it all looked very official.

Jack read what she had written:

Jack and Helen Alexander have been left an estate of $22,000 payable to them within a month of the above date of our letter.

The exact words of the letter have been erased through a faded memory over time but Jack thought this would never work. The banks aren't stupid; the old woman must be a con artist. He showed this letter to Helen. She said it was illegal and Jack could end up in jail with the old woman as a fraud.

"And then, I would be a jail widow," she said.

Jack always did what he was told, so Helen and he went and saw the bank manager, saying they only had $20,000 and expected to lose the property. It was unfortunate as they could have had the amount by selling what was on the place.

The manager said, "That is going to cause me and the bank some trouble as there are another four properties waiting to go ahead for you to finalise your sale, so they can sell to their prospective buyers, which would have been a big deal for the bank. Then there is another problem. Even if you did manage to get the deposit, how would you pay it off?"

"I can get a job at the local hospital as I'm a registered nurse and midwife and my wages would help pay the loan off till Jack gets the place up and running," said Helen.

"I'm sorry, Mrs Alexander, the bank cannot rely on you to pay the mortgage as you're a woman and you might get pregnant again. Then you wouldn't be able to pay off the loan."

It was extremely rare for Helen to get surly but she eyed the bank manager and in a stern voice said, "And what's the difference if Jack runs off with some floosy? We are partners in this enterprise and how dare you say, because I'm a female I am not financially responsible. That is discrimination, and I will take you and the bank to the new Discrimination Commissioner."

"Well, it doesn't really matter now," said an uncomfortable bank manager, shifting in his chair, "as you can't raise the deposit."

Helen retorted, "Yes, we can. Jack, show him the letter from the solicitor."

Jack sheepishly showed him the old woman's 'forged' letter.

"Oh, this makes all the difference," said the bank manager, his eyes lighting up after he read it. "Yes, on this correspondence, it is a letter of credit. We can go ahead with you buying the property. Why didn't you produce this before? It would have saved me a headache and getting a roasting from Mrs Alexander. Under the circumstances, with the bank wanting to finalise on the other four properties, I'm prepared to take a risk on you two and process the deposit and the mortgage."

As they left the bank, Jack turned to Helen, smiling and saying, "Looks like you're coming to jail with me and the old woman. Hope we don't have to share a cell with her."

"That manager made me so cross, as if to say I was not worthy as a human," Helen frowned.

"Well love, I'm glad he did because with your rare outburst and that illegal document we have, for the first time in our lives, have our own home and land."

They then drove down to Boonah to the real-estate office to sign the legal papers and all that went with it. They were now the owners of a 350-acre property on Lake Moogerah Road. Helen could only think, *Jack is amazing how he always manages to get what he really wants but, to be fair, I did put my penny's worth in, even though he always puts in a lot of work to get the result he wants.*

She was happy for Jack but she really didn't want to leave Shipfield. She was happy and secure in her hospital role as a bush nurse and the homestead that she liked, with all its modern comforts. She knew things were going to be tough but she had to believe in her husband because she was married to Jack and all his unauthorised ways. His family ended up doing quite well in their adventurous lives together.

When Jack looked at the property, he was only interested in the land. He should have paid a little more attention to the house but it was difficult at the time as the owners were in the house and he didn't like to snoop around.

"Oh Jack, there is no toilet, shower or hot water, not even in the sink," said Helen as they found out it emptied just under the house with no drainage. "That's where the awful smell was coming from when we looked at the house."

Helen was not a happy girl. Jack tried to help a bad situation and said, "Look at the beautiful views and Mt Edwards looking straight into our back door." He put his arm around Helen and added, "It's going to be hard love, for a while, but at last we own something, an asset and all this is now ours. Let's go for a walk."

The walk didn't help. The shower, they found, was under the high tank stand with a bit of hessian for a tiny bit of modesty. The toilet, which was about 50 metres from the house and not good for Helen with her condition, was in a tiny tin shed with a splintered wooden seat over a four- gallon kerosene bucket. Some newspaper was cut in to squares for toilet paper, punctured by a nail and hanging on the tin wall. The door might as well have not been there as it was hanging from its rusted hinges at a very peculiar angle and had not been closed for ages. Then there were the old farm machinery and parts of, goodness knows what, lying about that, just to have a shower or poo, they would have to navigate a minefield.

It was time to go back to work to Shipfield and give their notice but first, Helen went to the Boonah hospital and gave them her credentials and said she would be looking for employment within a month if there was a vacancy. She was assured there would be, as they were always short of registered staff.

They were only away for three days. The children were glad to see them back, after being looked after by Helen's Auntie Mac, who had never had children and didn't quite understand them. Helen went straight back to work at the Miles hospital and gave them three weeks' notice. They were sorry to see her go.

Jack, on the other hand, gave Reg three weeks' notice, which was not accepted as he wanted Jack to keep managing everything for him.

"Who is going to look after the horses? Who is going to maintain the shipment of cattle?" he asked.

"Well, I'm sorry Reg but one has to look after oneself and you have to accept my notice as I will be leaving in three weeks. I promise I will leave the property in good condition for your next manager, sorry Reg but that's the way it is."

And that was the way it was.

The property was well maintained; there was still a lot of tidying up and training the men up to looking after the horses and cattle, including the mixing of grains and the sowing of oats. The men were reliable, looking after everything while Jack was visiting the other proprieties but there were always things that needed fixing or the ordering of feeds for the horses when Jack got back. Then, of course, there was the paperwork, finalising everything and making an easy transition for the new manager.

A very busy three weeks indeed.

On the weekends, both Helen and Jack had a lot of packing up to do. Mr Norris down the road kindly lent them his big body truck with a crate on it, so Jack could take the horses down. Now there were a few. The three horses they had bought had foals. Molly, the draft horse, had an unexpected foal. Jack told the owner who said he couldn't handle Molly and a foal so he might as well keep them. He offered to pay but was declined because Jack had put so much work into their centenary celebrations.

And then there was Peter, an illegal foal, out of one of Shipfield's stock Arab mare that had joined with next door's Connemara stallion. Something mysterious must have happened one night. All told, nine horses were taken down to the newly bought property. Another trip that weekend was taking the sulky and spring cart down. It was a very tired Jack that Sunday night.

The following weekend, Jack took down some of their personal items, as well as a large Laminex table and the six chairs belonging to it, that Mrs Norris had given Helen, as well as a very old, vinyl, yellow and grey two-seater lounge, that was in good condition. Remember, our two had no furniture at all as it was always supplied. They did own the colour TV and the cabinet it stood on and a stool. All this went down in the truck. Helen, at night, had been very busy after tea, making two bean bags for the children to sit on while doing homework or watching TV. That is all the furniture they had.

The big day arrived. The children were excited, Helen not so. All the packing had been done, the homestead cleaned and polished, the sheds and the property were left the best Jack could possibly do. The house yard was mowed and garden weeded and watered. There were things the children were sad to leave behind, including the swing and gym set that Jack had made for them one Christmas, as they were cemented into the ground. The other was Deborah's favourite: a cubby house, too big and awkward to put on the truck.

Jack was sad to leave a very well-equipped tool room where one could make or repair anything. And Helen was the saddest of all to leave her nice homestead. As a matter of fact, when Jack had shaken the hands of his workers and thanked them and he and Damon climbed into the car ready to leave, Helen refused and stayed on the steps, holding Deborah's hand. Jack pleaded with her but she refused. He waited about 15 minutes then drove off, leaving them on the steps.

After driving a couple of kilometres down the road, Damon asked his dad what his next move was.

"Because you just can't leave Mum and Deborah on their own," he said.

Jack replied, "I think we shall sit here for a little while then go back and see if Mum is going to come."

They drove back to find them still sitting on the steps.

Jack opened the passenger side door and pleaded, "Darling, we do have to go. It won't be too bad."

A very sullen Helen walked down and hopped into the car, while Deborah got in the back with Damon. It was a silent, uncomfortable ride for some time, before Helen spoke.

"Darling, I didn't want to leave. I was so happy there."

"I know you were, but we do have to move on. I can't risk our future on Reg or the company. You know what happened to the manager on one of the northern properties. And what's more, if it wasn't for you getting upset with the bank manager and making me produce that forged letter, we would not have been in this situation now. Don't blame me, it's not all my fault."

She leant over and gave him a sweet kiss on the cheek.

"I know all that Darling, but it was hard for me to leave."

C.22

Yarramalong
1979

When they arrived in the township of Boonah, they had a lot of shopping to do: cheap beds and mattresses for the kids and for themselves, some linen. They had blankets and quilts, supplied by Jack's mum years ago, crockery and cutlery from Helen's dad, coming from unused wedding presents. There was also Helen's electric frypan, toaster and the all-important sewing machine.

Lots to buy with so little money. They had Helen's small savings and two months wages and holiday pay. Jack had a month's wages and holiday pay, plus $2,500 of savings. This went on beds and mattresses at Furniture Court, then to the electrical store to buy a fridge, washing machine and a kettle. They requested if these could please be delivered that afternoon as they had nothing at all in their new home.

Why didn't they have all this sorted out before they came? Probably because they were too busy getting loans and finishing at Shipfield. Helen bought some food to last a day or so and a very tired family arrived at their old, tired house.

The house was empty and bare, except for the laminex table and chairs in the kitchen and the two-seater lounge and bean bags and TV in the L-shaped lounge. There were also all the packed items in tea chests and cardboard boxes, which Jack hurriedly had put down when he transported it all a week ago.

Jack immediately checked the horses and cattle out, to see if they were okay and had plenty of water and feed. He then chopped some kindling and wood and lit the slow combustion stove. Helen, in the meantime, unpacked as many essentials as she could find to get everything started. The children raced around and explored and chose their bedrooms, then went outside to explore.

The house was built about 1887 and was designed with one large room, surrounded by verandas. Over time, the verandas were filled in to accommodate more family members and children. They were told that 15 people lived there at one time. Helen and Jack could not imagine how they could have all fitted in. The farm cottage, that's really what it was, had hoop pine floors, tongue and groove walls and high timber ceilings. The walls had never been painted except for two bedrooms, which were to be the children's rooms.

"Jack, you better ring up the phone and power people as, surprisingly, they are both connected, but who knows when they will cut it off and when are the people coming with all the gear we bought this morning?" Helen asked.

"Well, I don't know love but, first thing in the morning, I have to muster the cattle up, as Gordons, the trucking mob, are loading them tomorrow arvo for the sale on Wednesday and I also have to contact the harvester, which had already been booked by the previous owners," Jack replied. "Darling, you know I had to arrange all this as soon as the bank said we could buy the property, as we have to have the money by the end of the month and I bet it won't come as soon as the cattle and crop is sold. We have to fill our obligation to the bank or we are in deep trouble. What happens if the bank rings the solicitors and they have no knowledge of the Alexanders and an estate coming to them?"

"That's your problem. Mine is to enrol the children into the Kalbar State School and see the hospital to ask if I have a job and when I can start."

"I've got the stove going love. The children will be wanting their dinner soon," said Jack.

"And I guess you want it to?" came Helen's reply.

"Oh, if it is really convenient for you to scrape something up for your loving husband."

"You be very careful."

The couple had an uncomfortable night as none of the furniture arrived. The Boonah town business must have been on slow casual. The children slept on their bean beds; Helen and Jack slept in Jack's swag, which really only had room for one but they managed a few precious hours of sleep together.

Everyone decided not to have a shower and, surprisingly, the stove heated the water, which only worked from the kitchen sink, so at least they could have a farmer's wash. Helen had to escort Deborah to the toilet and Damon asked his dad should he come along and inspect the red back spiders under the toilet seat. Just as well, as the four-gallon kerosene tin was full, so that night, tired as he was, he had to dig a hole and bury the smelly contents. The first thing on his priority list, when they had some money, was a septic toilet.

Helen left early the next morning with Deborah to enrol the kids at the Kalbar school, then to the hospital to see if she had a position there and when could she start. She was told she could start the following Monday, as they were short of staff due to the school holidays and one member on maternity leave. Helen accepted the position and said she would be pleased to start next Monday. She really wasn't that pleased as she wanted time to settle into her new home and help Jack but they needed the money quickly, so a start on Monday it was to be.

Damon had decided to go with his dad to muster the cattle but first, there was a bit of maintenance to do, including clearing scrub from the old cattle yard and loading ramp, which was situated beside the old unused dairy. It took them much longer than they thought, so it ended up a bit of a rush to catch the horses and find the cattle in a property they didn't know. They were lucky as the cattle were all in one of the front paddocks which was clear of scrub and lantana being an old cultivation paddock.

They counted them twice as there seemed to be three extra head compared to what was reported. Damon asked if they were theirs and his dad said, "They are now."

They got them into the yard without any trouble as they were very quiet. Jack was pleased that they could be rested for a few hours before the truck arrived.

That afternoon, they were all busy as four trucks started to arrive, two with their gear they bought yesterday and two semi-trailers for the cattle. The cattle had to be loaded first; the gear could wait till the loading was finished as the furniture and electric gear was supposed to have been delivered yesterday.

The rest of the day they spent setting everything up. The washing machine went under the house where they discovered the laundry was. As the house was built on a hilltop, the back entrance had only two steps into the kitchen, whereas the front had 10 steps to the front door.

All the beds were made up and Jack found some hooks and wire to hang clothes on, while Helen did wonderful things with the large packing cardboard boxes for cupboards. This was the furniture in their three bedrooms. The start of their new home. No wonder Helen was reluctant to leave Shipfield, especially after they all had a cold shower under the high tank stand, which was a lot of fun. Screams and laughter coming from the shivering, nude family.

"My dear husband, it won't be fun for long. We better have something more civilised soon, as I start nursing in a few days' time and a decent hot shower is a must," said Helen.

"With the capital we have at this time, all I can do is put drainage under the sink as it's a health hazard, put a shower in the bath and connect the hot water from the stove," said Jack.

The cattle made quite a few hundred more than he estimated but agents' commission and trucking fees would have to be paid out of the sale. Damon thought his dad was mad buying a milking cow in calf. Jack told him, if the calf turns out to be a steer it was his but if it was a heifer, it was dad's and, not only would they not have to buy milk but they also could make some money from the calves the cow might produce.

They stopped at the hardware shop and bought PVC pipes, a couple of U bend traps and elbows, copper piping, a shower head and fittings and PVC glue, all that was needed for drainage and a shower for mum. They opened an account and asked if it all could be delivered to 688 Lake Moogerah Rd, Charlwood, as soon as possible.

As can be imagined, a lot of work and cleaning and fixing up was in progress for the next few weeks of the holidays. Helen was back at work and the kids in their new school. Deborah was excited but Damon thought it more important and interesting to help his dad than go to school, which wasn't very interesting at all.

Helen came home one night very worried.

"This town is not a good place to live," she said, "there are a lot of bad people here. There seems to be wife swapping, murders, robbers and affairs. Every morning I go to work, they are all talking about this person and that person and naming them. It's disgraceful."

Poor Helen, she had been in the bush too long and with

only the ABC to listen to. All the girls at the hospital were only gossiping on what happened the night before on the soapies, not what was happening in town.

Even though Jack had made a shower and drainage for the wastewater, Helen was still not happy coming home from night duty and having a cold shower, as all the hot water had been used. The stove that supplied the water wasn't working at night.

Jack had estimated selling the cattle would make $9,000 but with commission and trucking costs and the purchase of a milking cow, the agent's cheque was made out to JW&HB Alexander for $8,790, $210 short Let's hope for the family's sake the soya bean crop comes well over Jack's estimate of $12,000.

It did by just under $3,000 and that was after harvesting and commission costs.

Jack, in the last hours of the month, paid the bank the $20,000 they owed for the deposit.

The bank manager smiled and said, "I knew you would do it, Jack," and still smiling with a huge wink, followed by saying, "Lucky we didn't have to use that... er... letter, Jack."

Jack went cold in the stomach. But all was good. They were, with Helen's wage, paying off the fortnightly principal and interest on the mortgage. The manager was now a bit worried about income, seeing Jack had sold all the cattle. Jack assured him not to worry and promptly got up and left the manager's office, without looking back.

They had a bit left over from Helen's wage for food and stuff for the kids. The money from Jack selling the crops and cattle provided a small profit of $2,340, which was spent on a septic toilet, thank God. But there was not enough for Helen's gas water heater,

"Darling," Jack said, "It is the very next thing on the list."

Kenny and Sam called to see how they were going, the

following Saturday. They were amazed how much cleaning up had been accomplished in such a short time. Kenny got down to business.

"Jack, you must have life insurance on Helen. If something happens to her, you will lose the property. Insure her for enough to cover the mortgage and the children till they leave school. And what's more, you should insure the property and your personal items."

"Kenny, I haven't a razoo to spare," said Jack, "as a matter of fact, at the moment, we are living day to day. There is no way I could even think of paying insurance premiums."

"I tell you what I can do. I will write you two policies, payable within six weeks. If you can't pay by then, we may be able to work something out."

"Well, you better think of something as I doubt we will be able to afford anything, even in six weeks."

"Now, I guess you have submitted your plans to council for a camping and recreation business?"

"Do I have to do that?" Jack was surprised. "Can't I just go ahead? It's our property, can't we do what we like on it?"

"No, you have to have planning consent, so ask the council for the forms. The sooner the better, otherwise you will not be allowed to operate."

All this was a bit of a shock to Jack. He realised all Kenny was talking about was spending money he didn't have. He thought, *It looks like you gotta be a bloody millionaire before you can even start a small family business, why didn't the bank mention about planning consent?*

"I got some good news," cried an excited Helen, "Sam said they have unused wardrobes and chests of drawers lying under their house we can have."

The two girls had come into the room, smiling after their tour of the house and non-existent garden.

"Why are you looking so downcast, Jack?" asked Helen.

He told them what Kenny had said and felt at a loss.

"Well, let's have a cup of tea and a bit of lunch and we can worry about worrying later on."

Helen was the bread winner, paying off $80 a fortnight to the bank and what was left of her wage, they lived on and paid the bills. Things were tight, very tight but survive they did. Jack spent every day clearing rubbish, building a horse yard down the front and cutting timber on the place. He cleared the front government land beside their front entrance and talked to the people who ran the outdoor recreation grounds of the grammar schools, about what he was planning to do and if they were interested. He put in the planning consent to council and got knocked back. He redid another application and it was knocked back as well.

"What are you going to do Jack?" asked Helen, "We do have to get an income from this place or we are sunk."

"If all is lost, we can do our second option and that is, start up spelling and training stables," said Jack. "I know the industry and a lot of people in the industry, due to the work I did at Shipfield with the thoroughbred horses."

"But that's going to cost money too."

"Yes, I know but we start small and the paddock fences are good and I can build some shade sheds. I think it wouldn't take much to start getting some money in."

"Well, maybe but whatever you do, we cannot live like this for too long."

Jack received two phone calls, both from mysterious callers.

The first said, "Regarding your submission for a recreation centre. Put everything in it, like accommodation, restaurant and as much as you can think of. There are council elections soon and if you get the submission in quickly, it may be successful third time around."

"Who is this?" asked Jack.

"Never mind, just resubmit it." And he hung up.

The second caller asked if Jack was licenced enough to fly to New Guinea. The caller said he knew that Jack was financially starved and if he could pick up some gear from New Guinea and deliver to Cairns, it would be very profitable for him.

"I will ring tomorrow to see if you are prepared for a windfall."

Jack thought about it for a couple of minutes but knew, if he did it, he would be forced to do more trips. When the mysterious man called the following night, Jack gave him a very firm no and not ever to ring his number again. Later, talking to some pilots, they thought it was possibly gold they wanted smuggled, not drugs. He asked if any of them had been approached. They shook their heads in the negative, which really wasn't a straight no but it wasn't Jack's problem. He had enough of his own.

Then town planning came through and, officially, they were now a camping and recreation centre. There were conditions and improvements needed, of course, that had to be made but Jack somehow didn't see them. All he saw was a go ahead from council. Firstly, he gave permission to Brisbane Grammar school to camp there, as it was a stopping place for their hike up Mt Edwards. Jack said he wouldn't charge them for camping but if and when he got the horse riding going, he hoped they would use it. They said they would if Jack made it educational.

On checking newspapers and putting ads in for horses, he came across an ad for a riding school for sale at Greenbank, an outer suburb of Brisbane. He met Spike, a rough-looking character whose every second word started with 'F' or 'C'. He was a Vietnam returned serviceman and had a number of horses, 10 in all, ranging from 13 hands to 16, all part of his riding school he had hoped to start up, but couldn't get permission from council. Also, he did not have enough feed for them, so a deal was made.

Jack said he had no money to pay Spike but he had plenty of paddocks with excellent feed and he should be able to cover his debt in full, in six months' time. Spike said he needed the money now as his wife had given birth to twins. Jack said he really needed the horses but honestly, he was flat out paying the petrol to get there. Spike thought a while and said he was in trouble with the council and had to move the horses within a fortnight and a week had already passed.

"So, I'm stuck both ways," he said. "You look an honest chap, so I will truck the horses to your place as long as you take care of them. We will call it free agistment and I want to be able to come out any time and inspect them."

Jack readily agreed.

He had the horses; he had the riding yard built with two sliprails at each end. Who could afford gates? Now he had to get saddles and bridles. He had two saddles and the children had theirs. He needed another 12. He rang his old saddler friend, Bill Scholler, in Chinchilla, who Jack had done a lot of business with when he was running Shipfield. He asked Bill if he could supply him with 12 second-hand saddles and bridles, as he was starting a riding school but had no money. Could he possibly wait nine months for full payment?

Bill said, "Some graziers don't pay me for 12 months. Yes, if I can find enough suitable gear for you, I would be pleased to help you get started. I am coming to Brisbane in a fortnight. If I can get everything you want, I will bring them down and meet you in Ipswich."

"That's great. I really appreciate it more than you know. Thanks a lot, Bill," said a grateful Jack.

"Well, that's alright," replied Bill, "You have been a good customer over the years when you were starting up that breeding and training facility."

It was all happening. Jack was breaking in his young horses; the new arrivals, Spike trucked up to the property, had to be ridden to make them quiet enough for the general public. Damon helped on the weekends, riding the smaller horses. Deborah hadn't ridden since her accident but big brother was encouraging her in secret to start riding again.

Helen seemed happy, especially now she had a gas hot water system for steaming hot showers before going to work. She had made some good friends at the hospital but Matron Brent seemed a bit of a problem to her. Helen was used to doing everything in Miles as a bush nurse: from x-rays to plastering broken limbs, delivering babies and anything else required. At Boonah Hospital, she was only allowed to work in obstetrics and do just general nursing. She was a bit frustrated at not being allowed to use all her skills that she was proud of.

Jack had a vivid dream of a horse winning the Melbourne Cup. He scratched around and found $50 of the emergency fund he had hidden. As Helen was about to go to work this day, the first Tuesday of November in 1983, Jack handed the precious $50 to Helen and said, "I dreamt the winner of the Melbourne Cup. Could you please put it on this horse to win?"

Helen looked at Jack and said, "Are you mad? We can't afford to waste a precious $50 on a horse race just because you dreamt about it. I know you and your dreamings."

"Darling, trust me and put the money on the horse, please."

"Alright, seeing you asked me and you seem so sure of yourself."

Jack sat down to watch the race with excited anticipation. The race started. His horse left the barrier last and was trying to catch up to the other horses. Very slowly, it started to gain on the rest of the field. It was now on the outside. It was a battle but the horse was slowly pulling ahead. With less than 250 metres to go, the final three were coming down the straight but Jack's horse wasn't among them. *Never mind*, he thought, *it was worth a try.*

All of a sudden, on the outside, Jack's horse made a run and streaked past the leading three to cross the line first. Jack's horse had won. It was Kiwi at nine to one.

Jack was so excited. They were going to have money for Christmas. They'd be able to buy presents for the kids and spoil themselves, may be the pictures and a dinner out. Oh, it was what the family needed after going through such hard times.

Helen usually arrived home at 5.30pm. She was late and Jack thought she must be celebrating with some of the nurses. Jack was so excited and couldn't wait to see her to ask how much money they had won.

Jack was starting to get worried. It was getting dark but, to his relief, he heard the car coming up the driveway. She had arrived safely. Jack raced up to the car full of excitement.

"How much did we win? How much did we win?"

As a crestfallen Helen got out of the car, she confessed she didn't place the bet.

"I thought I was being a good wife and you would have been so pleased with me if the horse lost and you could have had the fifty dollars back." (Why was she late? Just putting off the bad news and doing some free overtime at work.)

The normal hug and welcome didn't happen. Jack was speechless. His dream for the family was shattered. He was dry in the throat. No matter how he tried, he just could not get his voice box to work for some time.

Now, our loving couple, like all couples, had problems. Helen never talked about herself, her thoughts or feelings.

(Helen was asked to contribute to this book about her life with Jack and her feelings about everything. She declined saying, "I don't like talking about myself or my feelings. I will leave it up to Jack.") Jack always did, except when he was upset.

As an example, after Helen didn't place the bet on the horse, he thought, *the poor girl must have been frightened out of her wits when she heard the horse she was supposed to bet on, won.* Jack knew he should have given her a hug and said, "It's alright dear, you thought you were doing your best."

But he didn't. He wanted to but the words and actions weren't there. They both did what they did. It wasn't good but love would eventually cross these emotional bridges. Well, it did for them.

At a much later time, Helen was worried about Jack; he had been working flat out since they came to their new home. Clearing, building, handling horses, working out marketing and signs and the money woes at night.

"Jack, you have to have a break, a holiday or you're going to get sick or injure yourself. You have lost weight and you look tired," she said.

"No, I'm ok love, I just had just a big day," he replied.

"No excuses, you are leaving this property for a week and that's that."

Jack succumbed to her orders. Not only in her voice but the look in her eyes told him he had no choice.

He booked himself into a motel at Surfer's Paradise and took a stroll around the place. It was very busy and crowded. He spied an interesting bookshop and rummaged around not looking for anything in particular, when he saw a book with the title, *Aboriginal Words and Placenames* by A.W. Reed. He bought it. He and Helen had wanted their property to have an Aboriginal name, so they could have a registered business name and, as yet, they hadn't been successful.

He then went shopping for food as eating out was out of the question with their budget. He did a bit of window shopping and went back to the motel. The next day he decided to go to the beach. Not being a beach or water person, his idea was just to walk along the sand for something to do.

He was shocked and amazed as he walked along the beach. He saw topless, young women sunbathing on the dunes. This, to a bushman, who had never seen such delights, couldn't see where he was walking and tripped over, horror of horrors, a young, topless sunbather laying in the middle of the beach. He apologised and tried to get up quickly but, in his haste, his feet were going so fast to stand up, he wasn't going anywhere. He eventually managed, apologised again and quickly walked away. The girl must have been in shock at the sudden occurrence and did not utter a sound, not even to accept the apologies.

Jack was not hanging around. He walked as far as Broadbeach and, to prove how physical and mentally tired he was, he just fell on the sand and went fast asleep. Now Jack, at home, would wear only shorts, a hat and his work boots and socks. Having an Italian grandfather, his skin hardly burnt; it just went brown. He had been working in the sun for months, so his body was used to the Queensland sun.

But on this day, he had just his shorts on and his big hat, no boots or socks. When he woke up at about five pm, his feet were burnt so badly they were red and swollen and he could not stand on then. He had to crawl across the sand to the roadside where he managed to flag down a cab. He asked to be taken to a bottle shop and purchased three bags of ice, then was taken back to the motel where he ordered a pizza to be delivered and wrapped his feet in ice. He rang Helen but got no sympathy.

She said, "Can't leave you by yourself for a couple of days before you get yourself into some sort of trouble."

Poor Jack spent a week there with feet wrapped in ice before he could safely drive home. Helen was horrified when she saw his feet, still red and blistered and the web between the toes still swollen. He got a tiny bit of sympathy then.

After searching and a lot of discussion, they decided on Yarramalong as the name for the property. It said in the book that it meant, 'the place of wild horses'. Of course, horses were not an original animal in Australia. When the Aboriginals first saw a horse, they noted their big teeth, 'Yarram' and 'along' meant wild country. Hence, Yarramalong, according to the book Jack bought.

Not being really experienced in advertising or business, it was found out, much later, that Yarramalong was too long for marketing and brochures, People could not pronounce it but, somehow, Yarramalong Recreation Centre stayed for a long time.

Jack found a large fork in an iron bark branch and bolted on old timber sleeper on both sides. Helen, with her artistic skills, painted Yarramalong on both sides and Jack cemented the trunk into the ground where it still stands 46 years later.

They were ready for business. The horses with fat, gleaming hides that were well brushed, including the manes and tails, and trimmed hoofs. Saddles and bridles were oiled and looking good with new saddle blankets. The horses were standing in Jack's new yard, looking a picture. From a shady tree, he had hung a large waterbag with cups for his new customers to refresh themselves. They didn't come. Cars were going to the dam but no one came for a horse ride to be relieved of some money. It was the start of the Christmas holidays and Jack stayed with the horses, hoping a customer would come along. He even had a pouch on his belt with change in it. Something had to happen.

He made seven large signs. Helen was asked to paint words on them in the most shocking pink. He then erected them on the road, the first one two kilometres up the road and then he placed the rest in large spaces, with the last one pointing to Yarramalong's entrance. It was the time in the news, when all the massage parlours were in Brisbane and the premier at the time, Jo Bjelke-Peterson, did not seem to recognise they existed. It was a big media blitz that went on for weeks. So, what did Jack do?

On the first of the running signs in shocking pink was written: MASSAGE.

The next sign said YOUR; the next BOTTOM; then running on PONY, RIDES, HERE.

A lot of cars slowed down and there were a lot of smiles from the passers-by but no customers, until they started to trickle in after Christmas day. Mostly from the caravan park that was very popular with campers. They even got a bit of overflow, where Jack offered them complimentary camping, as he had no facilities at the partly cleared camping ground beside the large water hole.

The horse-riding numbers started to improve, as one lot of guests/campers told others and they came. The council told Jack to take the signs down but they stayed there until the end of the Christmas holidays.

C.23

Devastation on Two Fronts

Business was slow but money was trickling in. Brisbane Grammar started to bring their students for horse rides. Two rides, consisting of 15 students per ride every Thursday, for a month. The other private schools, with their recreation centres at Lake Moogerah and Maroon Dam, started to make enquiries, as well as the Queensland Government Education Centre at Maroon. Their business was starting to look like it could be a success.

Now Brisbane Grammar School started another activity. While one group rode, the other group climbed Big John. There was a very large hoop pine tree on the property, about 30 metres high with a huge base. Jim Johnston, of Brisbane Grammar, thought it would be a good climbing tree. He asked Jack if they could use it to climb. Jack was not keen as he loved his trees and was in awe of this magnificent pine.

Jack said, "Alright, I will give you three climbs. If I find no damage to the tree, you may continue."

On his third inspection of the tree, he noticed, attached to the tree, on a lacquer board, written in large gold letters - BIG JOHN. *(Jack's other first name)*.

It worked like this; they tied a safety rope to each student's harness about a metre apart on each student. So, all students were connected to this one piece of climbing cord. Then they had to pick their leader to climb the tree and all had to follow the same way as their leader or there would be an unholy tangle. Then the leader would put a little rag doll, Daphne (Later on, it was Priscilla after Daphne fell to pieces), on the very top of the tree. Then, they had to make their way down, go for a horse ride, while the others who had finished their horse ride, had to climb the tree and rescue the doll. In the years of Yarramalong Recreation over tens of thousands of students had climbed Big John.

This activity was popular with a lot of schools. And, one by one, recreation teachers who move around, thought it was great and Big John became the name at a lot of interstate recreation centres for their climbing trees. Sadly, Big John was hit by a big bolt of lightning 40 years later, was burnt and did not survive.

Meanwhile, Jack and Helen wrote a submission to the Commonwealth Development Bank for a loan of $10,000 to build an amenities' block and to upgrade the road in the camping ground. They had very generous interest and long terms to pay back the loan. They got a call to say a representative would be out to inspect the property and to collect more details regarding their submission. It was all coming together for our loving couple.

It was a very hot 40-degree day with a northerly blowing; a very uncomfortable day indeed. Helen was at work; Jack had just finished a ride with some customers when he noticed billowing smoke apparently coming from the camping ground. He jumped into the old Ford station wagon, bought from an old pilot friend who owned a garage in Warwick, for a few dollars, and raced down. To his horror, the whole area of the camping ground was alight with flames, with the strong northerly wind causing them to race up Little Mount Edwards.

There was no way Jack could even attempt to put it out, the heat and ferocity of the fire made that impossible. He raced to the house, rang the neighbour, who was the local fire warden. It was to no avail. The only help was from a neighbour, a farmer called Kerkman from the opposite side of the creek. With his tractor he tried to make a fire break on the western side. He, eventually had to bail out of the tractor and run to safety as his tractor caught fire.

The other help was from Jimmy Johnston from Brisbane Grammar School. The Kalbar volunteer fire brigade arrived. Because of the hilly terrain with its gullies, the fire created two fronts. There was a western front heading for the house and outbuildings and the northern front heading up Little Mount Edwards and towards the small settlement at Moogerah Dam.

"Quick children, run and get the young horses out of the paddock behind the house and let them go in the front," cried Jack as he helped the fire brigade, finding water to try and help make a break around the house.

The children just got the horses out when a huge fireball came over the paddock they had just left, hit the large hayshed half full of useful grassy hay, with some useful farm machinery and completely burnt and gutted it all.

The saddles and all the gear for the horses was stored in a little fibro cream shed. These were now part of the asset that must be saved. Jack threw everything into the old Ford station wagon. He had a young volunteer who was helping. Jack picked up a well wrapped package in tar paper and threw it at the youngster, who caught it and asked, "What's this?"

Jack replied, "Gelignite."

The boy froze.

"Hang on," said Jack and threw another small parcel.

"What's that?"

"Detonators," was the reply.

The Tale Comes to an End

The lad took off with his parcels. What happened to them? Goodness knows. (What was Jack doing with gelignite? I'll tell you later.)

Jack, to keep the children busy, suggested they make cups of tea for the fire fighters. Jack was upset to see his children handing out cups of tea and biscuits to all the people who were standing around sight-seeing, doing nothing to help the area. Jack has never forgiven those people.

The house, the old, open garage / workshop, the cream saddle shed, the grain shed and an old small car garage were saved. Everything else was destroyed. This included the hay shed, fowl house, pigsties, other small buildings, 50% of the fences and most of the paddocks were badly burnt. What were the horses going to eat? He rang Helen and told her not to come home because of the smoke and devastation, that Jimmy Johnston said she could stay there the night and he would bring the children.

Jack believed the children hosing the walls of the house constantly saved it. When he stayed at the house that night, he could feel the timber walls of the house were hot to touch. Not warm. Hot. *It was a wonder the whole house didn't go up due to spontaneous combustion,* he thought. He patrolled all that night putting out spot fires and checking that all was safe.

The next day was Sunday and Helen got a few days off work and came down with the children from the Brisbane Grammar Outdoor Centre. She just couldn't believe how the house was saved with all the burnt destruction around. She, on this rare occasion, let her emotions go. Turning to Jack, she came into his arms saying, "It's awful, all the work you have put in and now there is months of clearing up. Darling, how are we going to survive?"

"We will and we must," said Jack with a strong voice and his conviction. It was the opposite of what he felt inside. "Darling, we have got each other and two wonderful children. We are blessed; this is a setback that will make us stronger."

Jack went down to the camping ground, reviewing the total damage caused by the fire. The worst damage was at the campground. Tears filled Jack's eyes. He just stood there in disbelief. His beautiful campground, with the lovely 100-year-old shady trees, was now desolate.

Some gums and ironbark were still standing, though damaged. Standing there by himself, he saw a dream collapsing. He just lost it, which was extremely rare for Jack. Then some interesting information came to him via Jimmy Johnston, who said a young man told him, "I didn't think it would be so bad."

Jimmy had said to the boy, "Why did you light it?"

The reply was, "My dad told me to."

Who would want to do that to me? a bewildered Jack thought. *I have not hurt anyone; I have no enemies. No, it was just an accident.*

The rest of Sunday and Monday the family started to clean up around the house. On Tuesday there was a call from their bank manager, giving his condolences about the fire and then followed by saying, "We have an offer for your property for what you owe and we recommend you accept it."

Jack said no way and hung up. He rang Kenny up about the insurance policy which he had managed to scrape up a premium for.

Kenny said, "Oh, I haven't lodged it yet."

"Why not?" Jack asked.

"I'm sorry, I just must have forgotten to lodge it, I have been very busy lately."

"So, we are not insured?" Jack's anger was rising.

"I'm afraid not."

Jack just hung up, desperately disappointed in his so-called friend. Some terrible thoughts start coming to his mind. A lad said his dad had told him to light the fire. The bank rang and said they had an offer for the place and now, he found out they have no insurance. There was something very dirty and ugly going on.

He mentioned his suspicions to Helen who replied, "That's ridiculous, it was all just a coincidence. Why would anyone do this to us?" Jack shrugged his shoulders saying he didn't know but something seemed a bit funny.

The next day, Tuesday, a car rolled up. A man in a suit got out of the car and introduced himself as Robert from the Development Bank.

Jack said, despondently, "We had, as you can see, a devastating bush fire on Saturday. I suspect the bank would not be interested in all this ruin."

Robert, a bloke in his late forties just smiled and said, "Bush fires can happen anywhere, just show me around the property."

Jack took him down to the camping ground. He had a good look around, asked where he was thinking of putting the amenities block and a few more questions about the camping ground. Then he asked to go back to the house where Helen supplied tea and a freshly made orange cake. He got Jack's submission for a loan out of his briefcase; he reviewed it slowly, while Jack's heart was pounding.

He then asked a few more questions and said, "We won't back your submission as it stands, but if you forward another submission asking for $20,000 instead of the $10,000, which wouldn't get you anywhere. I can see a need for an improvement of the road and you will need an amenities block. If you put in some more detail, including your marketing plan, which you outlined in your previous paper, I feel you have a very good chance of getting the loan as there are grounds for a facility such as yours in this district. I realise the fire is a bitter blow for you but these things happen to make you stronger."

"It's funny you should say that as that's exactly the words I said to Helen the other day," said Jack.

When he left, Jack and Helen hugged each other, as they regularly do, saying, "It's a recreation centre on its way."

Jack worked on the new submission that night.

Jack nosed around and found the father of the son that lit the fire and asked him to pay for damages. The man, a prominent, respected professional person in the Boonah Shire, just laughed at Jack.

"Go ahead and sue me, my son is just over 18. Sue him but he has nothing."

Jack walked out of the office. He was angry. No one should get away with such an act, as there would be consequences.

Jimmy Johnston, wrote an eyewitness account of the confession from the lad, saying he lit the fire as he was told to do so by his father. Jack took it to a solicitor to try and recoup money for the damages. The solicitor, hearing all the facts, said, "It's clear to me some people with influence want your property, as now it is extremely valuable. You are the only property in the shire that has changed from rural to recreation and that you can do anything with it now, makes it a profitable business for schools and tourist recreation.

"I know you want to sue and hurt these people but they are prominent in the district probably in Lions, Rotary and the Masonic clubs. If you take them to court, they will make you broke for life as they will delay any proceedings until you can no longer continue and then you would be up for all court costs," the lawyer advised, "Sorry Jack, I want your money but you haven't got a chance with these sort of people unless you have 10 times the money they collectively have."

"Thanks for your advice," said Jack.

He was angry. How could people ruin an innocent family because they wanted what they have. It was like a western movie. The rich, big rancher wanting to take over the poor sod buster's property as he had plenty of water or oil, so they rode down, shoot the family, and take over the property. Well, to Jack it was exactly the same.

Without going into detail, Jack had a hidden gift, similar to the Aboriginals. It's called pointing the bone or singing someone to death. Jack could not believe that just because someone had money and influence, they could do such a thing or, at worst, get away with it.

So, Jack sung this man whose son had lit the fire. Just before going to sleep every night, Jack recreated the image of that person in his mind and repeated, "You die, you die," until he fell asleep. The man died six months later. (That's Jack's story anyway.)

The truth came out 12 months later. Sam, Kenny's wife, confessed everything to Helen. Thinking Kenny was a friend, Jack told him about all his plans but had no finance behind him. He also had no insurance, thanks to her husband pocketing the premium. It was ripe for Kenny and his little consortium to burn the Alexanders out and start their own recreation centre.

Sam said she was disgusted with the whole thing and, once she learnt the facts, she left Kenny who had since contracted a sickness. She couldn't live with him any longer, not only because of the dastardly thing he had done but the kindness Helen and Jack had showed them up north She had also found out Kenny had sold all the goat skins Jack and he shot and salted, telling Jack they were not tannable.

So, there it was. Jack was right. It was a consortium of prominent people in Boonah who had decided to burn them out and take over their property. They had not reckoned on Jack and Helen's resilience and their determination to succeed with their plans for their recreation centre.

What was Jack doing with gelignite? I'll let him tell the story.

Working on clearing out the camping ground, there was one

section which was perfect for a roundabout for cars to turn around, instead of driving on the grass. But there was a problem. A huge iceberg-shaped rock was in the middle of the roundabout and had to be moved. I dug around it thinking I could pull it with the tractor that was left with the property. But no. I had dug down about a metre but I still hadn't come to the bottom of the rock.

There was only one solution and that was to blow it up but I didn't know anything about explosives. I wondered if the old man, Ernie Dicker, knew anything about explosives. Ernie was about 85 years of age, had coke bottle glasses to see and walked with a stick. He might know something.

Yes, he did and would be pleased to help me. I asked him where I could purchase such items. He said to go to the council and get a permit to use explosives, then they would tell him where to get the gelignite from.

"You will also need detonators and a good length of fuse cord."

I asked him, "Can I really buy all that stuff by paying a fee for a permit and know nothing about explosives?"

I went to the council and, after paying a nominal fee for a permit, I asked, "Where do I buy all the stuff that I need?"

The clerk said, "Follow me," and I did, into the council depot.

Then he went into the middle of the yard, unlocked a latch to a trap door and we walked down some steps to an underground storage area. He asked me what I wanted.

I told him, without a clue of what I actually needed, "Ahh, I need 12 sticks of gelignite and a box of detonators and a couple of metres of cord fuse."

These were handed to me without question and I was told the council would send me a bill for my purchases. I drove, very carefully, home. I just didn't understand how safe my packages were.

The day arrived. I picked up Ernie at his house at Lake Moogerah and we drove to the camping ground with the explosives.

Ernie summed up the situation, saying it would be an easy job seeing as I had dug deep around the rock. He grabbed four sticks of gelignite, placed a detonator and about two feet of cord to the bundle then, to my horror, he rammed it all into the dug hole as far as he could with his foot. I suggested getting behind a huge rock about three feet in diameter, about seven feet high and about 100 yards from the job, for a shelter. Ernie said it was not necessary; I disagreed.

We lit the fuse and it started to fizz and sparkle. I made it behind our cover but with Ernie hobbling, he didn't quite make it. I do have to admit that there was a barb wire fence we had to negotiate before reaching our safe cover. The gelignite went off. Well no, not really. It was a fizzer and blew a few shards off the basalt rock.

"We need more explosives," said Ernie. "Take me home now and go and get a bag of nitro fill fertiliser from the hardware/nursey store in town. Then soak a couple of pounds of the stuff with diesel and give me a call next week when it's ready."

We were at the rock again with four sticks of gelignite, a pound of soaked fertiliser and all rammed into the hole with 18 inches of fuse sticking out. We lit it and hurried to our safe cover. We waited. We waited some more. Ernie said the fuse had gone out and started to move from our cover.

I encouraged him back behind our shelter saying, "I think we should wait a bit longer."

"No, the fuse has gone out," and he proceeded to walk straight towards the rock.

I did a very large loop towards the rock, expecting to be blown up at any time. But Ernie was right, it had gone out. There was only two inches of fuse sticking out from the explosive package.

I said to Ernie, "You go back to our cover and I will light the fuse."

"No, two men must stay together to light the fuse," said Ernie.

I said, "No, you will not make it back under cover in time."

It ended up that we both lit the fuse. Ernie holding it, while I struck a match to it. It started to fizz; we only had seconds. Ernie couldn't extract himself from the hole. Did I leave him struggling to get out? I mean he was an old man of 85 years, he hasn't long to go anyway. I had stacks of years to live and a wife and children. Did I save myself and let him go to kingdom come, or did we both visit the kingdom together?

With my good heart, I dragged him out of the hole, helped him get to his feet and we hobbled to get to our predetermined cover. We didn't make it; we were thrown to the ground and felt a heavy blow to the stomach. The explosive noise echoed through the rocky gorge for some time. Rocks whistled past over our heads. We were shaken to the core.

Ernie remarked that he thought we might have moved the rock. We sure did. There were huge lumps of rocks for yards around. We found pieces even over our cover. Thank God, we were not there. It seemed that being close to the explosion, we were better off. Even though our bodies suffered the shockwaves than if we had been farther away, we certainly would have been hit by flying rocks. I drove a slightly shaken, old man back home, while I think I smoked four cigarettes in the last half hour, thinking I've got an almighty hole to fill.

Thanks Jack. You were lucky to survive, being the amateurs you were.

Life continued with school for the kids, hospital work for Helen and cleaning up and occasional horse rides for Jack. They were successful in their second submission to the Commonwealth Development Bank and work had to begin on the amenities block and cutting and grading a road to the camping ground. It was important to have both projects started and finished so more income could be made.

Yarramalong was slowly taking shape as a business enterprise. It wasn't going to make a profit for quite a while but, with hard work and ingenuity, it had to be successful. If it was going to be a recreation centre, one should do more than horse riding and camping. What other activities could one do to entice more people and groups to spend their money? And how could they let the world know they were here in this small country town 100 miles from the tourist centres of the Gold Coast and Sunshine Coast with their millions of dollars in marketing and advertising? What chance did they have?

C.24

Marketing and Activities

They paid a girl at the local newspaper to design and print their first brochures. They thought it was great but looking back on it, they were not the glossy, exciting brochure they should have produced. But then, they didn't have the finance. Wherever Jack went and saw a brochure rack in hotels, cafés or tourist information centres, whether legal or illegal, he just rearranged other brochures so his were at the front and at eye level. He didn't even ask. A bit rude.

His best idea was to prostitute himself. (No, not that!) He went and paid precious money for professional photos and a portfolio and tripped around to advertising officers and casting agents trying to sell his image. No way could they afford TV advertising, so why not meet the media people by doing commercial ads? Hopefully, there could be a payoff.

For a bloke with no experience but with some hide and desperation, Jack managed to be an extra in quite a few TV advertisements and documentaries. While doing this, he took their amateur brochures to the studios and passed them around to the crew and directors. It paid off. Not only did he make a bit of money from doing the ads but he also got people interested in the property for a great location. Some came and had fun horse riding and became regulars. Over time they had celebrities come and do shoots for their TV programs, like the show "Neighbours". The Solo Man made his ads in the creek, fighting crocodiles (pretend ones, of course. It's television, nothing is as it seems) and lots of ads and films were made over the years at Yarramalong.

There was more to come on this subject.

Meanwhile, Helen was busy with her nursing and enjoying it but she felt very uncomfortable working for the matron who, with her sisters, practically ran the hospital. Also, Helen felt all her experience and skills were not used and therefore, was frustrated daily, not being able to help patients when they needed her experience.

While Jack was being the... er... star, Helen was doing the school meetings, taking kids to their sports and music and dance lessons, was doing all the work of a good mother and wife. She started her new job as the pathologist at Boonah, working for two laboratories and also doing blood collections, driving around the district. Wait, there is more.

Jack was also learning orienteering skills, bush guiding and abseiling, while Helen was getting her canoe instructor's certification. How in the hell did they both manage it all?

Recap. All this took several years when Yarramalong was just beginning but, as the amenities block and road were finished and Jack had finished the clearing and sort of landscaping the two camping grounds, the extra recreation skills were learnt. The saddler and the horse bloke were paid off. Then, with hard work, no days off or holidays, their reward was loan rates on a now $200,000 combined business loan, rising from 10% up to 22% in 1986 to 1990. A killer blow.

They managed but how? All of Helen's wages went to pay

off the loan, while income from the Yarramalong Recreation Centre paid the essentials bills. When she could, Helen would ask the neighbouring farmers if she could pick up any vegetables left by the harvesters, such as carrots, potatoes, pumpkins, beans and whatever was available, which she did after work. She would then cut, dice or cook them up and put in the freezer. For meat, they bought just the cheapest mince. With all her efforts and cooking skills, even scraping spilled rice in the cupboards, she did a wonderful job feeding her family. Jack had locked up the cheque books and announced to the family that money was a non-existing commodity in the Alexander household.

Things were tough but, with hard work, determination and even frustration, they managed. Jack's training as a manager on properties had been a good education on keeping the books and an eagle eye on money coming in and going out and just plain managing the whole enterprise. Helen believed in Jack's ability to manage the finances and never spent money. Helen hated shopping and was very careful with grocery shopping getting only the bare essentials. She made all her own and her children's clothes and even a couple of shirts for Jack. They worked well together.

Jack, when he had a chance, visited public and private schools with brochures, which improved over the years from the originals. He typed up information on activities, programs, qualifications and the benefit of students doing outdoor education. It took a lot of time and Jack hated sitting outside the principal's office, the memories of doing so as a student gave him a churning stomach.

Everything was coming together but there were regrets. The children never had a family holiday together with both parents. When Helen could, she would take them to the Gold Coast for a week or to their Auntie Mack's at Coolum Beach. Someone had to stay at home as they kept Yarramalong opened seven days a week, 52 weeks a year! They could not afford to close down due to their debts and overheads and, of course, looking after now over 30 horses.

Through Jack's marketing, word of mouth and Helen's nursing and people skills, customers were schools, organisations, government and private and the general public. You would think with all that traffic they would be doing extremely well. But Jack and Helen were people people, wanting everyone to have fun and enjoyment on their property. They were not businesspeople and were a bit shy to charge the price they should have for the excellent service and facilities provided. It was not surprising that Helen sometimes conveniently forgot to charge some of poorest of the general public and Jack was no better, now and then letting a child or two of a family ride for free. But they paid their loans and bills. They educated their children and survived but never made any kind of profit in the 26 years they were there.

Another thing Jack and Helen did, was to get the Greater Brisbane Tourism Association off the ground. This incorporated seven local councils and a few private providers of tourism facilities. With finance from the councils and state government, a lot was achieved in getting tourism noticed in the greater Brisbane area. Jack was in an executive position and had contacts with the media, especially with Des McWilliams who, at that time, was the evening news reader at Channel Ten. He asked Des if it was possible to showcase some of the tourism places of the tourism association on television. Des said it would be impossible considering the program of the television stations. But he did try and managed to get a few seconds in a gap in the programs.

The board of the tourism association gave Jack the opportunity to discuss further with Des MacWilliams about showcasing tourism on television. It ended up with the Great Outdoors and now all television stations have produced their versions of the program, to advise viewers on holidays they can take, not only in the greater Brisbane Area but in Queensland, Australia and the world.

I think Des and Jack should get their due compensation having started all those great information shows. Thought I should mention it. Helen took over Jack's role later as an executive of the Greater Brisbane Tourism Association.

C.25

Bless the Horses

Yarramalong was the place of horses. A riding school. Not any riding school but the best Jack could make it. There was no bolting for home, as they were well-educated horses that knew their job. A lot of riding, training, study and research before any paying customer rode one of Jack's horses.

Jack spent hours riding each horse, getting them to know the three trails and always resting them at the same spots so the horses learnt these were stop areas and could go no further for a few minutes. That was to teach them, no matter what any frightened or overconfident smart rider might do, they stopped at these designated areas. Damon helped on the weekends, riding the smaller horses and ponies. A well-worked horse was a good, safe horse.

Another thing Jack did, which was very unusual and seemed a bit stupid. When no one was about and all the horses were mustered to the yard early in the morning, Jack would pretend to be the herd boss stallion. He would put on a very angry demeanor, his face was anger, his body stance was anger. He walked and ran around the horses, pretending to kick and bite them and boss them around, exactly as a stallion would do in the wild to control his herd. With this act of Jack's, surprisingly, they took him for their leader and were always devoted to him.

Of course, he loved them too: grooming them, rubbing them, always talking to them and saying how much he loved them.

There was always clean water for them to drink and the best quality feed when it was necessary in the winter or dry months. However, usually there was plenty of variety in feed in the 300 acres of Yarramalong.

The horses were happy and well-behaved but more needed to be done. Jack had now been riding horses for nigh on 30 years as a stockman and a qualified pony instructor of the British Horse Society. Even though their instruction ended with Olympic gold medal winners, and the queen and her children learnt their riding from that organisation as it taught dressage, jumping, and three-day eventing, Jack was not convinced it was the be all and end all in horse riding.

He took his faithful horse, Peter, who for many years was Jack's demo horse, down to the oval at the camping ground. For a week, Jack rode and analysed what he did to make the horse automatically do what he wanted.

After the week's training session, he rode some of the other horses and, lo and behold, they reacted to Jack's demands as Peter the demo horse had done.

Being in the saddle for weeks and months on end, not for a few hours but up to eight, even 14 hours, it was only natural that the body became attuned to the horse's movements. In other words, the rider and the horse were as one. That's okay but how did Jack teach it to beginners? That's the question and that is why Jack spent a week analysing himself and his riding.

He wrote down what he had found out and it became a beginner's guide to horse riding on trails and in the bush. Nothing was done about his research but it was there as you will find out later on. However, let's talk about Jack's customers, who they were, how they went, the incidents and the fun.

Starting with the schools, Brisbane Grammar, and a few of the general public, were the first group to ride at Yarramalong. One of the conditions was, it had to be educational. At the beginning, the horse's reins were attached to a hook of wire on the posts in the large riding yard. Later on, shady stalls were built. They were all lined up, groomed and saddled, ready for the ride. The 15 Year Eight students were lined up outside against the yard rail while Jack with Peter the demo were in the yard facing the students. This was briefly how it went:

"Good afternoon, welcome to Yarramalong. My name is Jack Alexander, and this is Peter the demo horse. I would like to give you a lesson before you get your horse and ride off into the sunset like John Wayne.

"When you are allocated your chosen horse, do not run up to it or sneak, just walk normally, talking to the horse just as you would meeting a person. Then, unhook the reins from the post and lead your horse to an open space.

"Now to get the reins over the horse's head, hold them and give the horse a rub on the nose, then take them over his head, doing it gently and while talking to the horse. He might not understand you but it helps him to understand your body language. Then watch closely. This is how you safely mount a horse."

Jack would show them on Peter, mounting, holding the reins, how to stop, how to turn, how to make the horse go, dismounting, thanking the horse for the ride and putting him back exactly where you got him from. Finally, taking the reins gently back over his head and putting them on the hook.

"Any questions?"

"Are the horses quiet?"

"Yes, they don't make a sound."

"Can we pick our own horse?"

"No, I will do it for you as I can look into your eyes and read your personality and match it with the horse's personality, so the good kids get the good horses, cheeky kids, the cheeky ones and the kids that have never ridden before get the horses that have never been ridden. Any more questions?"

Then Jack would look in their eyes and sort them out, not by the terror in their eyes, but by their body language.

"Now the ones that have never ridden, move to your left, the ones that have ridden a bit but not overly confident, move to your right and the ones that are confident, stay where you are."

The young students walked up to their horses. Some hesitated, some went straight up to them and some decided they really didn't want to go horse riding that day. But seeing it was a school activity, they had no choice, according to Mr Jim Johnston, the head recreation teacher of Brisbane Grammar's Moogerah Outdoor Centre. So students, whether they liked it or not, were lifted on to their horses if they couldn't mount by themselves.

Did you know horses have a sense of humour? As the students walked up to them, sometimes they would turn and look at the poor fellow and put their ears back or swish their tail or move to the side. I'm sure, after the riding session, they the horses would have a good laugh amongst themselves.

"Did you see the frightened look that kid had? Bet he shit himself. Hehe."

"No, what about when I went close to a tree and the kid thought I would brush him off? Hehe."

"Oh dear, the way they bounced on our backs, I'm sure we may have damaged their future family prospectives. Less humans, what ya say? Neigh, neigh."

After the ride, the excited chatter indicated most students

had to be made to leave their mount as they wanted to stay and pat and rub them. It was always the same, except for some rare exceptions, of all the people that rode the horses. It was claimed by the students that it was the best activity of their week's camp.

Jack realised what a good thing he was doing for city kids that had no idea of animals or country life. Three examples:

He was asked by a very nervous rider, "Do the horses cock their leg to have a wee?"

Jack's answer was, "Wait till he sits down to have a poo." Which of course didn't help the panicky rider.

Another time. "Oh sir, the horse has ripped his guts open and there are intestines hanging down."

"No son, that's his dick hanging down and he is showing off."

And yet another. "What's that funny sound coming from his belly? Is he sick?"

"No, that's just his penis rubbing inside his sheath. You can ask your teacher if you don't understand the words."

Talk about horses and their humour. Peter the demo horse, whenever a group of female students or, for that matter, any group of females were given a demo to ride when Jack was on his back, Peter would purposely unsheathe his penis to its full extent. Worst of all, he would, ever so slightly, move so it wobbled from side to side.

Jack tried to stop his exhibition by kicking and pinching him on the opposite side so the clientele couldn't see. But the demo would then be a waste of time as the prospective riders ignored Jack with their interest diverted to Pete's member. Jack tried many ways to stop this from happening but never had success.

Over the years that Helen and Jack were at Yarramalong, over 80,000 clients rode their horses. They were students from public and private schools, the general public, kids on remission, programs for disadvantaged children from Maroon

- the government recreation centre, rehabilitation centres, Endeavour Foundation for Down syndrome children. You think about it and they had them riding their horses.

The horses got to know the people. For instance, if it was St Lawrence school, Year 12 boys, full of testosterone, the horses followed their behaviour and would be very lively. Then again, if he had a nervous group or beginners, they were very docile. As an example, when Jack had the Down syndrome children riding, after a small talk they had to get their horses. There was screaming, yelling and running near the horses' legs, sitting down and all sorts of behaviours. Did the horses care? They knew what was on and acted very calmly, completely different from the Year 12 boys.

Jack was one of the first to use horses with children and adults with chronic disabilities. It took time. Of course, some were so disabled it would never be a feasible proposition. But if there was the slightest chance, Jack would do his best to give them a safe ride.

Sometimes it would take a few sessions or visits to be able to take those clients on a trail ride, but he did. He would tie a cord from the bit, through the two saddle Ds then on to the bit on the other side with enough tension so the horse thought the person had control, even though hands were everywhere hanging on to the pommel of the saddle or scratching their nose or whatever. To take them for an hour's safe trail ride gave, not only the clients a huge sense of achievement, but to Jack it was the ultimate joy giving to those that had limited ability. He was on a high every time.

Remembering a couple of adult mental health clients, after one ride, one of the men said to the other, "You thank Jack for a fun ride." The other said nothing.

"I told you to thank Jack for the ride or I'll hit you," said the first man.

Still the other said nothing and he got hit.

"I can't stand people that have no manners," said the first man, then he walked to the coach.

Meanwhile the chap that got hit said to no-one in particular, "He didn't give me time," as he followed the hitter into the bus.

Another one who thought he was a pilot of an aeroplane, even wore a captain's cap and talked constantly of flying, started to fly and fell of the horse, not hurting himself but kept repeating, "Quarter past two, quarter past two."

Jack was asking him if he was alright and helping him back into the saddle, he enquired why was he saying quarter past two.

He replied, "Quarter past two, time of accident. Need time for compensation."

Later on, there were riding safaris that went for three days in the surrounding countryside. Both for the general public, who were given the demos and the rules and schools, which had two-hour riding lessons the day before to make them safe before taking them into the never never. At first, Jack used a pack horse. Later, Helen would come and set up tents and have food already prepared for the evening meals.

There were a couple of frightening experiences for Jack on these school safaris. Both of these were at Johnstone's yards where they yarded the horses overnight. This day, as it was finishing with horses in the yard, the students from a private girls' school were putting up their tents and cooking their own meals on the one fire that had been lit. As part of the three-day exercise, they had to supply and cook their own meals. Girl's groups managed good hot tasty meals, while boy's groups brought chips, lollies, muesli bars and other such stuff. When it was a mixed group and the boys saw what the girls were cooking, they were so helpful, begging for the girls would give them some of their meal. They would just about do anything for them and, as normal, the girls had slaves for the rest of the safari.

Back to Jack. As the meals were being cooked, it started to rain. Just lightly at the start but, by bedtime, it got heavier. Jack normally slept in his swag under the stars but he must have known something as he had brought his little one-man tent on this trip.

He woke up in the middle of the night and felt water in his tent which, to him, was strange as he didn't think it had rained that much. Then he felt himself physically rolled down the slope, inside the tent. The whole area was flooded. It was black and dark. *Where was the opening zipper?* He could not find it. *What was happening?* He was locked inside what felt like a plastic bag in a raging surf.

A good stockman always carried a knife. He found it and slashed the tent to get out: cold, soaking wet, no clothes except for wet underpants. Could he go up to the female teacher's tent or students in the condition he was in? No. He got some damp saddle blankets and huddled with his horses. Bless his dear Helen, who came round very early to see if everything was alright after the heavy storm. She drove Jack home for a hot shower, change and a quick breakfast and drove him back to the camp as the girls were getting up and starting a fire for their breakfast.

Jack found out what had happened. As normal, he'd set his camp well away from the students and, as it so happened, a dam had burst its banks with the students well above its reach but our Jack was below and copped the full force of the water as the bank gave way.

Another incident happened at the same spot but at a different time. It was with a school group of boys, rather energetic and it took a bit to quieten them down. Jack, in his swag, well away from the school tents and students, had just gone off to sleep when a strong loud voice said, "Identify yourself."

Jack thought it was one of the kids mucking about and said, "For God's sake, get back to your tent, shut up and let me sleep."

The voice spoke much louder, "Identify yourself or cop the consequence."

"It's Jack from Yarramalong. Who is this and what's your problem?"

"Police here, I know this chap, stand down."

The local copper walked up to Jack, asking, "What are you doing here?"

"As you can see, I have a school camp here. Can't you see all the tents and the horses in the yard? Mr Johnstone knows we are camping here, so what's wrong with you?"

"Your campfire was reported and we have a murderer been sighted in Aratula. He murdered two women at a horse ranch west of Brisbane."

"Well, you could have saved all your trouble if you had just rung Mr Johnstone, instead of getting a squad from Ipswich because someone had a sighting of a campfire."

Jack was angry. Not only was he woken up because of the incompetency of the local police but if he had got out of his swag and stood up, he could have been shot by a nervous constable.

Jack asked, "Would you mind leaving our campsite with your crew now and I will report this ridiculous incident to your superiors?"

Jack snuggled back down in his swag as the police left but he didn't go to sleep. Helen was on her own on a horse place and a murderer had been sighted in the district. He thought he had better saddle his horse and make sure she was safe; he knew the track well, even at night but it would take a couple of hours to get there. Then, if Helen had heard the news about the murder and Jack woke her up in the early hours of the morning, you could bet she would have the shot gun beside their bed and Jack could get shot. He gave that idea away.

Then Jack's imagination started to interfere with his sleepy mind.

What if we search the foothills of Mt Edwards and found the murderer? He wouldn't stand a chance. Knock him out by swinging the stirrup iron then tying him across the saddle and, like a good western, arrive at the police station with the criminal tied to his horse with Jack leading the possie of the student boys. Just like in the western movies, a great news story and advertising for Yarramalong.

Alas, it didn't happen; the murderer was found in another district.

Because of their business, Jack became prominent in the tourist and outdoor industry and knew big changes were coming, in regard to regulations, insurance, registered guides and leaders and, the big one, insurance.

Jack was at a national conference on the outdoor industry in Canberra and met another delegate from Tasmania who knew about problems with the horse industry. Jack showed him what he had written about safe horse riding.

The chap said, "I'll read it tonight and tell you what I think about it in the morning."

Next morning, he said to Jack, "You have copied this nearly word for word from the American Association for Horsemanship Safety and Education."

Jack was shocked. What he had written was straight from his head and not copied at all. He informed his colleague it was his own work and had never heard of that association. He would find out about it. It was agreed and suggested that he bring any findings about the association and whether or not they could provide benefits to Australia in the same industry. It would be put on the agenda at the next conference.

Jack wrote away and paid for the manual of Horsemanship, Safety and Education and after reading it thoroughly from cover-to-cover, Jack was amazed and surprised that it was so similar to what he had written. So, he went to the United States to their conference held near Lake Erie. He qualified as a trail instructor and pack leader and arranged for one of their instructors to come to Australia and run clinics.

The instructor came out, ran clinics in all states, paid for by the Camping Association of Australia and trained instructors in all states. Now adopted by all state governments, the rules and regulations for horse riding in Australia covered all aspects of the horse industry. This is something Jack is proud of: initiating this safety program for horse riding in Australia.

A few famous horsey comments:

"Ony an aviator or an equestrian has a right to look down on others."

"Always look a gift horse in the mouth."

"Horse sense is the ability to say neigh."

"Fools breed horses for men to ride."

C.26

Rocky Road, Near Death
Helen's new Life

Yarramalong Recreation Centre was growing quickly. Jack had to employ a full-time riding instructor/guide and a casual maintenance man but that was enough. Jack was doing the horse rides, (you now needed two riding guides to take a trail ride) plus organising the school groups, plus marketing and going to meetings. He was also looking after the general public camping site. It was all too much.

Of course, after work, Helen was busy with customers and working on the weekends but it was not enough. Jack needed her full time on the property. The business was half hers, why did she keep her job at the pathologists? At the beginning, her wages and job were vital getting Yarramalong started and on the road to success. But after five years, the property was paying for itself and Jack was paying staff much more than what Helen was bringing home. He desperately needed her full-time.

Our two lovers had been on a smooth bitumen road up to now. That road had now turned to gravel with a few potholes. Jack's argument was, it was half her business, why didn't she help run it? Helen's argument was, "I love my job, why should

I leave it and be told what to do every day by my husband? Everything seems okay with the centre and he has two staff so I will continue to enjoy what I'm doing."

The desperate plea from Jack for her to stay, as Helen went to work every morning, was ignored and the loving relationship started to break down. Arguments started about little things. Jack tried to keep his frustration and anger in check but sometimes it spilt over. Of course, Helen, as always, kept to herself, never explaining anything, hoping Jack's 'tantrum' would end sometime.

But Jack, working 18 hours a day, seven days a week, had another problem. His darling children, who he loved so much, eventually left home. He would always wait for the school bus to bring them home, to enjoy their company. Damon always helped with the horses and Debbie always helped her dad get dinner ready for when mum came home.

But they left. Damon went down to the Gold Coast to start his carpentry apprenticeship and Debs started her business degree at Toowoomba university. Did they keep in touch with their depressed Dad? No, they were enjoying new friends and places. Who could blame them?

What happened to a man who was overworked, unhappy and thinks he has lost his loving family? He got sick. Jack, would you like to tell about your near-death experience?

If I have to.

I was flat out doing horses, rides, cleaning the amenities block, looking after the campers' needs. Helen had taken a week off to run a teenagers' holiday, which we did in the September school holidays.

It was a hot day, running around trying to do everything that had to be done. When finished, I started to make myself some dinner. I just didn't feel right and thought I must have had sunstroke.

I couldn't finish my dinner and thought I would have a cold shower and lie down. That didn't help, either. I just felt funny. That's all I can describe it as but, somehow, I felt like I could collapse, but what from? I didn't have a fever or pain, I just felt very uncomfortable. I laid down and tried to go to sleep but that was a failure, I should drive the two kilometres to Helen who was down with the holiday kids. But what if I collapsed on my way down? Then I would be denied any help whatsoever.

In desperation, I took the chance and drove down to the camping ground and woke Helen up in her tent.

I said, "Sorry love but I don't feel so good."

She didn't check me out, just got dressed and woke the recreation student that was helping her, saying "Jack is not well, I'm taking him to hospital." Then she said, "Let's go," as she entered the car.

We drove up to the house and told me to get dressed as she was taking me to the hospital. I protested saying, "I'm not sick enough to go to hospital, I just feel funny."

"Do as you're told, we are going to Boonah Hospital and that's that." I didn't realise, but Helen had noted my diaphragm was up to my chest and that something was seriously wrong with me.

The doctor at Boonah Hospital hardly looked at me and said, "I will arrange for him to be admitted to St Andrews hospital immediately, I'll call for an ambulance or would you prefer to take him there yourself?"

Helen said she would take me as he gave me a morphine injection.

"What's that for?" I said.

"It's for your pain."

"I haven't got any pain."

"Well, for your benefit, I'm giving it to you anyway."

The drive down to the hospital was okay except poor Helen was getting driving instructions all the time from me. We arrived at the emergency entrance, where a smart suited doctor took one look at me and said, "I think we should operate immediately."

The image I had was of the doctor standing on the steps sharpening a carving knife.

Not on yer nellie was I going to be cut up. I said, "I'm not having an operation till you tell me what's wrong with me."

"I suppose you want a second opinion," he said rather shortly.

"Yes," I said. It was around 1am on this particular Thursday morning.

After a while, another suited doctor appeared and confirmed with the other doctor that indeed, I should have an operation straight away. I couldn't understand why they wanted to cut me open when they didn't know what was wrong with me and why was the only treatment an operation? I refused. They put me in a single room with my own bathroom and did some observations.

I woke up a few hours later in excruciating pain. It was indescribable. I suffered from bad migraines but these pains now felt like they were killing me. I now had tubes in my arms and a catheter. Drugs were killing me. My body was shutting down due to the pain and drugs, so for four hours, I was in terrible agony, then there were four hours of drugs.

I was dying on the Sunday. After Helen had finished the kids' camp, she was told by the doctor that there was a good chance I wouldn't survive the next 24 hours and to be prepared for the worst. She brought my darling teenage children to see me; they were beautifully dressed in their best clothes to visit their dad for perhaps the last time. I didn't want them to see their dad practically naked with tubes coming out of his body and bottles of human fluid hanging from the bed frame.

What I said to them next, I have always regretted to this day. I said, "Get out! Get out of my room," and they left. If I had died, that would have been their last memory of me.

Helen had my mother and my sister ring me but I could hardly *speak to them, I was so weak. I was told by the doctor that the man in the next room had died from the same illness that I had.*

"And that's what?" I asked through pain spasms.

"You have septicaemia."

Google said the mortality rate for septicaemia was over 50%. For abdominal sepsis, which I had, it climbed to 72% and approximately 30% survived after the first year of hospital admission. And I'm still here.

The nursing care, at that time at that hospital, was shocking. They left me for dead: no comfort, no washing, no shaving, just rushing in with water or drugs and observation. At one time, I lay in horrific pain under the bed, with my finger on the help button. No one arrived for half an hour as they were at afternoon tea.

How did I know it was half an hour? Because I timed them, as I had to keep some sort of brain function going. Also, sick and dying as I was, I would wait till two in the morning, when all was quiet, gather my bottles and stuff and hobble into the shower. It was the only thing keeping me alive to feel the lovely, warm water pouring all over me. I really couldn't wash or dry myself but it made me feel refreshed and alive. The Sunday night that I was supposed to die, I was having my regular two o'clock morning shower, when my doctor walked in. Seeing the bed empty, he must have thought I had been taken to the morgue, and he thinking he had been up all night to make sure is the patient was alright. Then he heard the shower going, busted open the door, looked at the poor creature showering and said in a loud angry tone, "Yer fucking dancing in the shower," and slammed the door and was gone.

By Monday, I was starting to feel a tiny bit better. On Tuesday, I cried all day. It must have been my body in total relief from the infection. Wednesday, I was still very weak but slowly feeling my old self again.

On Thursday, the doctor on his regular visits said, "You can have the tubes taken out this morning, including the catheter. It could have come out on Tuesday but I wanted to teach you a lesson for dancing in the shower."

He went on to say, "If we operated on you last Thursday, it would have been a touch and go operation as your body was so infected and swollen, it would have been a very messy and dangerous operation to perform. But you being such a cantankerous, head strong and tough individual, you accurately did the right thing and let the infection take its course. You may go home Saturday then get your strength back. You will need to get your damaged gall bladder taken out as it was the organ that caused the problem."

I went home and back to work. No sick leave for the self-employed. Until I met our family doctor in the street a few weeks later.

"What are you doing in the street? You are a walking time bomb. Ring up and get you operation done now."

He frightened me so I rang up when I got home and was booked in for three days' time.

At the hospital again with Helen, at five in the afternoon, prepped and shaven for an early morning operation. I just didn't want to lay there for the next 12 hours worrying about my virgin torso being violated. So, I asked the nursing sister if Helen and I could go to the pictures. She said, "No, you are already prepped."

I insisted so she said, "I will ring the doctor."

The answer was, "Let him go to the pictures; it will be safer for the hospital and staff. Tell him not to eat anything at all and be back as soon as the film is over."

With my hospital gown tucked in to my clothes, to the pictures we went. I don't remember which one but we both enjoyed it. As we sat outside the hospital, I had my very last smoke, kissed Helen and went into the slaughterhouse.

They cut me open from close to the centre of my chest, nearly down to my right hip. Eventually, the doctor wanted to check out all my organs. Gall bladder was out, a few days convalescing and

Helen was back at her pathology job. A week after the op, I was shoeing horses. It was a bit painful with all those stitches but when it's gotta be done, it's gotta be done.

Thanks Jack. That was an ordeal you went through now let me now finish their story.

Nothing had changed much. Helen was still at work, Jack was still trying to do everything but the incident gave them a big fright. Jack wanted a proper holiday. He hadn't had one since eight years ago when he burnt his feet. He used to be interested in the characters, the Beagle boys in South America from the Donald Duck comics and he wanted to go to South America. It was not a popular tourist place in 1989. Helen agreed and Damon took his holidays to look after the place with Joanne, our great horse instructor guide.

It was a small adventure group traveling to South America. First stop was Buenos Aires, Argentina and they loved the old, wide city roads and the tango dancing on each street corner. Meals were cheap as was everything else. The American dollar was king in a country that was experiencing 100% a day inflation.

Jack and Helen then took a flight to La Paz, Bolivia, where Helen enjoyed the Mata de Coca tea. Jack got very sick on it. It was complimentary, given by the hotel to help with climate sickness but Jack vomited all over the hotel foyer and was crook that night. Was it the tea or the climate? Jack came good later the next day but Helen and the rest of the group kept drinking the tea and were giggling, saying things they really shouldn't. They must have been half drugged. They loved the Witches' Market and the top-hatted women with their large skirts.

Then they took an interesting trip to Lake Titicaca, which bordered Bolivia and Peru, an unforgettable train ride in Peru, to Puno then on to Cuzco. They visited Machu Picchu in the Sacred Valley of the Andes Mountains, with its outstanding produce, everything large and delicious. Then they experienced a terrifying bus trip down the most dangerous road with gravel turns and twists, where they all thought they were going to die. They finally arrived safely at Cocachacra in the province of Islay in Peru.

They fell out of the bus, thanking God for still being alive. Some passengers were in shock and a bit delirious. Next stop was Arequipa and a bus ride through the Atacama Desert. It was officially the driest place on earth receiving no rainfall, whatsoever. Bones and skulls of soldiers and armies long past, who had perished trying to cross the desert, could still be found in the sand. Why was it important in this story?

The bus stopped for lunch and Jack ate something and he was immediately sick. He went behind a huge boulder and stayed there for a while trying to recover, then went back to the group. Neither the bus, nor the group were there. They had all vanished.

He crawled back to the road but found nothing. He was stranded in an inhospitable desert, no water and nothing to survive on. In 40 degree celsius heat, there was nothing Jack could do except wait in the hope a vehicle would come along. It would be a long wait as no vehicles had been seen once they left the Arequipa area. Finally, Jack saw a bus emerging from the heat haze. It was going in the wrong direction but then, he realised, it was his bus coming to look for him.

The bus driver had not checked and counted his passengers. Helen had thought Jack got on the bus but was sulking in the back seat as she wouldn't swap sandwiches. Thank God she didn't. Jack's must have been old meat or something. If Helen had it, she would have been gravely ill as her ileostomy would have not coped. As it was, Jack was very sick for the next three days with bad gastro. He missed out on seeing most of the famous geoglyphs, the Nazca lines and wondering if he would survive.

They took a frightening flight by Faucett Airlines to Iquitos. There they would go down the Amazon by boat to Leticia, in Colombia. The saw giant water lilies and many little villages. Helen was shocked that what they saw, was not natural jungle but regrowth from logging and clearing.

One passenger said to a chief of one of the villages they stopped at, "It's a disgrace what you people and your governments have done to this country: logging, mining and clearing all of the natural Amazon."

The reply was, "You rich tourists have made all your money from mining, logging and clearing, why shouldn't we? We are poor and will never be a tourist like yourself. We have to make a living somehow." A very embarrassed tourist had nothing to say and just walked away.

Helen caught the first piranha fish. She had to be quick as they bite the line in half as soon as they come out of the water. What scalpel teeth they had. Jack managed one but Helen managed three. They ate them for tea. It was an interesting boat trip as they saw lots of interesting wildlife, including pink porpoises and caymans.

They always moored the boat at night, usually at one of their tiny jetties made for the tourist boats. They were now on the Colombia, Peru and Brazil borders, when things started to happen.

At midnight, voices were screaming and there was the banging on cabin doors. *Levantarse! Fuera!!* Get up! Get out!!

Jack opened the cabin door to see what was going on. He was confronted with a very young solider with cross belts of ammunition over his shoulders and chest, holding a very lethal gun. He motioned for him to stand aside. In the meantime, Helen came out, putting a light gown over her nightdress. She was also instructed, like Jack and all the rounded-up passengers, still in their night gear, and the small crew of captain, cook and deckhand, to march off the boat into the jungle.

Spanish was spoken rapidly and loudly. A lot of shouting was going on. The captain was the most vocal. Who were these people? What did they want? These are innocent tourists, what right have you to round up my customers in the middle of the night? Jack guessed that would be the sort of things he was yelling.

There were six of these young terrorist soldiers, all heavily armed, marching them through the jungle on a small dirt track in the middle of the night. They had been kidnapped! The track was lit up by the moon but there were lots of shadows from the trees and brush. Were there snakes or anacondas or deadly spiders they might be stepping on? Where were they taking us? What's going to happen to us? We are going to be robbed and murdered or held for millions of dollars for ransom. This, Jack imagined, would have been going through the minds of the tourists.

Jack was in the lead behind the guiding soldier with Helen close behind. She was not going to lose sight of him. The crew at the back were still voicing their angry disapproval. The other tourists in the line were being pushed along, not physically, but by voice and gestures. They were marched for about an hour. There were too many thoughts by the group to think of time.

They came to a large, unpainted, timbered house, a few steps and a veranda which opened into a large room. There was quite a long counter and behind this was, Jack guessed, the leader of the kidnappers, with soldiers standing erect each side of him, ready to use their automatic weapons at his slightest command. Jack, being in the lead, watched the guards intently and if he saw the slightest movement of the eyes or body, he would duck behind the counter, not thinking of his wife who was just behind him.

The captain, still verbalising in loud Spanish, came to the front, speaking to this officer/leader. To Jack's dismay, he was holding all their passports, then with a lot of Spanish and gestures, handed them all to the leader.

The captain turned and said quietly to us, all in good English, "I'm sorry, I don't know what's going on but I suggest you don't talk, sit down on the floor where you are while I negotiate with this officer and get you back to the boat as quickly as I can. I don't think any harm will come to you."

He thinks, that's no guarantee, thought Jack as his and Helen's hands came together for security and comfort. Helen leaned into Jack and whispered, "Have you thought of an escape plan yet?" Jack just held his finger to his lips and did a quiet ssssh.

The sun came up. Luckily, they were in the shade all the time but it was still hot. Everyone was getting restless, going from one bum cheek to the next on the hard floor. Some of the women in night dresses, with no knickers on, like Helen, had to be conscientious to keep their legs together. Very difficult, sitting on the uncomfortable floor. Small bottles of commercial water were handed to them all by the boat cook, which was badly needed, but there was no food. The captain and the leader disappeared into a joining room and the two guards were changed by two more. The young soldiers who walked us off the boat came and went but there were always a few, as well as the ones behind the counter, keeping an eye on us.

If someone spoke, one of them got up and stood beside the perpetrator glaring, yelling, *Callarse, callarse.* Shut up, shut up. They knew that word by the end of the day, as it was difficult to sit for such a long time and the Spanish words were heard often.

The sun was going down and the captain came out of a room and said, "I still don't understand what they want but I suggest you all slowly stand up and find your way back to the boat. Help yourselves to food and whatever you need. We the crew are being held here."

They all got up stiffly, some having difficulty after sitting for such a long time and started to find their way back to the boat. This time, Jack was at the back of the group and, as they were walking onto the veranda, the captain shouted, "I don't think they will shoot."

A funny sensation ran up and down Jack's spine as he followed the group into the jungle.

They managed to find the boat, just as the sun was setting. The first thing they did was raid the galley for food. Helen and two other women decided to cook a meal for all of them, as Jack and others searched for snacks while the meal was being prepared and cooked. The skipper and crew arrived back at the boat about 9.30 that same evening and asked each of them individually to come up to the bridge and sign a statement about what happened and how they were treated. As they signed it, one of the passengers next in line witnessed it.

The captain was still angry about what had happened and he would, with our statements, make one himself and send a copy to his boss as well as to the President of the Colombian Government.

The passengers noticed, when they got back to their cabins, all their belongings at been rifled through but nothing was taken. What they were searching for or what the kidnapping was all about, remained a mystery to this day

That was their big adventure after visiting places in Brazil including: Manaus, Brasilia, Salvador in the state of Bahia and Rio, then it was back to Argentina with a visit to Iguazu Falls and finally returning to Buenos Aires, then home.

Damon and Joanne did a marvellous job looking after the place, while Debbie was busy studying in Toowoomba. Helen went back to pathology and Jack back on the horses and running Yarramalong after a great and needed holiday.

Finally, after much not-so-patient waiting, the question

came to Jack. He had his answer well prepared. Rarely did Helen ask a question. Her thought was, if you wanted me to know something, you would tell me.

The question?

"If I did come home, what would I do?"

"Well, it's up to you but it would be great if you looked after the camping customers, the groups and do the activities and you would be paid the going rate and superannuation, as I know you like having control over your own money," Jack said. "That would be your half and responsibility of Yarramalong. While I would do the horses, administration and marketing as well as maintenance. With no interference by either party how they run their half of the centre. How does that sound?"

Phew, it was agreed without question.

It was the best thing that happened. Helen loved her job, really loved it, besides nursing, it may have been better. She thrived in her role.

In the ATV, with the little back covered tray, she would go down and sell fresh milk, bread and ice. She also hired out the canoes and the wood for fires and had lovely chats, cleaned the toilets and checked the rubbish bins for Jack to empty. She did the same mid-morning and, in the evenings, would chat away to everyone and be shouted a wine every now and then. This was during the weekends and holidays with the general public. She ran two teenager holiday camps, one at Christmas and one in September, where she camped with the kids. In the meantime, Jack had a big indoor centre with a large kitchen and a little shop built.

After getting her hygiene cooking certificate, Helen started to cook for the camping schools and the teenager camps. She also had her canoe instructor certificate. In her spare time, she studied fun game books for children and adults, orienteering, guiding and made a program of all the eatable plants residing at Yarramalong. There was also a bird book, which anyone who was interested, could add to the list. They had a lot of twitchers come and build their hideouts to add to the list but only those birds seen within the Yarramalong boundaries. It's believed that 109 birds had been spotted at the last count.

Helen had her hands full with all her activities looking after everyone, did a bit of nursing when needed for a camper or child. Anything serious would have been dealt with at the local hospital, which was extremely rare. It was usually a parent not keeping a close eye on their children, such as a child burnt at a campfire or a child swinging a large stick around and clobbering their sibling. All in all, Helen had a ball and tried to think of interesting, fun things for all that came to Yarramalong.

C.27

Happenings and Incidents at Yarramalong

There were always funny things happening at Yarramalong, well for Jack and Helen, at least.

Like the dad who tied a guy rope from the family tent to his car, then later on drove off to get more beer, while his wife was having a nap in the tent. It was to the amusement of all, even the wife, who was unhurt, thought it was funny. There were a few words to her husband, not fit for children's ears.

Two girls turned up with a tiny one-man tent. One girl was very masculine, with short-cropped hair and dressed like a man. The other was delicate in a pretty dress and curly long hair. As they were standing beside this tiny tent, Helen asked them, "Did you two sleep in that small tent?"

They both nodded a yes and Helen, in all her innocence, said, "You must have slept on top of each other."

Often, they had people coming from the other side of the creek, which was not the Alexander property, pinching their canoes without permission. Helen caught one man and accused him of stealing.

He replied, "I'm just having a lend of it."

Helen noticed a very expensive Fat Boy Harley Davison bike on the bank.

"Well then, you don't mind me having a lend of your bike?"

He replied, "If you could ride it."

Helen said, "Don't go away, I'll just get my helmet and leathers."

The canoe was promptly brought back to its right place and the man took off. This was typical of the way Helen dealt with people.

Another time, one of the campers informed Jack, "Those foreign men over there," pointing to a group of five around a campfire, "they are a bit strange. One of them kept guard while the others slept and we think they barbequed some of your possums."

Jack went over to them, had a friendly yarn, then had a walk around the area and found some guts and possum skins. He went back and said, "I believe you killed and ate some of our possums. We don't like that behaviour here. I kindly ask, when you have cleaned up your campsite, including the guts and skins, that you leave."

Which they did but put the guts and skins, unwrapped, in the rubbish bins which Jack then had to deal with.

Then, what about the bloke trying to cut a large gum tree with an axe. Jack always maintained their campground was National Parks. In a way, it was, since they joined the boundary with them.

He rode up to the man who was busily chopping and said to him, "That's a very expensive tree you're chopping. It's a $2,000 fine for chopping down a National Parks tree. I am now forced to fine you for that sum."

As Jack was talking and bluffing the camper, guess what he did. He was bending down, gathering up the wood chips and trying to put them back where he cut them out of the tree. Some people!

They had a military court martial on the campgrounds. The military sometimes had their adventure camps at Yarramalong, where it was a bit of recreation and a bit of volunteer work on the property. It so happened, two soldiers went to the pub in a military vehicle to get more supplies. The problem was, the sergeant, who was licenced to drive the vehicle, was too inebriated to drive it back, so an unlicenced corporal had to take the driver's seat, where he rolled it on the property. Hence the court martial.

Two officers arrived to conduct the proceedings and set up their desk and chairs under a shady tree in the middle of the campground. The two defendants were separated, one each end of the camping ground, told not to speak to each other and write their full statements regarding the occurrence on the Saturday night last.

A shouting match started.

"Hey Bill, what time was the accident?"

"How would I bloody well know but what was the date last Saturday?"

The two officers shouted their warning not to speak to each other but they continued to do so. Jack, who was cleaning the toilet block, was highly amused at what was going on. It was like a good comedy show. It really was a serious event; the sergeant lost his stripes and was downgraded in pay, while the corporal was given discipline duty.

It was Christmas time. They had a group of kindergarten children having their Christmas party at the campgrounds. There was excitement and anticipation of Father Christmas arriving. One of the parents dressed in a Santa costume with a large bag of toys, climbed into Jack's spring cart beside Jack, with dear old Major pulling it.

As they rounded the last bend of the track, coming into the

area, where the children were singing Jingle Bells, Santa stood up in the cart. He pulled out a huge, brass school bell from his toy bag, which he rang enthusiastically and loudly, yelling, "HO, HO, HO!"

Dear old Major got such a fright at this sudden unexplained, loud noise. There were only two things a horse might do. Bolt or come to a dead stop. Without warning, he came to a dead stop. Father Christmas shot out over the cart rail with the bell and bag of toys. Jack noticed the size nines written on the soles of his boots as he disappeared over the front.

Were the kids upset about Father Christmas's fate? The burst bag of toys, with all its contents spread over the field, got more of their interest as they were checking for their names written on the tags than poor Santa's health.

After calming the frightened horse down, Jack picked up the dazed, costumed parent and asked why in the hell did he ring the bell. He thought it would be fun. Fun. Jack still chuckles at those size nine boots disappearing over the cart with the wearer in them.

Next to Yarramalong, as mentioned above, there were national parks and a gorge between two mountains: Little Mt Edwards and Mt Edwards. Now, this gorge, with Reynolds Creek running through it, supplied by Lake Moogerah, had a steep slope of smooth basalt rock called Flag Rock. You could walk along it with care to the lake. There were two teachers, at separate times, who broke their ankles while walking along on the rock. Ambulance officers thought they already had slight fractures and, walking on an angle of between 30 and 45 degrees for a kilometre or so, aggravated the fracture. Jack had to rescue one in a canoe, paddling down the creek to waiting ambulance officers, the only way to get help.

Helen had guided school children and others through the

gorge on Flag Rock many times, without incident. But she had to rescue a few that decided to walk the gorge on their own, who felt unsure and frightened to continue after reaching the very steep part.

What people tend to do when frightened is climb the rock towards the top of the mountain. This is a highly dangerous thing to do as there is no escape that way. This happened to a middle-aged portly chap who was stuck. Helen, with no experience or training whatsoever in ropes and rescue, found a suitable rope, climbed to where the panicked man was, tied the rope around his waist, with some kind of knot. Then 50-year-old, ileostomy survivor, Helen, lowered him down to safety by getting herself in a good sitting position on the rock. Jack wondered what would have happened if she had slipped. It could have been no more Helen.

Another time, the message came from a neighbour that his son went down to the gorge to do some fishing and he had not returned for dinner that night. A search with the SES and Jack, failed to find them. The missing boy arrived for lunch the next day with a surprise. A girlfriend. They had been...er... cuddling at the top of little Mt Edwards and nowhere near the search area.

One of the sad things about running Yarramalong were the breakups. Regular families coming every holiday for years, Helen and Jack, especially Helen, would be devastated that loving families, who they got quite attached to, had broken up. They never could understand how perfectly matched couples or so it seemed, separated.

Sometimes the wife would bring her new partner and children to camp, other times it was the husband alone with the kids or with a new partner. It seemed so wrong. Sometimes an awkward situation would occur, when one with the new partner and kids would be camping and then, the other separated partner turned up at reception with their new partner and kids wanting to camp. Helen was always very diplomatic, something Jack wasn't. She always made a difficult situation find a good compromise, suggesting something like, "We are so sorry, we are booked out for a wedding" or "I will ring a great place for you to stay this weekend but don't forget us next time."

One sad situation was a regular visiting family of mum, dad and two kids: a brother and sister, who Helen and Jack always called 'the family'. The children were probably seven and nine years of age when they started camping at Yarramalong. When the breakup occurred, they were in their teens. Overall, there were about nine years of regular visits to Yarramalong.

The father, a professional man, came with his children and told Helen his wife had left him after 15 years of marriage as she was always pining for her teenage boy friend she had left behind in England. So, she went back to England and became his partner. A year later, a Harley Davison pulled up outside reception with the rider that could only be described as a biker with the leather jacket and chains, tattoos, earrings and rings like knuckledusters on every finger. He was the complete opposite of her separated husband and, on the back of the bike was the ex-wife.

Yarramalong became famous with overseas customers. One chap, a world traveller, came with his daughters for quite a few years. He had been to all the resorts and amusement parks in the world and voted Yarramalong as the best place of all.

An English couple hired a campervan and came to Yarramalong as recommended. They stayed for a week then returned to London. They told Helen they were going back to England but leaving the campervan for their mature-aged daughter who had been touring Europe. The daughter came and spent a few days at the campsite then left with the camper van to explore the Sunshine Coast.

Helen and Jack were shocked to see the parents, along with the campervan, a few weeks later. The parents had been notified by the police their daughter was missing in some forest in the Sunshine Coast area. So, they stayed for a couple of weeks then, hearing no good news, went back to England. And as far as anyone was aware, she has never been seen again. It had been speculated that she was murdered but a body was yet to been found.

School camps were where our couple had a few experiences. They supplied the campground and facilities as well as the activities they were registered to run. Plus, Helen cooked all the meals. A very busy lady indeed. But students were under the control of their teachers.

Two of the main reasons schools loved to come to Yarramalong were the horse riding and, to be more honest, Helen's cooking. No expense was spared; everything was home cooked from main meals, sweets, cakes, scones and biscuits. She had two casual helpers to help prepare the meals.

Helen called vegetables by different names. For example, pumpkin was "Yarramalong's yellow delight" or silver beet was "rainbow's delicious greens". You get the idea. The kids loved their dinners. It was surprising how many students had never had home cooked meals, including some of the younger teachers. It was rare that food was left on the plate.

It surprised Helen and Jack how many children were on medication and/or allergic to this and that. For example, a child would say, "I'm allergic to cow's milk."

Helen would say, "Well, you can't have chocolate blancmange then as it's made out of cow's milk. You may have stewed apples instead."

"No, it's only if I drink milk out of a glass. It's alright if I have blancmange and stuff."

Over the years of cooking, the list got longer and longer of kids with allergies. One letter from a parent read that her son was allergic to mosquito bites: *and where he is bitten, it itches and small lumps appear.*

The Tale Comes to an End

Teachers did an incredible job. We all make mistakes, like the teachers who guided a group of students up Mt Edwards, brought them back safely, then had their dinner. Jack had a call from the caravan park on the other side of the lake at about 8.30 that evening.

"We have six students that we believe are from a school that is camping at your place. They say they got lost."

Jack drove over, picked them up and took them down to the camp. The teacher was cross at them and said, very shortly, "Go and see Helen and see if she can give you a feed. You shouldn't have gotten lost."

As the kids went to see Helen, Jack looked at the teacher and said, "I think it may be an idea now to gather all your students and check if there aren't any more lost."

The reply was, "Do you think I should?" 'Nuff said.

What about the one that decided, seeing as it was in the program, that the students should cook their lunch in groups of five as a camping exercise in the bush. Great idea but to have six flaming fires with no clearing around them at noon in 40-degree heat with a 50-knot wind blowing, was not the smartest idea.

Thank God, Jack noticed the smoke before an uncontrolled bush fire erupted. He helped the kids put their fires out and mentioned to the teacher, in his not so friendly voice, to have a better thought-out safe program in the future while camping in the bush.

A teacher came up to the house late one night and gave Jack two phone numbers. He asked that he ring those numbers, which were of two parents whose children were participating in a school camp. He said to tell the parents there had been no accidents, their children were quite alright but it was vital to come to Yarramalong by 10 the next morning to discuss a matter that was important to their children and to themselves. He also told Jack to hold the parents at the house till both sets of parents arrived, then they were to go down to the camping ground together.

What was this all about? Helen knew, as she was down at the camping ground tidying up the kitchen for the next day. A teacher told her what had happened and Helen suggested the best thing was to go up to the house, see Jack and get him to ring the parents as the camping ground was in the gorge and there wasn't any phone coverage.

As the teacher had been walking past the tents, checking that the students were settled down for the night, he noticed at one tent, there seemed to be two feet apart, pointing to the sky and two feet together, pointing to the ground. Grabbing four ankles, he pulled the owners out of the tent, to the great embarrassment of them all.

Did you know glad wrap with a rubber band is not a safe condom?

Another incident. At Yarramalong, there were two campsites: the main one and the island campsite. It only became an island in a big flood. Two different schools were camping: a girls' school at the main campsite and a boys' school at the island campsite, about 1500 metres apart. It was discovered during the night, the boys had sneaked over to the girls' camp site. There followed a strong discussion between the head male teacher and the head female teacher. She wanted the boys camp to go as boys could not be trusted. An inquiry was held and Helen and Jack were the so-called referees.

After a lot of blaming and student interviews, it so happened the girls had smuggled in wine and cigarettes, hidden in their pillowcases and sneaked over to the boys' camp and invited them over for some fun. Of course, we all know how weak boys are when conned by the fairer sex. As it ended up, both camps ended up joining in the activities and it resulted in a great camp.

A teacher came down with a group of boys from the

camping grounds to go horse riding. Jack noticed a fading red palm print, embedded on the teacher's cheek.

"Er, what happened to your cheek?" Jack was hoping there was no funny business happening down at the camping ground with the teachers.

The teacher explained, "As you know, the days have been very hot, so have the nights and very uncomfortable for sleeping. A young female student teacher staying with us, set her camp well away from where the boys were camping. Evidently, with the hot humid conditions she decided to sleep on top of her sleeping bag with only her panties on.

"Meanwhile, a huge goanna was feeling very hot and felt like some moisture and salt. He climbed on to the sleeping student teacher, laid on her chest and started to lick the sweat off her face. She woke up, one eye at a time opening and saw a huge monster face and a long string-like tongue.

"The frightening experience made her panic and she ran screaming down to the boys' camping area, which woke the boys as they glimpsed a topless woman sprinting past their tents."

The teacher had grabbed her, put his arms around her to stop the panicking student teacher from running over the bank into the creek and also to cover her from her half nudity. He had asked what caused the mad panicky flight. She told him about the goanna licking her mouth. He had laughed, taking his arms from around her. She still in shock, slapped his cheek hard with the open hand. Hence the fading imprint on the teacher's face. The embarrassed student teacher, with arms folded over her breasts, walked back to her camp, looking neither to the left or right, as a few dozen eyes followed her self-conscious progress.

The Army Adventure Training came again but this time with a carton of fluorescent sticks. They found out a scout camp was coming that late afternoon. So, a couple of army wags thought they would have some fun. They both undressed to their undies, broke the sticks and one used the liquid to paint the top part of his body and the other painted the bottom half.

It was a late arrival with parents bringing their scout sons to the camp. It was dark in the gorge but all of a sudden, an army chap shouted out, "Oh my gosh, look at that. What in the hell is that?"

Everyone looked up and saw a pair of greenish legs running, with a green torso chasing them. Jack knew what it was but he still got a fright. A couple of dads jumped in their cars and drove off at speed, telling their petrified sons, "There is a reasonable explanation for everything." Good on yer dads.

The army chaps helped the scouts put up their tents and invited them to their campfire. Jack can't remember if they told them about the body chasing the legs.

Jack had to get some of those fluorescent sticks. He bought plastic spiders and all sorts of creepy things, doused them in the liquid and stuck them in trees and bushes in the dense spooky undergrowth along the creek trail. This was done to enhance the Moonlight Champagne ride they had started to do. But it was all to no avail as everyone was so busy looking where they were going, all they saw were the horses' ears in front of them, even though Jack reassured them the horses could see in the dark and knew the trail well. It didn't help.

"Would you like to go firewalking this evening?" The woman in charge of long-term unemployed teenagers asked.

"Yes, that would be interesting. What time and where?" enquired Jack.

"Be on the island campground at 6.30 this evening and don't eat anything beforehand. The hungrier you are, the more you're aware of your body," were the instructions.

"Helen, want to come down tonight and do some fire walking?" asked Jack.

"Why do you want to get yourself involved in something that stupid?" answered Helen.

"Because I don't want to see anyone burnt or the place set on fire. I think we should go."

"Alright I'll go, it should be interesting," answered Helen.

Jack was a bit cross when he saw a pile of his wood, that he had trailered from a sawmill, as complimentary firewood for the campers. They had taken the lot. The pile was about one metre 30 centimetres high and two metres in diameter. The woman in charge lit it up.

Jack whispered to Helen, "She will pay for this."

Then the session began.

"Write down on this piece of paper, all your fears and problems then read it out, then throw it into the fire and watch all your problems be destroyed."

Helen and Jack were in a circle of 15 problem kids and partook in the exercise, including where everyone had to take shoes and socks off.

"Now, since you were a child, you have been taught that fire will burn you and that your brain now automatically tells you fire will burn. You have been given preconceived ideas about a lot of things as a child, which are not true."

"She is talking a lot of rubbish," whispered a sceptical Helen.

The instructor went on about how to handle fears and problems and how they could be overcome. She continued on in this theme till the pile had completely burnt down, leaving hot, burning coals. She then put on a leather apron and face shield and raked the coals into a small pathway about three metres long and about half a metre wide, with a bucket of water at the end, in case a burning coal got caught between people's toes.

Then they were told they did not have to walk on the burning coals. A decision had to be made and there was nothing wrong with either choice. *Argh*, thought Jack, *the exercise was for them to make a personal decision and that the fire walking was just a ruse*. Wrong Jack.

"Now, I want you all to stand up and form a circle," said the woman.

They all did in their bare feet, except Helen.

The instructor continued, "I want you to chant this: *release your mind and see what you find, release your mind and see what you find* and continue with this chant."

Then the instructor, minus the leather apron and face shield, walked across the red-hot burning coals. *So what*, thought Jack, *her feet are probably covered in thick calluses or some special stuff to stop them from being burnt.* Then she suggested the kids have a go. One did. Plonk, plonk, she walked along the fiery pathways. No burns. Another couple of kids did the same thing. Jack thought, *if those street kids can, so can I.* Helen grabbed his shirt.

"Don't be so stupid, you're not doing this. It's all wrong."

Jack shrugged off Helen's grip and stood at the start of the path of hot coals, with the kids still chanting, *Release your mind, see what you find.* The coals were a glowing red with little blue flames licking out from under them. The heat coming off was so hot, he could feel his willy burning.

"This is ridiculous, I'm not doing this," but the kids did, so he started to walk on hot coals.

It felt like walking on styrene beads. He stopped and looked down at the wonder of himself walking on hot coals. He shouldn't have stopped and he walked very quickly down to the end and said to the instructor, "You, you have burnt my feet."

She hugged him and said, "You have lost your inner child, go into yourself and control that naughty child."

He said he had done it; she released the hug and Jack hobbled over to Helen.

"I want to go home now."

"You have burnt your feet, you silly boy. You'll get no sympathy from me."

They went home and Jack put his feet in the bathtub, filling it with cold water, then went to bed to sleep. After a short time, his body started to aggressively shiver.

"If you're going to carry on like that, you can go to the spare room," said an annoyed Helen rolling over. So, Jack did and his whole body shook and shivered. He thought it was probably shock.

Two days later, Jack went to the doctor. The instep on the left foot was slightly burnt and so were the bottom of the three toes on the right.

"And how did you burn your feet?" enquired the doctor.

"Fire walking," said Jack.

The doctor shook his head and said, "There is nothing I can do for you, off you go."

Poor Jack, no sympathy for a burnt sole.

One last thing in this chapter. Snake Gully. It was a section of a narrow-dried creek bed next to the running Reynolds Creek. Snake Gully was covered with vines, bushes and trees, very enclosed but just enough for horses to pass through.

Jack mentioned to his riders, "We are now going through Snake Gully. Be aware and if any snakes fall on you or your horse, just brush them off."

It actually did happen. As Jack had just finished his spiel and was leading a group of students through Snake Gully a student cried out, "Sir, a snake has fallen on me but I did what you said and brushed it off."

Thank God, it was just a small harmless green snake.

But that wasn't enough for Jack. He managed to buy a four-foot realistic plastic brown snake. He wound it around a branch just higher than a rider's head on a horse. If a rider was annoying Jack, he would say, "Watch above your head," and smile at the shocked reaction of the rider.

Sometimes, he would stop at the branch, put his hand near the fake snake's head and talk to his riders but most times they couldn't tell him, "Jack, your hand is inches away from a deadly snake."

Sometimes, they were just lost for words or they would tell Jack back at the yards how he was nearly bitten by a snake. Gosh Jack, you just had to have fun with your customers. The snake's demise happened a few years later when a couple of New Guinea natives chopped it to pieces. Jack never found another snake like that one.

There were plenty more incidents in the 26 years Helen and Jack ran Yarramalong and they loved it. It was a good business but not a profitable one. As any profit was spent in upgrading equipment, horse costs and replacements. But they did get a fair living from it, bringing up the children and surviving some very difficult times. Jack and Helen preferred to give excellent service rather than charge what they should have for what they provided.

But what about Helen and Jack? As mentioned, Helen loved the kids and the campers and they loved her but Jack wanted to sell. He was getting tired, not so much the campers and horse riders but the ever-increasing red tape, licencing costs always increasing and having to be registered for this and that. But what worried Jack the most was insurance. Lawyers and solicitors always egging on the general public to sue. And being told by their insurance solicitor, "Jack, you're running a place for the general public. Just cop it." The hide.

Now we have heard a lot about Jack but what about the quiet, loving, smiling Helen? Besides her winning trophies for her dress making and making her daughter's beautiful wedding dress, as well as some excellent applique, when she decided to do something, Helen did it and didn't give up until she had done her all.

The Scenic Rim Region is set in the foothills of the Great

Dividing Range and is surrounded by world heritage-listed national parks such as Main Range, Border Ranges National Park and Lamington National Park. Yarramalong is near the Main Range and Cunninghams Gap.

Helen had read a little comment in The Guardian, the local newspaper, that a power company, called East Link, was going to run transmission lines across the Scenic Rim from north of Cunninghams Gap to the Queensland and New South Wales border, then onwards.

Helen was incensed. How could they run those huge, steel towers across her wonderous, beautiful mountains? She put an ad in the local paper asking the locals to help her form a committee to stop this outrageous blight and eyesore on the eastern side of the Main Range. She asked Jack to chair the committee.

A committee was formed but, admittedly, not as enthusiastic as Helen was. These were the days when any sort of pollution or damage to the natural environment was not a big issue as it is today, with global warming on everyone's mind. It was decided to get facts together, detailed research and present it to the government's Minister of Mines and Energy, Tony McGrady. And if they were not able to see him, then a protest outside parliament was suggested.

Helen did most of the research of the adverse consequences that could occur if the project went ahead. They did not receive a meeting with the minister, so a small protest marching outside parliament house went ahead with signs reading: STOP EAST LINK.

Of course, the action was not successful. But that did not stop Helen. She persisted until the minister reluctantly gave her an interview, which ended up with the minister agreeing to meet Helen at the Governors Chair, in the Main Range National Park, named in honour of Sir Charles Fitzroy, Governor General of the Australian Colony. Other notable visitors there, had been Sir George Bowen, Lord Lamington and Aldous Huxley's grandfather. May I mention Jack and Helen Alexander as well?

The meeting went well and the Honourable Minister, Tony McGrady, said what a beautiful site it was and yes, it would be a disgrace to put transmission towers across the face of the Main Range of the Scenic Rim. Then he confessed that they had two sites for the lines. The other was from Toowoomba through Warwick, then on to New South Wales. He also mentioned that Helen's detailed, excellent submission was more favourable than the abuse and fruit-throwing of Warwick protesters. As far as this writer knows, they did not even put in a submission.

The Scenic Rim, or more precisely, the Main Range, thanks to Helen, was saved from those horrible steel towers which can now be seen over farmland in the Southern Downs. Today, everyone admires the beautiful Main Range, a great tourist attraction. But sadly, her efforts behind keeping this beautiful view have been easily forgotten.

Jack was doing thousands of rides with less than a half percent of injuries needing medical care. Even though, at his own expense, he brought horse safety and education to Australia, which had been accepted by every state in the country, his insurance overnight went from a $3,000 premium to a $30,000 premium, which was impossible to sustain.

It was decided they both needed a good holiday. They discussed where would be a good place to go and Jack decided on Antarctica.

Helen said, "That's impossible. Darling, you have to book at least two years ahead and even then, it's very expensive."

Jack found a voyage of discovery, Antarctica on the Norwegian liner, MS Nordnorge. He rang up the cruise line and was told, "I'm sorry sir, we are fully booked for the next two years."

"Well, could you put us on the cancellation list then?"

"We don't have a cancellation list, sir. No-one ever cancels on these sorts of trips."

"Told you so," said a smug Helen.

Jack retorted, "You think you're soo clever. Get your warm gear ready, we are leaving in a few weeks' time."

Helen laughed and went to finish sewing a pretty blouse with the material Jack bought her for Christmas. Jack was tired; he needed that holiday and Antarctica was where they were going.

He rang the number every morning and afternoon. He put on his superior, no-nonsense voice saying, "I am Mr Jack Alexander wanting a vacancy on the Nordnorge sailing on Friday, February 13th, 2004."

He got the same answer every time.

"Sorry, no vacancies."

This went on for a week, same question and same answer. It was exactly seven days later when, as usual, Jack, in his no-nonsense voice, was asking for a cabin on the liner, when he didn't receive the usual answer.

"Sir, we are pleased to tell you, we have just managed a cabin on the Nordnorge for next month. We will need payment received in the next 24 hours.

Jack said, "Payment will be made in that time and thank you most graciously for acquiring a cabin for us."

He couldn't wait till Helen came home from work to tell her the good news.

"Darling, remember I asked you early last week to get your warm clothes together for a cruise to Antarctica? Well, as promised, we are leaving next week so you better let the hospital know. We need to have doctor's certificates to say we are healthy and the appropriate needles and everything else we must do."

"Yea sure," laughed Helen. "There is no way you could get a cruise that quick but then, it's you Jack. Are we really going? Fair dinkum, Jack, is it on?"

"Sure is, my lovely. I have to go to the bank first thing in the morning to pay and we better see if we can get an appointment with the doctor. Have you enough ileostomy supplies for a month or more if we are shipwrecked?"

"I will place an order now but I will manage and anyway, that's none of your business. What are we doing about Yarramalong?"

"Well, we aren't doing horse rides now and there are no schools booked in yet and Damon comes home every weekend. Roy, our groundsman, can check the property during a couple of weekdays. But we have lots to do so let's have a cuddle now and a good night's sleep, as we are going to have a very busy five days."

They did have a very busy time with long distance flights to Buenos Aires, then to Chilé and then to Puerto Montt, embarking at 1700hrs. Breathless, they made it.

It was a wonderful trip; the scenery was spectacular, not only the Chilean Fjords but the Antarctica. It was awe-inspiring. The whole cruise finished on 26th February, a 14-day cruise both Helen and Jack needed so desperately.

A couple of incidences must be mentioned. They managed to get off and walk around the tiny island of Cabo de Hornos which only shipwrecked sailors visited and very few tourists, because of rough seas. This time, however, it was calm.

Breakfast and lunch were buffets and the evening meal was in the dining room. All meals could only be described as delicious. The buffets were set on five tables, at least five metres long and holding food from every land: European, Asian, American, South American, Spanish, you name the food, it was there. Now Helen was a stickler for fresh vegetables and lots of greens; she kept her family very healthy and did her utmost to keep them so.

The first breakfast, Jack just had to have his cereal with fresh fruit and muesli, every morning, wherever he was. Dear Helen, wanting to keep him regular, popped a few prunes on his cereal. Lo and behold, while eating his breakfast, he bit into a prune and the seed, breaking the filling and half a tooth, with the nerve dangling down. Guess who got the blame. Doesn't the wife always? Poor Jack, no more delicious foods, just boiled eggs, jellies and anything that can be swallowed without chewing. There was no dentist on board, so what did he do?

He had a packet of chewing gum. Why? We don't know. Jack never had chewing gum. He would pack the hollow in his tooth, morning and night, with the gum. It was all he could do. Helen was very sympathetic and always chose soft food for him throughout the whole cruise. Later, it was found out, if he'd a little birthday candle, he could have put the warm wax into the cavity. Jack now carried a birthday candle in his toilet bag.

The other memorable event on the trip, besides the great talks and information about the seas and wildlife, which were always told with enthusiasm and excitement, was the scenery and their two dining guests, Marit and Harold. They had a table for four assigned to them. Helen and John were already seated when they saw a couple walking towards them. They looked at each other, thinking, *I hope those two don't sit with us*, but they did.

Marit was slightly older than Helen, frumpishly dressed, with long, greying hair tied in a bun, not quite contained in the two knitting needles stuck cross ways. She had a kind face with a lovely personality. Harold was conservatively dressed in a suit and a tie. He was a schoolteacher in Norway. Marit, his wife, they learnt later on, was a famous psychiatrist who travelled around the world giving lectures.

Well, they had a ball. Jack and Marit didn't stop telling jokes: dirty and otherwise, yarns, exaggerations and lies for the whole trip. They tried to outdo each other. The four of them had tears from laughing. Helen and Harold looked on, laughing in amazement as their two partners swapped yarns. Other passengers wanted to join their table; the waiters had smiles on their faces. It was really a fun time for the four of them. Later on in the trip, Marit invited them to Norway for a visit. And that's another story.

Even though they had a fabulous holiday, as soon as they got home, the weight and worry were back on Jack's shoulders. He was tired of it all: seven days a week, 52 weeks a year, for 26 years, with only small breaks here and there. Can you blame him wanting out? But Helen was happy and did not want to sell.

It took quite some years but sell they did. Selling the good, dependable horses broke Jack's heart and to this day he still remembers them individually. He was so tired he practically gave the property and equipment away. They had just enough to buy a house and some acres. Both he and Helen were terribly disappointed Yarramalong did not continue as an outdoor recreation centre.

C.28

A Fresh Start
2005

Did our couple retire, lay on the beach, drinking cocktails, go to the theatre, play golf and relax? Not on your nellie. Helen went back to nursing. It took her months to get over leaving Yarramalong, the clients and having games with the children. Jack was happy, the heavy burden was lifted off his shoulders.

He volunteered, working for Beacon for a few years. It was a volunteer organisation funded by big companies Australia-wide. The organisation introduced industry into schools and schools into industry. It was a worthwhile project but it was a pity it wasn't funded by the government so all schools could benefit from the importance of transporting students into industry. Kids often finished university and apprenticeships and could become disappointed in the career they picked, instead of really getting the proper inside information while at school.

Busy, busy Helen, besides nursing, became deputy chair of the local chamber of commerce, put herself on the Greater Brisbane Tourism board and did fantastic quilting and sewing to win many prizes. Then she joined the Garden Club and became secretary of the 80 members for a small town like Boonah.

Helen surprised everyone, especially her husband, by starting to tell the odd joke. It became a regular segment of the club's proceedings. She even told some risqué ones.

Even though Helen always had a smile on her face and had a happy disposition, her joke-telling was a surprise to all. Jack was not quite sure if she understood a lot of them but she laughed in the telling, which made everyone laugh. They all loved the segment, even if a few elderly men approached Helen saying they were embarrassed by some of the jokes, while the women wanted more of the risqué ones. It was poor Jack who had to find a joke for the next monthly meeting, which become quite a chore.

After leaving Yarramalong, they rented a house. Jack liked the idea. Nothing to look after and they could invest the proceeds of their sale and travel the world. Not so Helen. She wanted a house of their own to feel secure, instead of not ever knowing the landlord's intentions.

So, Jack suggested she find a suitable affordable place to live, thinking she will never find one, being so busy. He wasn't going to help as he wanted to rent.

"I've found the ideal place," said Helen, coming home one evening. "It's not on the market yet. Come on, Jack, come and see it now."

"What now? It's nearly dark."

"Don't procrastinate, let's go, it's only 10 minutes away."

They went. As they drove up the 500-metre private road, Jack thought, *No way we will be able to afford this.* Then he saw the previous owner had built a free standing, one-metre-high, natural stone wall around the two-acre garden. He wasn't impressed.

Helen, full of enthusiasm, said, "It's double brick, no maintenance, no painting, there is nothing you have to do."

Jack thought the three-bedroom house with a great office,

a large bedroom with ensuite and a big open fireplace in the lounge room, was pretty good but he just ummed and erred without any real statement. He also noticed the large doorways and handrails in the two bathrooms and toilets.

As an excuse, he said to Helen, "This home is for old people. Notice all the handrails and wide doorways for wheelchair access? We are not buying an old people's home."

"Oh, don't be so silly, it's not an old people's home," said Helen. "When it was built, the idea was to make it suitable for when or if their elderly mother came to stay. Anyway, what do you think?

"I'm so excited. This place is just right for us. Lots of trees, no neighbours can be seen and the garden is beautiful. There is a bore, a dam and four 700-gallon water tanks, so there is stacks of water."

"Are you the real estate agency or the seller?" asked Jack. "You certainly have done your homework but I want to see the place in the daylight and have a good walk around before we decide."

"Jack, it's well within our price range, please don't be difficult."

"Love, it's a huge investment but after a good look around and discussion on the pros and cons, I think it might be a proposition."

A few days later, they saw the property in full daylight. Jack was still being difficult.

"Look at all the rocks. The place will be crawling with snakes, especially with that dam in the garden, probably full of frogs to feed the snakes."

After a good inspection and a walk around the property, he gave in but he said there must be a satisfactory building and white-ant inspection. Helen gave him the biggest hug and a loving kiss.

"Thank you darling, you have done the right thing."

As it so happened they did. As the world financial crisis became a reality and if they hadn't bought a house, a good asset, all of their investment from the sale of Yarramalong could have gone. Thanks to Helen and her persistence, they had done the right thing, and yes, he did congratulate her that she was right not to rent but to buy.

But Jack wasn't that happy. The place was 30-acres of unusable scrub and rocks and, being on one block, it could not be subdivided. Jack didn't want work. He'd had enough of physical hard work and wasn't keen on having to maintain fences, firebreaks and weed control, but Helen was happy and the property was a good buy.

Helen still busy nursing and committed to her community obligations. Jack had given away his Tourism, Horse council and camping/outdoor positions and started a weekend job at Silk Road, a camping and clothing shop, which sold the best gear. During the week he still volunteered for the Beacon Foundation. Well, enough said about what the busy couple were doing, let's concentrate on their holidays, adventures, and stories.

Jack, why don't you tell us about the drowning that happened in North Dakota, USA.

Helen and I were visiting our friend, Michelle, who lived in Medora. We had met at the conference of the Horse Safety and Education, where Michelle and I were accredited as Horse Trail Guides. I thought Michelle was a real cowgirl. She could ride, shoot, gamble and do anything a man could do (nearly). She ran the horse-riding school in the Theodore Roosevelt National Park, which was set in the Badlands of Medora. Helen and I had the privilege of staying in Theodore Roosevelt's original wooden cabin, where the bison were grazing near our front door. The cabin also overlooked a magnificent view of the Badlands.

We were yarning at the corral when, all of a sudden, riding through the cotton trees towards us was a cowboy. He looked like he was straight from a western movie. Dressed in a tartan shirt with a cow hide vest, a string bow tie, a pair of chaps, tall cowboy boots with spurs and the cowboy beaver skin black hat. Attached to his saddle and saddle bags was a rifle in a holster with a lasso hanging from the horn. He was leading a pack mule.

As he approached us, I said "G'day." and Michelle said, "Hi." Helen said nothing as she couldn't believe what she was seeing.

"Can you take me mule," he said in a slow drawling voice. (He took a few minutes to think before he spoke. I know I should sometimes).

I took his mule and put it in the horse corral, as he rode back from whence he came. As he left, he said, "There's been a drowning."

We glanced at each other with puzzled looks on our faces.

"Did he say someone drowned?"

The cowboy returned now leading a horse. I asked him who had drowned.

He replied in his slow drawling voice without any expression, "Me partner, he drowned."

Michelle asked him if she should ring the National Parks and he replied, "Yep."

Saying nothing, we three just waited till Michelle came back.

"Jack, you and I have to saddle our horses and follow the Little Missouri River down to the Parks boundary fence and see if we can spot a body or anything unusual, then to ride over the butte, (hill/range) and report to the Parks."

So, off we went through the cotton trees and rode along the banks of the river. It must have been cold as there was a small ice flow. We scanned with our eyes, gave each other a start when one of us would shout, "There he is," but it was only dead branches sticking out of the water or washed-up logs on the bank. We saw no evidence of someone drowned.

Meanwhile, Helen left with this strange cowboy, asked him if he would like to use the phone. The answer was, "Yep," so she led him to the tack room and showed him where the telephone was.

He rang a number and said, "There's been a drowning. Me brother, he's drowned."

Silence as someone was speaking at the other end of the phone, then a "Yep." He hung up the phone and walked back to the horses and pack mule, waited, until a large gooseneck horse float arrived and picked him and the livestock up.

"Did he say anything at all to you?" I asked Helen.

She replied, "Nope," imitating her visitor.

Back to me and Michelle. Michelle wasn't sure which butte we had to climb. (Remember it was the Badlands where crooks and people who had wandered there, had never been found.) I saw a trail going up a steep hill.

"Is that the trail?" I asked.

"It could be, let's give it a go."

The trail got steeper the more we went. It got so steep, there was no turning back. It was like climbing a cliff with air each side of us. My horse started to slip a bit. I think it was my fault as I wasn't quite used to the Yankee saddle and wasn't balanced right, like in my good old Aussie stock saddle.

We eventually got to the top of the butte, realising we had just transversed a bison track, not a regular trail. At the top, we found a couple of long ancient poles and a very old fire pit with a lot of animal bones. Michelle thought it may have been an Indian camp of long ago. Who knows? But now it was twilight, about 9.30 pm.

We loped the horses across the top plain for some time. It was the most beautiful experience: the sun just gone, the steady beat of the hooves, everything jelled into one with the fabulous landscape before us. Ahhhhh. We came to the end and found the rangers waiting for us with a horse float. They took us back to the ranch where I related the whole experience I'd just had. Helen told me about her strange experience with the Dakota cowboy.

We must have slept soundly as we didn't hear a thing, as lo and behold, a huge marquee had been set up with chairs and stools and tables, early that morning. On the table were all types of pies: apple, blueberry, pear/apple, cakes and, of course, the inevitable coke and coffee. They must have been busy that night, baking and setting up. There were pickup trucks belonging to about 20 people. It was like a party, instead it was refreshments for the searchers: relatives and friends of the drowned man.

Two frogmen entered the icy Little Missouri River with big knives in hand. We were told the current was so strong that the frogmen held hands. Then, with their knives in their other hands, they dug into the bed of the river to stop themselves being swept by the current.

A shout came. "We found him," said a frogman surfacing from the ice-cold river.

Someone called the undertaker, who arrived in a pickup. It was the drowned man's wife, who was then told it was not her husband but a river snag. Helen and I felt awkward as we didn't belong there. So, after a coke and pie, we left the scene.

Thanks Jack, I'm sure you have a few more stories to tell.

Michelle had lent them her brand new Celica sports car to tour a small part of the USA. They got strange looks as everyone had pickups and Japanese cars were rarely seen, if at all. They visited Montana, Yellowstone National Park, Wyoming, Mt Rushmore, South Dakota and back to North Dakota. A fabulous trip with awe-inspiring scenery. Dropping off Michelle's car after a good clean and wash, no damage, a present and a thank you, they still didn't know what happened after they left. Did they find the man who had drowned?

Michelle filled them in. It was a few weeks later, they found the body. It had been preserved in the icy waters and his pockets were full of sand, which had kept him down. The two brothers had been going to set up a camp the other side of the river. One said they shouldn't cross and the other said it was alright and started out. It was said the current was too strong and deep. The mule got into trouble with the lead rope caught around the rider's leg, causing him to fall into the river.

Our couple caught the train to Seattle where Helen wanted to see Deborah, as she was living in Canada, and the famous Butchart Gardens on Vancouver Island, which was an hour or so ferry ride from the city. Jack went down to the ferry office to buy the tickets and asked the shop assistant for two return tickets for tomorrow's ferry to Vancouver Island. And seeing it was in Canada did she want their passports?

"Oh no, that's not necessary," she said, "it's only a day trip. A driver's licence is only required for identification."

So, early the next morning, they were ready for the ferry, Helen reminded Jack, "Have you got the tickets and passports?"

Jack told her he had the tickets but the girl said passports were not required, only drivers' licences.

"Jack, we are going to another country. We must have our passports."

"Listen to me, I was told it was only a day trip. Passports were not required and I'm leaving them in our room safe, that's final. If we stop and keep arguing, we will miss the ferry. As it is now, we had better move ourselves."

Which they did and just as well, as they were the last to embark.

They arrived at the Vancouver customs.

"Passports please," said the customs official.

"Er, we were told we didn't need them seeing it was a day trip," said Jack.

"You're in Canada now. Have you got your passports or not?"

"No but I've got a copy."

"We don't take copies." He signalled with his finger and an armed guard with a military-type gun escorted them into a small white room with the guard locking them in.

Helen was angry, no furious. With tight lips she said in a voice Jack had never heard before, "I told you we had to take our passports."

She didn't have to say anything more. He could see and feel the seething livid anger in her face and body. He had never known his darling, smiling Helen to be even slightly angry but this was very new to him. He knew he had better keep quiet.

After a couple of hours locked up, they were escorted by an armed guard on to another ferry which was full and about to leave. They had missed seeing their daughter and the fabulous Butchart Gardens she had been dreaming about for years.

They sat on the only bench seat left on the ferry. Jack tried to make light of a dangerous situation as they were on their way back to Seattle.

So, he said, "Make yourself comfortable, as we will be on this ferry for a long, long time as we don't have a passport into Canada or into America. We are without a country, therefore, we will have to spend the rest of our lives on this ferry."

Helen didn't think Jack's statement was amusing. She just sat bolt upright, silent all the way back to Seattle. When they got to the American border, the immigration officer said to Jack's nervous statement, "Through you both go, it happens often on these day trips."

Helen stormed back to the hotel. It was strange behaviour for Helen, who never held a grudge or was angry for more than five minutes. Under these circumstances, there was a good reason.

Jack went straight back to the ferry booking office and wanted to see the manager. He told him what happened, how they had missed seeing their daughter and the wife's dream of seeing the Butchart Gardens. He asked Jack who told him only a driver's licence was required for identification to go to Vancouver Island.

Now an Aussie is not a dobber but, in this case, the troubled Jack pointed to the girl and said it was her. The manager went over to her, had a conversation, came back, apologised, saying she was new in ticketing and he would refund half the fare. Jack didn't think that was fair. They should have been refunded the lot but he was a foreigner, so what could he do? Except buy Helen a posy of flowers, a box of chocolates and a night on the town. I think he was forgiven but every now and then it got brought up at dinner parties.

Things started to change. Helen went from general nursing to working in the dialysis unit, which she loved. She got talking to the same patients every second and third day. But Jack was worried about the long hours she worked, her drive of 45 kilometres one way and getting home at 10.30 at night. Helen never used a mobile phone or computer. It was the same with her brother and sister; they just couldn't work them, even after having lessons and instructions. Goodness knows how Helen managed the dialysis machines but she did.

Jack's weekend job at Silk Road, which had sold, was finished and the time volunteering for the Beacon Foundation was over. Jack decided to become a First Responder for the Queensland Ambulance Service. After a lot of study and practical tuition, he was on the road driving his own car, supposed to be accompanied by a partner, but rarely was. Whenever comms called him for a job, an ambulance would be sent. They could arrive at any time, from 10 minutes to over an hour.

Jack was on call 24 hours. He attended car accidents where some were fatal, search and rescue operations, home calls, weather, an asthma attack, a choking, suspect heart attack, falls off ladders, in the kitchen, the bathroom or whenever a person could not stand on their own two feet. But, unfortunately, aside from the above, Jack was shocked. He thought people called an ambulance if they were dying or had a serious life-threatening injury. However, 80% of call outs were not urgent or life-threatening cases, where people could have seen their GP.

I will only mention two of the 100's of cases Jack attended to, over nine years. One, he was called to a woman who was haemorrhaging at one in the morning and who lived 60 kilometres away. Jack went as quick as he could, no speeding or sirens, just the normal road rules in the private car as was allowed.

He thought, on the way, what he could do to stop the bleeding. He arrived at the house, and a woman came out with an overnight bag and said, "Let's go."

Jack enquired, "Where is the woman who is haemorrhaging?"

She replied, "It's me," and showed him a half circular cut on her thigh that had stopped bleeding and was obviously self-inflicted.

After getting the whole story, Jack called comms and told them the situation but was informed the ambulance was on its way and would be there shortly. Jack told the paramedics what he had learnt from the woman, that all she wanted was a lift to Boonah to see her boyfriend.

The paramedics said, "Fine, we won't be stopping at Boonah. We have come from Ipswich, which was over 100 kilometres away. We will take her there and she can find her own way back."

That was three trained men, an ambulance fully stocked and a car, just so a person could get a lift. A waste of good resources.

Two. A call for a suspected heart attack to a property where a man was lying distressed in a van. Jack checked his blood pressure, his temperature, his blood sugar, his blood oxygen levels and all seemed normal. The ambulance arrived and Jack gave his report and told the paramedics he could find nothing wrong.

"Well, we will check him out again," which they did and found nothing wrong with the distressed man.

The older paramedic glanced around the property and asked the man, "What's going on here? There seems to be a lot of cars and a marquee set up. Is there a party going on?"

The man replied, "It's a wedding."

He was asked, "Are you one of the guests?"

"No," he answered, "I'm the groom." Poor bloke he was having a panic attack.

Then the paramedic said to him, "Listen very carefully, as your response to my suggestion will affect your whole life. My suggestion to you is this: we can take you to hospital to be checked out or we can give you a couple of aspirin and you can go ahead and get married."

There was a long pause, then the man said, "Could you please give me a couple of aspirin?" Jack often wondered if the man had made the right decision or not.

Damon was having a lot of trouble with his wife, unbeknownst to Helen and Jack, until his neighbour rang up and said, "I don't know you but my wife and I are very worried about your son, and we feel we should inform you, that Damon is having trouble with his wife and is very distressed. We feel he might harm himself."

Jack said, "Thank you so much for letting us know; we will handle the situation immediately."

Jack rang Damon, who lived in Gladstone over 500 kilometres away, that night. He said he needed a break and was going for a trip to Longreach, would he like to come along?

Son said yes and, in a couple of days, they were heading for Longreach. They argued, teased, expounded questionable knowledge and had a good time; it was never just dad and son, it was always two mates that enjoyed each other's company. Jack did not bring up the conversation the neighbour had with him but suggested they go on a holiday.

"I see there is a motor bike tour in South Africa and trips to the wild animal parks, what do you reckon?" said Jack.

"Well, I do need to have a holiday. I've never had one, I'll think about it."

As Jack was dropping Damon off at his home in Gladstone, he said, "I have a message from Mum. She said to tell you, if you're not happy, to do something about it."

Damon replied, as he walked away, "Dad, I'm not a happy man."

A week later, he rang up his dad and said, "We are not going to South Africa. I found a new trial motor bike tour of the Dakar Rally course, a couple of weeks before the rally starts."

"Okay mate, whatever you think will be good. You arrange everything, plane fares, the tours and all the costs and I will forward you my share to your bank account."

Jack knew that even though Damon was an excellent builder, as far as organising himself at doing anything, other than building and horse-riding, he was hopeless. So, he said he would be in it, knowing full well it wouldn't happen.

For a 65-year-old bloke to ride from Huntington, England, through France, Spain, Morocco, Mauritania, the Western Sahara Desert, Senegal and Dakar, then on to Gambia, on a motorbike was crazy thinking. Three weeks later came the information from the tour organiser, cost, fees and all the itinerary. We were to be at the starting destination at 7am Greenwich Mean Time on 1st December, 2007.

Jack nearly fainted. He bloody well did. He just couldn't believe it and now he was committed. *My God, I will never come back alive,* he thought. It was on. They flew direct from Brisbane at 41 degrees celsius to London at a freezing eight degrees. Helen got herself off to Sydney to be with daughter, Deborah, who was having her third child after a successful delivery of Jack in 2004 and Alex in 2006. Their third grandchild, Matilda or Tilly, was on her way in January 2008.

The men stayed in London for a couple of days and, after some confusion and disagreements, they managed to get themselves on a train north to Huntington, then overnight at a hotel nearby. Next morning at 7am, they were picked up by car and transported to the tour starting point at Station Farm. It may be of interest to know that our two Aussie fellows were so rugged up with thermals, down jackets, neck warmers, balaclavas plus their waterproof riding gear, they looked like the Michelin man. They were so heavily dressed, they could hardly walk, let alone carry all their gear needed for the next month. The reason being, it was freezing. There was sleet with the first blast of the first week of winter in Great Britain.

At the farm there were six riders, including our two Aussies, plus Lee the guide, Jason the mechanic and Alan the cook, with nine brand-new Dakar 650 motorbikes waiting for their riders. A handing out of papers and hastily copied maps, a few limited instructions and to pick and check their motorcycles over, a hot chocolate drink and then, without warning, our leader just took off and everyone started following him. Jack was last. He was trying to catch up as they whizzed down side streets and lanes.

Five minutes after the ride started, Jack felt and heard a clicking sound. Gosh, he had forgotten to fasten the chin strap on his helmet. Could he stop, take of his thick motorcycle gloves and his liner gloves and try to do the fiddley catch up with his cold fingers? Yes, he could but he would lose all the other riders. Safety first. He stopped, taking his two sets of gloves off and did his helmet up. *Blow them*, he thought, *if they didn't check if everyone was ready and I get lost, it's their own fault and they jolly well can come and find me.* Jack sped, hoping to catch up and, surprisingly, he did, just as they were coming out of a side road on to the M11 highway to catch the Dover/Calais ferry.

As they sped through the traffic, the leader changed lanes all the time and the riders had to follow his manoeuvres, as most of them didn't have a clue where they were going. They knew where the ferry terminal was but, other than that, they weren't sure how to get there.

As they were speeding down the M11, Jack's right side mirror came loose and was flapping in the breeze. He tried to tighten it but it was difficult as his right hand was needed for the throttle. The problem began with all the lane changing. The mirror was useless as it couldn't be fixed, so Jack's only alternative was to look behind him to see if it was safe to merge. As he did, the fine woollen balaclava slid inside his helmet and rendered Jack blind amongst all the traffic, doing at least 100 kilometres an hour. A predicament for our Jack. A quick turn of the head, a straightening of the offending balaclava and back again with the riders. Note well: never wear a balaclava under your helmet. Jack never did after that incident.

They met up with another three riders who came on their own bikes and they were all so pleased to catch the warm, dry ferry. They took off all their saturated gear and drank copious amounts of coffee. But it was on again, leaving the ferry in the rain and freezing cold and this time in the dark. It was to be the most frightening ride in Jack's life that night. Dark, heavy rain, where he could hardly see out of the wet visor, riding on the other side of the road, Jack just followed the taillight of the next rider. Their leader was not concerned about his riders, not once checking them again to see if they were all there. It seemed his main concern was to get to their motel in Senlis, which was just outside of Paris, as soon as possible. All the riders on that wet night trip, agreed it was the most terrifying trip they'd ever had and were sure they would die.

It was a group picture taken in the rain at the Eiffel Tower which should have been crowded with tourists, sellers and hawkers but all Jack saw was a small mangey dog and a broken umbrella rolling down the road. They were wet and cold all through France and Spain. They had troubles getting ice off their tents in the Pyrenees and it was a miserable ride with no sightseeing, just straight down the autoroutes then autopistas. They crossed the Gibraltar Strait by ferry to Tangier in Morocco which now meant they were on a completely different continent. They had a couple of rest days at Marrakesh, then headed into the western Sahara Desert along the coast road continuing on to the Morocco/Mauritania border.

The border was just a collection of small tin sheds, like enlarged bush dunnies. The group spent time there checking passports and registrations etc. Their leader, who spoke fluent French, handled it all as the riders waited, then he told them to go ahead to the Mauritania border with an Arab guide, called Bennie, to help them navigate the three-day crossing into the real Sahara Desert.

They started to cross no man's land, which no country owned. Bennie raced up and informed them this border crossing in no man's land was full of mines. Great, as the team had already covered a third of the trip and had wondered about all the smashed cars and overturned and squashed trucks. Jack informed the group he had his first aid certificate and that it would be in their best interest for him to stay at the back of the group, which he did. Thank goodness, Damon was second last.

They all made it through with all their limbs. Then there was another long wait for Lee, the leader, to go through the whole process of passports and registrations with the Mauritanian border officials. They had finished the whole border check and were, at last, on their way. But no, there was now a military roadblock. A suggestion from a soldier to please leave their bikes and proceed into the barracks, which were behind a high concrete wall.

They found themselves lined up against this wall with a few Arabs. Ahead were two officers sitting behind a desk under a large palm tree with a soldier sitting down behind a machine gun. Jack whispered to Damon, who was beside him, to turn a bit and see if there were any machine gun bullet holes in the wall behind him.

Damon whispered back, "I'm not going to move a muscle."

Having a surname starting with A can be a blessing sometimes and a curse other times. Bennie the guide was on the other side of Jack saying, "They are indicating they want to interview you first. Don't hurry, just walk up to them normally. I don't think you have anything to worry about."

Jack walked up not feeling his best. The senior officer, whose uniform was decorated with lots of medals, ribbons and bars, said in good English, "Passports and all your papers please."

Jack found everything in his pockets and handed the lot to the officer. As the officer was going through everything, he handed something back with a hint of a smile saying, "You might need this shortly." It was his small, folded sheets of lavatory paper.

He then scribbled some notes and said, "Please send your next companion up here." They all thought they were going to be shot, but it was the military checking up on the border force officers, as they were very suspicious of the government.

Through lots of adventures and all unscathed, they reached where the Dakar Rally was to finish the race. They had large timber frames for the marquees, a lot of signs and a lot of natives building little huts to sell their souvenirs to tourists.

Unfortunately, they heard the rally had been cancelled due

to suspected kidnappings and military interfering. Yes, they had been stopped a lot by the military and the police, but they were always nice with a genuine smile, just asking for their papers and sending them on their way.

They caught the ferry from Senegal to Gambia, where they stayed for a few days in Banjul. The riding group started to break up, some wanting to get back to families for Christmas. Jack, Damon and a couple of others stayed for Christmas as they had too far to travel to even to think of getting home in time. Meeting a few other travellers in their camp, they decided to have a Christmas party. Jack's job was to buy a goat kill and dress it for the pot. Damon's job was the fire for cooking. Two English blokes, who travelled over the Sahara in a Mercedes Mogul truck as they traversed around the world, had all the cooking gear. Two others supplied the beer and two more got the vegetables and ingredients for the great feast.

The blokes in charge of buying the beer, bought a half pallet load of cartons. The drinking started as soon as the beer arrived. The cooking was a bit haphazard, the vegetables were not prepared as they should have been but they had a very merry time and Christmas lunch was ready by 5.30 in the evening, some edible, some not. But the surprise of the whole day was when Jack brought out a whole large Christmas cake. Baked expertly by Helen, it had travelled from Brisbane, through France and Spain, over to Morocco and into the Sarah Desert, Senegal and Gambia. Protected by the lives of Damon and Jack, it was still moist and voted by all as the best Christmas cake ever and Jack seconded that.

There was a long flight to Gatwick airport, a bus to Heathrow and a very long flight to Brisbane, where Damon left for Gladstone and Jack left for Sydney and back to his darling, Helen. The arrival back in Sydney was exciting. He hugged and kissed Helen, who met him at the airport with their two grandsons, Jack and Alex, and a very pregnant daughter, Deborah, who couldn't wait to shed her load of baby number three.

Helen had had a great time while Jack was away. She had done Christmas shopping with her daughter, had fun and games with the grandsons, loving her job cooking for the family and giving her daughter the rest she needed. They'd had a huge Christmas Day with all of Stephen's, Debs' husband's, family but she did miss her Jack terribly, as there wasn't any communication between them from leaving Brisbane until his arrival back in Sydney.

(A lot more detail of their adventures on that Dakar tour could be told, but that would take up a lot of pages, and this story really is about Helen's and Jacks life.)

C.29

Adventures and Heartache
2015

Our couple had spent over 35 years without long weekends and holidays and they were making up for the lost opportunities. They visited their friends from the Antarctic cruise in Stavanger, Norway. They stayed with them for a couple of weeks and had a fantastic time. They showed Helen and Jack around the southern and mid Norway regions. They leant against the moving boulder, climbed Pulpit Rock, looked down on the Lysefjord and travelled on different ferries down other fjords and around the many islands. They also saw the sheep coming down the hills to be loaded on to the boats to go to their winter pastures. Or was it summer pastures?

After a great time learning the history and seeing the awesome sights and scenery of their beautiful country, Jack and Helen reluctantly said goodbye to their hosts and caught the m/s Finnmarken from Bergin to Kirkenes, a seven-day voyage along the coast of Norway. They crossed the Arctic Circle, saw the Northern Lights with their wafting colours of pink, purple, blue and other not-so- bright colours in the mix. It was fascinating to see them getting brighter and dimmer as they slipped away, then another set of the lights would arrive.

The boat m/s Finnmarken was more of a delivery ship that stopped at every port and unloaded and loaded freight, which gave Jack and Helen time to visit these little towns, sometimes in daylight, sometimes at night. It was a very comfortable ship. This time, Jack enjoyed all the food, without tooth trouble as had happened on the Antarctica voyage.

The boat was not a large tourist boat with casinos and floor shows but had interesting programs about the sea life, the towns and the history, well delivered and very informative. It wasn't as good as the Antarctic cruise. They should have left that one to last. It was a long flight home and back to Jack's volunteering with the Queensland Ambulance and Helen with a new job at the dialysis unit of the Ipswich Hospital.

Another coastal trip they did was on the Silverseas Line, a small tourist boat that left Vancouver to Alaska and back. It went through Prince Rupert Sound up to Juneau and Skagway. They did a bus trip up the Yukon trail where the gold miners, under shocking conditions, slaved away to get the yellow stuff. Men and horses died in the hundreds for that metal.

Jack and Helen did a canoe trip at the top White Pass Summit and had a very wet rafting trip, having to catch the train back, saturated. It was a good trip but not as good as Antarctica. When back in Vancouver, Jack had no option but to book a ferry trip to Vancouver Island so, at last, Helen could feast her eyes on the wonderful Butchart Gardens.

Jack walked around with her and knew he was hurrying, so said to her, "I'll go and wait in the reception while you can take your time to have a good look around but no pinching any plants as they won't be allowed back in Australia."

He was extremely patient waiting, as he wanted to make up for the last time, they, for some 'unexplained' reason, couldn't visit.

Marit, their Norwegian friend, contacted Helen and wrote:

Do you realise we are both having our 50th wedding anniversary in the same year, a week apart. Why don't we meet in Northern Vietnam to celebrate.

So they did and had a great time doing the tourist trail of Halong Bay, reached the mountain regions of the border of China - a long train trip but worth it, dining, sightseeing and just having fun. It was their last overseas trip.

So, therefore, they decided to do the Australian Tour. Jack had already ridden his motorbike solo around the coastal road of Australia after he did the Dakar ride. As a matter-of-fact, Jack has done quite a few solo rides in and around the country and is still doing so.

They saw, advertised on the internet, a 2002 Landrover Defender, for sale in Adelaide, completely kitted out with a bed on top. There was no more to do on it except buy some food, linen and fuel and they would be able to live in it for weeks, rain, hail or shine. Just the best thing to travel around Australia in without towing.

But it pains me to tell you, Jack had been noticing little differences in Helen. She didn't seem to walk like other people her age; she didn't move her arms while walking. Things just didn't seem right. They did the doctor visits, the specialists, the MRIs but there was no diagnosis. Jack studied the internet. He didn't like what he thought. No, it couldn't be. Helen missed out on all her teenage years, surely she wasn't going to miss out on her retirement years.

It all came to a head when they went down to Melbourne to celebrate Helen's 70th birthday with her sister, brother, nieces and nephews. While they had their celebration dinner in an old, converted fire station, now an upmarket restaurant, Jack noticed Helen was not interacting like normal. She should have been happy, laughing, joining in the conversation and having fun but she just sat there, solemn faced, eating her meal.

Jack excused himself and went to the toilet where he cried and howled like a little kid. He had suddenly realised he was going to lose his most precious love, not now, but gradually. As he tidied himself up and left the toilet, he met his favourite niece.

She said, "Jack, are you alright? You look terrible."

"Don't tell anyone, it's our secret but I'm sure Helen has Parkinson's."

It was confirmed by her Brisbane GP who she had visited every six months for the last 15 years. Jack rang her before the appointment and said he thought Helen had Parkinson's. After the consultation, the doctor confirmed it with her.

"Helen, I suspect you have Parkinson's and I will give you a referral to a neurologist." The woman should have picked it up at least 12 months before.

Helen didn't have the normal Parkinson's. She never had the shakes. She just started, very slowly, to decline over the years. The drug, Levodopa, (Manopar) replaced the dopamine that the brain was lacking. It made a big difference. They did trips in their Landrover Defender, along the Oodnadatta Track, The Mereenie Loop Road to Kings Canyon and Ayers Rock, the Birdsville Track, up to the Mitchell Falls, where Helen did the walk up to the falls, Home Valley and all the walks along the way, Cape Leveque, Broome, Halls Creek, down the Tanami Desert Road to Alice Springs, across the Plenty Highway, then Birdsville and home. Dear Helen walked to all the sights with only one walking pole and they had fun on all their trips.

Helen eventually had to give up driving and doing nursing and Jack gave up volunteering for the Queensland Ambulance.

One event worth mentioning. Jack drove the Defender from Brisbane to Darwin, left it at the long-term airport and flew back, saving Helen the long drive and a month later they flew to Darwin to pick up the Defender to do their Gibb River

Road trip. Now Jack had backed the Defender up near the wall of the carpark.

They were tired after arriving at midnight from the long flight and decided to sleep in the Defender in the car park. Now Helen had a bit of trouble walking up the ladder to the rooftop bed, so Jack helped her by walking up the ladder with her, then actually getting into the bed Jack pushed her bum in and helped with the legs. It sounds difficult but they had their method. Both were cuddled up asleep when a strong voice yelled:

"Police here, come down and identify yourself."

Jack thought they may have been in trouble for sleeping in the car park. Once he climbed down the ladder to face the two policemen, one of them said, "You have somebody up there?"

Jack said, "Yes, it's my wife."

In an accusing tone, one of them said, "What have you done to her?"

"Nothing," said Jack, then yelled, "Helen, wake up and poke your head out the door." He realised by the police's manner, something was really up.

"What's your problem?" said a sleepy Helen as she poked her head out.

The two policemen looked at each other then smiled.

"See, you have backed up near a security camera," one of the policemen said, "and it looked like you were handling and pushing a dead body into your vehicle, so security called us."

Jack explained that his wife had difficulty getting up the ladder. The two police said, "Have a goodnight," and left.

Our couple now couldn't go back to sleep, so they took off and drove to Katherine and had a late breakfast with Damon, who worked there.

It's not necessary to go into detail over the next 10 years, but I will mention a few of their struggles, As the years went by, things were getting more difficult for Helen. As an example,

Helen would have some material and a pattern out on the table to make a blouse, something she could make beautiful within a few hours. Now it would lay on the table for weeks as she tried to figure it out.

It killed Jack to see it lying there. He tried to help as he knew the fundamentals of making things from watching Helen and giving suggestions on collars and sleeves, but to no avail. With the garden she could not cope for long working in it and it was the same with her cooking. Her three loves were slowly taken away from her.

Helen has always kept everything to herself, never expressing her feelings, never showing any frustration or getting angry because having this dreadful disease. Very slowly, Jack had to take over looking after her, ending up doing everything for her 24 hours a day.

Their children and friends kept saying to Jack, "You can't keep looking after her, you will have to put her in a home."

But Jack felt it was his job and no one else's to look after his beautiful wife. But when the falls and mini epileptic fits started, it was getting very difficult for Jack to be there for her. She would be in her comfortable chair and Jack would say, "Don't move, Darling, I'm just going to the toilet," and he would just get there and there would be a crash.

She would be laying on the floor having gotten big bruises on her body. He would rush in and say, "Sweetie, why didn't you stay in your chair?"

She would answer, "I just wanted to get you a cup of coffee."

At bedtime, Jack would put whistles and bells beside her special bed and say, "Ring me if you want to go to the toilet."

She would do the same thing, get up, fall, hit her head and get more bruises.

Her excuse was, "You need your sleep after looking after me all day. I didn't want to disturb you."

Anything she did was for Jack, never thinking of herself.

They did have help from My Aged Care but it was very limited. When they ended up with a package for level four, Jack asked their provider how much care they could give Helen.

"We can give 20 hours of care a week," was the answer.

But that left Jack 120 hours on his own, trying to look after Helen. It was thought, My Aged Care was to keep people out of retirement homes. He knew he couldn't look after her properly or care for her any longer.

Helen went into Wongaburra Aged Care, 40 kilometres from their home, for respite and, gradually, as a permanent resident. It broke Jack's heart, but he knew he had no alternative. He would visit her every second or third day and was always excited to see her. He asked them to lift her in the hoist and put her in the wheelchair. Then they would go outside of the home and talk about everything and nothing, as he wheeled her through the park with the lovely trees and green mown grass, to the Beaudesert Information and Craft centre on the hill.

There they would go in and Helen would feel the material and craft displays for sale, with Jack slowly wheeling her around so she could enjoy everything. Then the information centre would serve them coffee and scones and cream and they would have a lovely hour or so away from the home.

Jack hated leaving her. He would stroke her hair and give her a cuddle and kiss, then just walk out the door, not looking back. He couldn't. If he did, he wouldn't' be able to leave. It was always a dreadful trip to a lonely home. Sometimes, he rang his daughter for a yarn but it was always the same.

Deborah, Jack, Alex and Tilly came up from Sydney to the Information Centre, where they set up a table and decorations for Helens 80th birthday. (Eighty years old, wow, 62 years with an ileostomy, all the adventures, work and putting up with Jack. It showed what an incredible woman Helen was. Just fantastic).

Jack wheeled her over after the girls at the home dressed her up in her best clothes that Jack had brought down, made a girlie fuss of her with makeup and hair and they all had a good time. Helen was in the greatest of spirits when they arrived at the information centre.

It was lovely to see the smiles and welcomes and Helen was enjoying it all. They sat down for coffee and birthday cake but before the cake cutting and presents, Helen turned to Jack saying, "I want to go back."

As Jack wheeled her back to the home, she turned her head to Jack, and said, "Darling I was having such a lovely time but something just comes over me."

Jack said, 'It's that bitch, Mrs Parkinson."

Back at the home, they had a birthday lunch for Helen, then she went back to bed where he left her and joined Debs and the kids back at the information centre.

In their last 20 days together, Jack still wheeled her up to the information centre for scones and coffee. He knew her time was close and arranged for the Boonah Hospital to have a private room so Jack could be with her till it was time for her to leave him. On his last visit to Wongaburra, Helen was not able to go for their usual outing, so Jack stayed with her, holding her hand and stroking her hair, which she loved him doing.

As he got up to leave, she looked at him with the most loving eyes and said in a quiet voice, "Jack, I really love you."

"I love you too, darling." And then he walked out the door, never to see her again.

The ambulance pulled up to take her to Boonah but she decided the night before she wouldn't go and passed away.

C.30

The End of the Tale

It was cloudy on this particular morning. Jack and his family were worried that it might rain but the clouds parted and the sun shone as it knew it was Helen's Memorial Day.

It was held at Mt Alford Lodge, a place on top of a hill, surrounded by the mountains of the Scenic Rim. It was all as it should be: beautiful gardens with lush green lawns, all so scenic with the majestic vista of the mountains. Helen would have loved it. They expected around 30 guests, but over 80 arrived, parking their cars and walking up to the outside area where the memorial was to be held. Jack was astounded by all the people who attended from such a small country town. Helen would never have believed it. She would have been so embarrassed.

It was a lovely memorial with Jack speaking about his love and the life he had shared with his beautiful wife who had always been his heroine. Deborah spoke about her love for her mother and all she had accomplished, with Damon standing beside her for support but too emotional to speak. Grandson, Jack, spoke about his wonderful memories of his grandmother and so did Tilly, her granddaughter. Alex called her his favourite grandma.

He had everything ready for his talk but, like Damon, emotions dried his throat.

Other speakers shared wonderful memories of Helen. The talks were not long and the guests gathered after the formalities and talked about their memories of a lovely lady. Jack was asked by some of the guests if he noticed some birds were singing during the official part of the proceedings. Another thought, it was a sign when a rooster crowed once. Poor Jack, he did not notice these sorts of things. He only noticed all the wonderful people who came to pay homage to his heroine and the mountains that surrounded this magnificent memorial for Helen.

A few months later, after discussing with the family, it was decided to spread her ashes on to Mt Edwards. A mountain which she had gazed at from her back door every day. Watching the mists snaking through the gorge and over the mountain in the winter, the storms and rain in the summer as if washing the mountain's face, the sun shining on its unique features in the early mornings. They were the symbols she always saw driving home.

How were they going to spread her ashes on that mountain?

Jack managed to contact the local aerodrome and spoke to people there. How could he spread his wife's ashes on Mt Edwards? A phone call a week later asked Jack to be at the airstrip Sunday morning with Helen's ashes, and so he was.

An old 99 Cessna aircraft, which was used in the Korean and Vietnam wars as a spotter aircraft, was sitting on the tarmac. It even had bullet holes in it. The plane was a two-seater, one behind the other. Jack sat in the back seat and a man came up and said, "Could you please hand me Helen?"

Jack gave him the box of ashes. He returned shortly with a bag tied with string at the top.

"Put this on your lap, holding the top of the bag tightly," he said, then from the bottom of the bag was a cord which he threaded through the window of the aircraft and tied it to the strut.

The pilot hopped in, gave the safety instructions and made sure Jack was holding the bag and had his seat belt on.

"So, you want to spread your wife's ashes on Mt Edwards. Where exactly do you want them?"

"Just on top of the tree line below the cliff face please," answered Jack.

They took off and flew on the eastern side of the mountain.

"Lucky we have an easterly wind," said the pilot. "When I count down to one, throw the bag out of the window,"

"One."

Jack threw the bag out of the window and the cord attached to the strut pulled the bag open and a white ball of ashes came out like a little, fluffy cloud. Then, like a mist, the ashes spread out over the treetops. It was truly a wonderful sight to see. Jack was not sad, in fact, he was happy that his Helen now had Mt Edwards as her memorial for eternity.

Now what about Jack? He felt like he had been dumped by his girlfriend, after 57 years of companionship. But he was pleased that Helen was at peace. No more changing, no more accidents, no more pain, no more putting up with that bitch Mrs Parkinson. But his life had changed forever.

He acted in a Monty Python radio play, as the Scottish Dr Farson for the Boonah play group. He went and visited his son in Darwin then joined a cruise from Darwin to Broome. It was very difficult for him, as all the passengers were early retirees and Jack was the only single person aboard. It was hard to see all the couples together having fun and talking about their excursions and what they had seen. Jack tried to join in a bit but felt like a stranger interfering. He wanted to get off after a few days but it wasn't the sort of cruise to get off early. The cruise did show him he had to get out, meet people and do things.

When he got back, he decided to do a tour of Tasmania, leaving his home in Queensland on his motorbike to Victoria to catch the ferry across Bass Strait. He spent a week riding around the Apple Island and did the return home, doing quite a few thousand kilometres at the age of 82.

Then he took a flight to Perth to see his brother Mike and wife Brit and attended their son's wedding, then hired a car to see some of the south of Western Australia before flying back home. Damon came down and spent three weeks with his dad over the Christmas period before returning to Darwin for his university job. That was the year filled in.

Jack, to this day, is trying to live up to Helen's mottos, riding his pushbike to keep fit, mowing lawns, treating Helen's garden with love and having coffee and dinner with friends. Jack is also helping John write this autobiography.

Helen should have the last words with some of her favourite sentences in this story, as a women should:

"Enjoy this day you have been given and have fun."
"If you are not happy, do something about it."
"Oh, just get on with it."

The Final

The End of the Tale

G,day, this is Jack. Remember I wrote at the beginning of my first book, "A Lie in The Tale," something like this: "I was on my way at last, an adventure of the unknown that lay ahead."

Well, I was on my way again, an adventure into the unknown. I wasn't quite sure how the journey began but I was in a beautiful field with the greenest of grass, dotted with buttercups, daisies, snowdrops, in fact there were flowers everywhere. I couldn't name them all but they were outstanding in colour and beauty. I thought this must be heaven.

There was a young lady attending the wonderful blooms. She must have heard me coming and started to glide towards me. She was alluring with such a happy loving smile. When she was beside me, she gently took my hand, saying in a delightful voice, "You're home now, Jack."

The peace and love I felt as we walked together towards a radiant sunset of happiness and love.

The End.

www.ingramcontent.com/pod-product-compliance
Lightning Source LLC
Chambersburg PA
CBHW011128070526
44583CB00023B/2950